THE YOUNG MIND

Co-edited by
Professor Sue Bailey and
Dr Mike Shooter

BANTAM PRESS

LONDON • TORONTO • SYDNEY • AUCKLAND • JOHANNESBURG

TRANSWORLD PUBLISHERS
61–63 Uxbridge Road, London W5 5SA
A Random House Group Company
www.rbooks.co.uk

First published in Great Britain
in 2009 by Bantam Press
an imprint of Transworld Publishers

In all case histories names of people, places, dates, sequences or the detail of events have been changed solely to protect the privacy of others. The authors have stated to the publishers that the contents of this book are true.

A CIP catalogue record for this book
is available from the British Library.

ISBN 9780593061381

Addresses for Random House Group Ltd companies outside the UK
can be found at: www.randomhouse.co.uk
The Random House Group Ltd Reg. No. 954009

Typeset in 11/15pt Minion by
Falcon Oast Graphic Art Ltd.

Printed and bound in Great Britain by Clays Ltd, St Ives plc

6 8 10 9 7

We dedicate this book to all children, adolescents and young people growing up in today's challenging and changing times. We hope it will help them – and those who support them through their emotional struggles, particularly parents, teachers and all those with a caring role – to grow into mentally healthy young adults.

Contents

Acknowledgements ix
Foreword by Professor Tanya Byron xi

Introduction 1

Part One: Growing Up

1. Understanding Child and Adolescent Development 7
2. The Brain and Brain Development 49
3. Coping with Problems 53

Part Two: Parenting

4. Parenting and Families 59
5. Parenting Skills in Adolescence 97

Part Three: School

6. Choosing a School and Problems at School 115
7. Children with Special Educational Needs 142

Part Four: Emotional Health

8. Emotional Health and Well-being 151

Part Five: Serious Disorders: Context, Causes and Effects

9. Abuse, Neglect and Domestic Violence 163
10. Worries and Anxieties 175
11. ADHD and Autistic Spectrum Disorders 184
12. Culture and Society 210
13. Dealing with Loss 218
14. Drugs and Drink 232
15. Eating Problems, Weight Problems and Eating Disorders 242
16. Tics and Obsessions 251
17. Mood and Behaviour: Psychosis, Schizophrenia, Bipolar Disorder and Depression 263
18. Self-harm and Attempted Suicide 282
19. Antisocial Behaviour: Conduct Disorder and Delinquency 292
20. Mental Health of Young Offenders 302
21. Sexuality and Sexual Problems 310
22. Atypical Gender Development in Children and Adolescents 319
23. Sleep, Fatigue and Chronic Fatigue Syndrome 328
24. Trauma, Stress and Adjustment 338

Part Six: Treatments and Therapies

25. Treatment for Children and Adolescents in Child Mental Health 349
26. Transition to Adulthood 360
27. How to Get Help 365

Editors and Contributors 370

Index 379

Acknowledgements

THE ROYAL COLLEGE OF PSYCHIATRISTS would like to acknowledge the contributions from all the psychiatrists, health professionals and College staff who took part in the production of this book. We would also like to thank the team at Transworld Publishers, who supported our vision in publishing the first book to encompass all aspects of the young mind.

Foreword

GROWING UP IN TODAY'S SOCIETY is tough and competitive. There are times in all children's lives when they need understanding, support and advice. But all too often adults feel powerless, and may be unsure about what to do and when to do it.

In my experience as a child mental health practitioner, I have found that it is natural for parents to worry that they are not doing the right thing for their children. Children are often very secretive about their social and emotional lives, and sometimes it is hard for parents and teachers to recognize when things are going wrong.

Some children are also born with developmental and behavioural difficulties, such as autism or Asperger's syndrome. In these circumstances, parents often feel that it is their fault and don't know where to turn for help.

There are hundreds of parenting guides and books on different aspects of children's physical, emotional, psychological and social development. The sheer volume of conflicting information and advice can leave parents feeling confused and less expert in raising their child.

This is the first time that all the complexities and anxieties about bringing up children have been brought together in one essential and reliable guide. It gives practical advice on growing up, parenting and families, school, emotional health and social problems. It also tackles issues that many people – both adults and children – find difficult to talk about. This includes things going wrong in families because of abuse, neglect or violence; gang culture; sexuality; and what happens to young people who end up in trouble with the police.

This valuable book discusses the emotional difficulties that children and adolescents go through at different stages in their lives, such as depression or anxiety, in a straightforward and open way and each chapter signposts you to further help and support. It will also help people to understand the normal development of children and their families. It is aimed not only at parents, but also teachers and young people themselves.

I feel confident that this family handbook, written by experts in child and adolescent mental health – professionals who have spent their working lives dealing with the problems that parents and children face – will be essential reading at many different stages in your life.

Professor Tanya Byron

Introduction

NO ONE WOULD BLAME PARENTS for being scared by the figures. Hardly a week seems to pass without reports of the emotional struggles our children, adolescents and young people are going through. Take, for example, the stories plastered all over the media in the first few weeks of 2009.

A survey carried out for the Children's Society in the UK showed that little has improved since UNICEF declared two years ago that Britain was the least happy place for a child to be raised in the Western world. Researchers at SANE were shocked by the discovery that 1 out of every 9 young people has attempted serious self-harm as a way out of their distress. Families in South Wales were shown to be still reeling from the suicides in and around Bridgend over the previous year. Dietitians swung between worries over how obese our adolescents are becoming and worries about how anorexia is affecting younger and younger age groups. And in one issue of a national newspaper, official figures noted that rates for teenage pregnancies are rising; nearly a quarter of a million children truant from school every week; and the DNA of over 2 million children is now stored on the national database and police computer registers.

In the midst of all that, is it any surprise that many parents – untrained for the job, stretched by financial worries, and often isolated from family and friends who might have given them good advice – are left wondering if they can ever get it right? Is their young child's unruly behaviour a sign of hyperactivity? Is their teenager's moodiness a symptom of dangerous depression? Is their daughter's latest food fad part of an incipient eating disorder? Is her first relationship a prelude to pregnancy? Has their son's skirmish with the law launched him on a criminal career? Will they be marked down as the sort of parents who produced a hooded young thug?

Professionals can sometimes become confused by it all too. Consider the following scenarios. At one end of childhood, a two-year-old boy is referred by the family doctor to the local mental health team because he won't do as he is told. He screams blue murder when he is restrained, slaps his mother in his temper and has a sly dig at his baby brother when her back is turned. The parents are exhausted and have begun to row with each other. The GP wonders if he needs that 'magic bullet', Ritalin.

At the other end of childhood, a shy fifteen-year-old girl with few friends, who has been the butt of verbal bullying in the past because of her academic success and early sexual development, has become increasingly withdrawn in class. Her first boyfriend has ditched her and her mother is worried because there is a history of depression in the family. Her father and schoolteacher feel that she will 'snap out of it in time; it's just a phase she's going through'.

In point of fact, the assumptions in both cases are probably wrong. The behaviour of the two-year-old is fairly typical for a child of his age, flexing his muscles both physically and emotionally, frustrated by parents alive to the dangers in the world and taking out his feelings on a younger sibling of whom he might already be jealous. What the parents need is reassurance and some handy tips on how to handle him, not referral. In contrast, the fifteen-year-old girl may well be slipping into a clinical depression, the sort of quiet despair that is suffered by one or two teenagers in every secondary-school class is rarely referred for the specialized assessment and help it warrants because of attitudes that play down its significance.

Until an event like the loss of a boyfriend proves the final straw.

But how are parents and professionals to be sure? How are they to understand the behaviour, mood swings and social patterns of the young people in their care? This book aims to help them with exactly those dilemmas. It is not intended to be another scare story, nor is it meant to be dismissive of the worries of either adults or young people themselves. The vast majority of parents will get by in raising their children as best they can through all that life has to throw at them, and the children will grow up to repeat the process with families of their own. Some parents will need some outside help when things get too tough for them to cope on their own. Some young people will have been born with difficulties – or will develop them in the course of their childhood – that are sufficient to require professional treatment.

The book helps to distinguish between these layers of concern, beginning with what lies at the centre of it all – the stages of child and adolescent development that are the foundations on which life is built. With these in mind, we can work out what range of behaviour could be expected from a child at a particular stage and what might be so far outside it as to be 'abnormal'. It explores what natural resilience and vulnerability individual children might bring to any situation and what skills the good-enough parents will need to carry them through it. General concepts that are often bandied around, like 'emotional well-being', are explored with reference to the many contexts in which children live – home, school and community. The sort of symptom clusters that may result from things going wrong are discussed, the packages of help that might be available and how to gain access to them.

Finally, it is appropriate that the book should end with a word about self-help – what children, adolescents, young people, their parents and families can do to help themselves. For the message of this book is as much about empowerment as it is about problems and their treatment. Despite all those scary statistics, most young people will emerge unscathed into adulthood and their parents will be able to take pride in a job well done. All of us have the chance, along the way, to acquire a better understanding of that sometimes complex, frequently confusing, and always intriguing, exciting and wonderful phenomenon that is the young mind.

Dr Mike Shooter and Professor Sue Bailey

Part One

Growing Up

1 Understanding Child and Adolescent Development

CHILDHOOD HAS BECOME AN INDUSTRY. Walk into the psychology section of any bookshop and you will find the shelves groaning under the weight of textbooks on child development, each more confusing than the next. Switch on the television and the channels are full of pundits telling us how children should be brought up, all piling guilt on the parent's head. Open the newspaper and we are at once fascinated and appalled by tales of disaster and cod-analysis of the effects it might have on the minds of children involved. The advertising agencies have prospered on pandering to the needs of children, or to needs they did not even know they had. Our schools, our playing fields, our whole society is geared to the success of one developing child pitted against another – whether we do it by measuring height on the kitchen wall, by exam results or by the scoring of goals.

And what are we to make of all this? How might we seek reassurance or identify problems, as parents struggling to understand our own children's behaviour or as teachers anxious about the behaviour of someone else's child?

The one thing all these books and programmes have in common, of course, is the telling of stories. Stories are important to all children and to those involved in bringing them up. We tell stories to our children as a way of stimulating their imaginations and cuddling close to them, in every sense. We tell stories about our children to other parents, often embellished by a little imagination of our own, as a way of proving that we too are good-enough parents (a phrase invented by the paediatrician-cum-psychotherapist Donald Winnicott to emphasize that we do not have to be perfect). And the experts are re-telling those stories, distilled from years of watching and listening, testing out what theories might be learned from them and reproducing them as 'evidence'. This chapter is not another textbook but an attempt to make those stories a little more accessible. If it sets the scene for the chapters that follow, or inspires you to further reading, then it has done its job.

Watching little Issy

All of us, watching our children and grandchildren grow up, are experts by participation in our life stories; so let me begin with one of my own. I have been lucky enough to have four children and to have had a share in bringing them up, with the same triumphs and tribulations as everyone else. Now they, in turn, are bringing up children and one, Isabel, lives so close by that I have had the privilege of seeing her grow up at first hand. I have watched her eyes first focus on her mother's face and the signals of love that passed between them. I have seen her mother's sleepless face in the morning and her father, out all day, struggling to establish himself as a parent too. I have watched them both trying to cope with an inquisitive child exploring the world with new-found legs and running into the everyday dangers of house and garden. I have shared in the rows about breastfeeding, dummies and bottles, and in the joys of bedtime rituals that protect her against the ghosts and goblins of fairy stories, the more frightening the better!

Now I listen to 'lectures' on the latest bit of knowledge Issy has discovered and marvel at the imaginative world she inhabits in her play. I am amazed at how she copes with the minor disasters of passing hurts and the major disasters of death and upheaval alike – asking questions through her tears, getting honest answers, trying to puzzle it all out. I feel for her confusion, between joy at her baby brother's birth and anger at having her nose put out by the attention her parents pay him. I am happy that she is developing first friendships outside the family. Soon I will share in the mixed emotions of her first days at school, as growing up, it seems, means growing away. And so it will go on into later childhood, the ups and downs of adolescence, young adulthood and beyond.

Implications: the journey

If any of that rings a bell, it is because there are common features to all child and adolescent development and to the experience of it in families, however unique their particular stories may be. Above all, there is the sense that this is a journey, a progression from an immature to a more mature state of development over the course of time. The great paediatrician-turned-child-psychiatrist Robert Coles, who spent a lifetime listening to the stories children told him, likened this to a 'pilgrimage' – children journeying through everything that life had to throw at them, actively seeking out some distant goal. We may not know what that goal might be or how close each child might get to it, but the direction of travel has entered our language. Watching an adult behaving childishly, we might wish they would 'grow up'. Listening to a child speaking like an adult, we might wonder at them having wisdom 'beyond their years'.

But the journey is not simply a linear one; the experience may become a circular pattern that is repeated from one generation to the next. Physically, this is obvious. Already little Issy is seen to have her mother's mouth or her father's eyes, and this is not just a way of establishing their ownership of her. There are real familial features that are handed on from parent to child and are instantly recognizable in family photographs; but so are more complicated behaviours too. I can see that little Issy is already taking after one parent or the other in the way she approaches life, just as others may have spotted how my own children, Issy's father included, took on some of my own personality.

Like it or not, our successes and failures may be imprinted on our children, and on their children in turn, in a repeated cycle. As the poet Wordsworth said, 'The child is father of the man'.

Schools of thought

How can we judge whether this development is going well or not? To start with, there are lots of ways of looking at a child's development depending on which school of thought the writer belongs to. Some of these have more scientific evidence to back them up than others; some describe wide variations of normality from one child to another. But all of them have something valuable to say about the landmarks of growing up. To list them all in detail would take up this whole book, so here are just a few examples.

Physical development

All parents will be familiar with the signs of physical development – from the primitive postural reflexes of the newborn infant, to more purposeful reaching out to examine objects (including bits of the baby's own body), sitting up, crawling, walking, the simultaneous development of all the senses, through to the complicated hormonal swings of adolescence and the growth of secondary sexual characteristics that mark us out as clearly male or female with all that that entails. We are familiar with them because the good-enough parent watches out for each milestone along the way, and the doctor and health visitor monitor their progress by examination and investigation.

But parents can be unnecessarily worried by comparing their child too closely with the next. Some children, for example, may walk as early as seven months, whereas good crawlers or 'bottom-shufflers' may not walk until well into their second year; and yet no difference can be found in their later years. And we are all aware, even if the advertising industry is not, of the variability in the onset of puberty between girls and boys, and between individuals within the same sex. One glance at the pupils in the first year at secondary school will show just how wide this can be and the real unhappiness it can cause for those who develop early or those who feel left behind. Undressing for PE can be a nightmare for both.

Cognitive development

The picture gets a little more complicated when we look at a child's cognitive development – how the growing child forms an understanding of the world, its functions and relationships that is intimately connected with other skills like language. The Swiss psychologist Jean Piaget (drawing inferences from watching his own children) has had enormous influence on our view about the ages at which children develop such concepts as 'object constancy' (the realization that things do not cease to exist just because they are out of sight); 'causality' (the link between an action and what happens as a consequence); and 'generalization' (using previous experience to solve new problems). His detailed observations have formed the basis of a whole battery of tests, using toys, pictures and books, to assess everything from the one-year-old's ability to recognize objects by name to the adolescent's ability to use abstract reasoning. Even adults may be psychometrically tested when applying for a job these days!

And yet, however useful this is as a framework, we know that it cannot be the whole story. Children do not learn staccato fashion, with a whole new layer of understanding suddenly open to them overnight. Their understanding is affected by how adults and peers interact with them in play and other social situations, helping them to experiment with ideas, master skills and rehearse for new situations with imagination and fun. There may be one or two 'eureka' moments in a child's life, but most concepts are learned by asking questions, mulling over the answers and asking more questions – a process that can drive the best of parents up the wall but is essential to the child's cognitive development.

Psychosexual development

In other words, children do not learn in a vacuum; they are prey to everything that is going on inside them and in the world outside. Now Sigmund Freud, the founder of psychoanalysis, was convinced that children pass through successive stages of psychosexual development that dominate their thoughts, feelings and behaviours at every point. They erect typical 'defences' against the anxieties of each stage that might at best colour their later personality or to which they might 'regress' under trauma. An 'anal' personality, for example, might be obsessed with pernickety detail, giving ground grudgingly as if still stuck in the battles over potty-training!

Whatever we think of these ideas and those of Freud's followers and rivals, they have entered our everyday speech. We talk of things going on in our 'subconscious', beneath the level of our awareness, and how these can suddenly (and embarrassingly) break through in our conversation as 'Freudian slips'. We talk of 'repressing' unwanted thoughts, or of someone being 'repressed' if they do not seem able to release their feelings, enjoyable or otherwise. We describe people as 'neurotic' if they are dominated by their anxieties and have distorted ways of dealing with them; as 'egocentric' if they always look to themselves; and as having an 'inferiority complex' if they are always putting themselves down. And we say that someone has a greater or lesser amount of 'libido' – their share of sexual desire. Biologist as he was, Freud thought that his concepts would one day be found to have biochemical roots in the brain. But as yet they remain articles of faith, useful and attractive though they may be.

Psychosocial development

Psychosexual theory tends to treat children as passive beings, unaffected by relationships with the important people in their lives; but we know that these complex interactions are crucial to their development. Erik Erikson, like Shakespeare before him, divided life up into the

Ages of Man. He described 'tasks' that are to be accomplished at each stage and reflect what is happening in the world about them. Thus, in the first year of life, a child learns from the intimate relationship with his mother the balance between trust and mistrust. This will allow him to form satisfactorily close relationships in later life while retaining a healthy suspicion as a defence against manipulation. In his second year, the child develops a sense of self-assertiveness, as opposed to shame and doubt, gained in the way he receives praise or disapproval from his parents for bowel and bladder training and wider behaviour. The battles this may involve are typical of the 'terrible twos' described below.

The older child learns to use initiative to achieve all sorts of exciting things, rather than feeling too guilty or frightened to do what he wishes, and passes on to the formal learning of knowledge and skills in school upon which his future self-esteem will depend. The adolescent's task is to sort out his identity vis-à-vis parents and peers, what sort of person he is and what he believes to be worth fighting for – a clarity of role but with enough flexibility to cope with change. Unfortunately, Erikson's ideas of later adolescent independence were largely economically based – moving out of the family home into college, a job and a house of one's own – and are simply unrealistic for many young people today. Families may have to allow them to grow into adults in the same house where they were once treated as a child.

Attachment theory

You might think that the story of children's development is even more of a two-way process than this, and to prove it we need go no further than the first years of life and the critical relationship the child forms with her mother. This is the core of attachment theory, about which so much has been written in recent years. It was first based on the observation of baby monkeys and their mothers, but it has had an enormous influence on human childrearing practice.

Attachment theory begins with the premise that we are all social animals with an innate (inborn) need for intimate relationships. The security of such intimacy starts, as always, at our mother's knee, with a good-enough parent who knows just how to respond to her child's demands, with just the right amount of promptness – not so soon as to discourage any independence, not so late as to cause her to despair of ever being heeded at all.

From this base, the securely attached child may explore the world and the strangers within it and greet her mother with affection on return. The insecurely attached child may be clingy from the outset, afraid to explore and meet strangers and angry with her mother when reunited; or she may appear completely indifferent to her mother's comings and goings, snubbing her in favour of the strangers themselves. All parents may have struggled with echoes of this, without any suggestion of abnormality, and may experience it again in the grief of bereavement in later life. But more than this, it has influenced the way society has come to understand the potential impact of early deprivation and it has changed the way we handle enforced separations like going into hospital. Thanks to pioneers like John Bowlby, mothers may now sleep alongside their babies in the paediatric beds, and babies with their mothers on the adult ward. Children are saved from emerging with feelings of abandonment which could undermine their relationship with the mother there and then, and with mother figures later in life.

Spiritual development

Study of the spiritual development of children and adolescents was frustrated for years by its association with religion, but it has now come to be seen as an important component in its own right. Having said that, I have to admit that the key elements – the growth of self-awareness, sympathy with others, and a 'transcendence' of both to a universal code of values – remain vague. Some writers have preferred it that way, feeling that spirituality has a will-o'-the-wisp quality that would be destroyed if it were pinned down like more mundane physical or cognitive development. Others, like James Fowler, have plotted seven stages on the way to 'selfhood' that give a direction and a purpose to life. These are built around the concept of faith, but in a much broader sense than religion.

Thus the infant is said to develop a 'primal faith' in the trust established with care-givers and a growing awareness of others outside the family. The young child, stimulated by stories and not yet controlled by logical reasoning, has an 'intuitive faith' that is protective against threatening forces in the world of fairy tales, of witches, ghosts and magical spells. The older child has a more 'literal faith' that is anchored in his ability to think more logically, order the world in his own head and understand what is going on in the heads of others. The adolescent is able to bring together the many aspects of development into a coherent set of beliefs, from the security of which it is possible to tackle a world full of people with very different ideas: 'conventional faith'.

Although this may be hampered by too rigid a timescale on the one hand and rather airy-fairy language on the other, the idea of spiritual development does seem to capture a quality within human beings that has always been important in the East. In the West, it is helping to fill the gap between medical explanations of illness and our personal experience of it. But despite the universal nature of its key concepts, it is likely to differ greatly from family to family, culture to culture, and one social group to another. What it means to a Muslim child on the streets of London may be very alien to a West African adolescent from the tribes of the Ivory Coast.

The complexity of stage theories

So where have we got to in this Cook's Tour of the schools of child development and the gurus at the heart of each of them? To begin with, it will be obvious by now that these are all stage theories, in which the developing child reaches particular milestones or completes particular tasks at particular ages in life, and then passes on to the next in a steady progression of increasing maturity. These are achievements about which children and their carers can be justifiably proud, though this can easily slip over into a competition to see whose child can move from breast-feeding to solids to steak and chips the quickest! But useful though they may be in giving us a general idea of how well a child is doing, life is much messier than this.

We have already seen that physical development like puberty can be a very variable event. There is no big bang in the lower forms of secondary school as all pupils break through the puberty barrier together! No one has told their hormones that the advertising industry has decreed that by this age all adolescents are supposed to be sexually aware and active. Similarly, our intellectual understanding of the world may be influenced as much by what goes on around us as purely by age and IQ.

Take, for example, the child's understanding of death. True, the younger child may not clearly grasp its permanence. He may still expect a dead animal, or grandmother, to return – even if he has been allowed to see the dead body and been involved in the funeral and burial. True, even an older child who is angry with a dying sibling for taking up so much of their parents' time may think he has caused the death in some magical way by secretly wishing it in his heart of hearts.

But young children who have experienced death in their family and have been included in the rituals and emotions of grieving, and have had things explained to them in straightforward language that avoids confusing euphemisms like 'gone to sleep', may have a better grip on it than older children who have never experienced it or have been excluded by overprotection and forced to fill in the gaps from their imaginations.

In other words, perhaps we should think of these stages as bundles of different tasks, the bulk of which may be achieved at a particular age but some of which may be done earlier, later, or not at all. This will vary according to the child's circumstances as much as to individual drive, in quite a normal way, though we can see that a crucial step missed at one age may come back to haunt the child at a later date. The child and family who have 'failed' to deal with separation anxieties early on may be more than usually thrown by the move up from a small, local primary school where mothers are in and out of the classroom daily to a huge, impersonal comprehensive school a bus journey away.

On a more positive note, too great an emphasis on the content of each stage may hide the fact that the most exciting things often happen at the transitional points between stages as children pass into adolescence or adolescents into adulthood. Families are well aware of such transitions and the flexibility that is required of parents to help their children through them. Professionals, however, have often ignored them in the past. Paediatric teams who have treated children for years may be tempted to hold on long after they have developed into adults and should have moved on. Social-work teams, exasperated by adolescents' behaviour, may pass them on to adult services precipitately or leave them to nothing at all. Many are the children with physical or psychological problems who have fallen down the gaps between child, adolescent and adult services with disastrous results.

Life gets still more complicated.

At first glance, all these schools of thought may seem to be in conflict, though we can see that Fowler's stages of spiritual development owe a debt to both Piaget and Erikson. Look closer and you will see that they actually dovetail, at crucial points in a child's life or over time, helping to explain different aspects of the same process.

At any one time

Take, for example, two periods of difficulty with which parents will be very familiar – the 'terrible twos' and 'adolescent turmoil'. Each involves a mixture of pride in achievement and anxiety about what it may involve. How that mixture is resolved will colour the future confidence of child and parents alike. And all the schools of thought have something useful to say about it.

Most two-year-old children will have found their legs, quite literally, and will have the physical ability to explore the world beyond their mother's knee. This will be accompanied by the biological urge to do so. At the same time, the child will have mastered cognitive concepts like object constancy – the discovery that a brick dropped over the edge of the table still exists though it may be out of sight. This not only allows a mother to go to the lavatory without her child feeling that she has deserted him for ever, but also allows the securely attached child to go off through the door in the confident expectation that his mother will still be there when he gets back.

But the world, of course, is full of dangers that the child cannot yet know about, so the good-enough parent must offer some protection. Parents must allow their children to explore their surroundings, picking them up and dusting them off each time they come a cropper, but within an envelope of safety. 'Don't touch the fire . . . don't play with plugs . . . don't kick the dog!' So there develops a battle between freedom and frustration that leads inevitably to temper tantrums, often on both sides. Many a child has been referred for treatment at this point, when all that is really needed is reassurance that his behaviour is a normal part of development. And the most important lesson for both child and parent to learn is that love survives our anger.

So, too, with many aspects of adolescence. Strange things are happening to the adolescent's body as his hormones surge around the bloodstream during puberty. The once brazen child may become secretive about his developing sexual characteristics and confused by his emergent sexual feelings. In the struggle to establish an identity of his own, he must be different from his peers yet the same as everyone else; he must take on his parents as role models and simultaneously despise them for making compromises with their ideals – for having feet of clay. And this 'ambivalence', this state of uncertainty, shows itself in emotions and behaviour. Rarely do adolescents think, feel and act along one consistent track. Rather, they swing backwards and forwards between pairs of opposite thoughts, feelings and actions over very short periods of time.

It is a process that bewilders parents, exasperates them and may convince them that their son 'must be schizophrenic, Doctor, because he's got a split personality – he's nice one minute and nasty the next. He doesn't seem to know his own mind'. And it may prove just as difficult for doctors and nurses treating a sick child in hospital, who quite rightly demands an adult role in decision-making one day and regresses into a tearful childhood on the end of a needle the next. In point of fact, the adolescent at the centre of it all may be just as confused and frightened by it as anyone else. There is not much use propping him up against the wall and asking why.

Over time

If childhood itself has become an industry, so have broad concepts to do with child development, like 'emotional literacy'. There are conferences dedicated to the subject, with experts on emotional literacy comparing its application in different cultures around the world. The phrase rattles around the corridors of government departments and has permeated the school curriculum. There are courses on emotional literacy that award certificates to teachers whose job it is to develop it within the classroom. It has come to be seen as a major component of mental health. But what do we mean by emotional literacy? Is it just the absence of mental ill-health, or is it something positive in its own right? There are as many definitions as there are writers on the subject, but let me add one of my own.

The emotionally healthy child, it seems to me, is one who emerges with a balance between her internal needs and an external appreciation of the needs of others in three key areas. First, the ability to know (recognize, label and own) her own emotions, and to know (recognize, label and appreciate) the emotions of others. This is the ability to work out when someone is angry, miserable or frightened, both from what they say and from things left unsaid, from the tone of their voice, the way they look and the subtleties of gesture, and to respond appropriately – the 'theory of mind' that children on the autistic spectrum find so difficult (see Chapter 11). Second, the establishment of a clear identity of her own while respecting, and being interested in, the identity of others with whom she comes into contact. And third, the development of enough concentration to pursue what she wants from life with motivational drive, yet being able to strike compromises with the equally valid and often conflicting wishes of everyone else.

From this emerge the three broadest components of social living – the three 'Cs' of Communication, Cooperation and a Concern for others. But the building blocks for all this are rooted in the physical, cognitive, psychosocial and spiritual aspects of development, working together at every level of growing up.

The 'jigsaw' of assessment

So how can we put all this together when trying to assess the meaning of a child's behaviour, how normal or abnormal it may be? Everyone has their own structure for doing this; mine is a jigsaw that brings together the various influences from nature (what a child is born with), nurture (how a child is brought up) and life events (what happens to a child along the way). Only by completing the whole picture can we fully understand the behaviour at the centre; and only then will we be able to work out how best to help a child with a superimposed mental health disorder.

Individual characteristics

The framework of child and adolescent development that we have been discussing will tell us what a child of this age ought to be wrestling with, what issues will be important to him and therefore how he might be expected to behave, within broad parameters. But what of this particular child? The genetic loading passed on from parents to their children may produce similar characteristics in brothers and sisters, but children can differ markedly even within the same family. Just ask a mother who has given birth to a grizzly baby after one with a more sunny temperament, or a restlessly active child after one more content to sit in his highchair and watch the world go by! These are different children, from different parts of the spectrum of normality, demanding different handling skills. And on the top of this come all the myths and realities about birth order – the oldest child secure in her sense of responsibility, the youngest child doted on by everyone, and the middle child who has to fight for any sense of status in the family.

This comes close to saying that children are different in their 'personality', but this is a word that is difficult to apply to adults let alone children, who are still developing and who may change dramatically from one age to another: 'She used to be such a mouse of a thing but look at her now'; 'I don't know what's got into him – he was our problem child but he's turned out so mature!' Certainly we should avoid saddling children with a fixed and often stigmatizing label like 'personality disorder'.

Instead, we should be looking for the positive strengths in children and helping them to fulfil their potential, whatever sort of people they are. Which brings us to the question of coping styles. There can be no doubt that some children cope better with adversity than others, though the greater the adversity the less important a factor this will be. There are some life events, like bereavement, that will shake the strongest child to the core and it is no disgrace to 'break down' in the face of them. Expecting a child to keep a stiff upper lip has led to all sorts of problems in a macho society where big boys don't cry and feelings are suppressed, which may explode later in less healthy ways.

Nevertheless, we need to account for the fact that some children with the most wretched family and community starts in life not only survive but prosper. Conventional research says that such strength might be due to a warm and loving environment, a good IQ, success in school and a supportive network of friendships. But these are just the sort of things that, by definition, are likely to be beyond our disadvantaged child. The good news for teachers and family friends, wondering how they can ever counteract the child's background, is that just one relationship with a significant adult can help. A relationship that treats the child in a loving and respectful way, that treats her as worth knowing for her own sake, may innoculate her against more malign influences. When things are at their worst, now or in later life, the child may draw upon the memory of that relationship and be comforted by it.

Events and experiences

It is tempting to think that the connection between life events and the effect they have on children is a simple, causal one. Things happen, the child musters his coping mechanisms in the face of them and survives or not, with varying levels of trauma, depending on the severity of the experience and the degree to which it is destructive to the child's life. Early deprivation, for example, the disruption of all those vital parent–child experiences in infancy, can lead to serious psychopathology in later life. Parental death or divorce; neglect; physical, sexual or emotional abuse; parental mental illness such as puerperal psychosis, which can ruin a mother's ability to care for her child; substance misuse, which might cause a father to fly into terrifying rages; natural and man-made catastrophes that tear a family apart – all these can have a devastating effect on a child's development.

At the extreme end of the spectrum, many writers have looked back at the early history of violent offenders and tried to pinpoint the moment when their normal development was derailed; more specifically, how early deprivation might have led to the behaviour of the 'psychopath'. There can be few more controversial words than this in child development. We shudder to hear it used, thoughtlessly and harmfully, about children whose behaviour parents and teachers simply find puzzling, frightening and impossible to deal with.

In its proper sense, the word just means someone with psychological problems, but it has come to describe a particular set of features – a deceitful and manipulative character, repeated impulsive and often aggressive behaviour that gets the child into fights with peers and adult authority figures, a reckless disregard for danger, an apparent lack of remorse for the damage such behaviour may cause, and more specifically a triad of developmental problems (such as bedwetting), fascination with fire and cruelty to animals. The label is stigmatizing, implies that it is all the child's fault, and carries an air of hopelessness about it.

Quite apart from the danger of applying a static label to a still developing human being, we should be asking where the problem really lies. Do we have a problem teenager? Or do we have a problem background that has evoked such behaviour by a combination of upbringing and deprivation? Or a problem community attitude that scapegoats the teenager and rejects him, rather than trying to help child and family in their continuing vulnerability? That, of course, could take us on to the issue of poverty and the influence of broken-down housing estates on which such families might be living, but that is not for this chapter to assess.

In reality, the relationship between life events and child development is much more complex. We have already seen that different children have different coping styles, strengths and vulnerabilities, and that this may be dependent on how supportive those around them are as much as on their own individual characteristics. What's more, the equation may even be the other way round. Children and adolescents of a certain temperament may have more events in their life than others. It is easy to see that a daredevil, risk-taking child may have more accidents; but how some people may be more accident-prone in a wider sense is mysterious though well documented. 'Poor woman . . . her life is full of tragedy . . . it always seems to happen to her.'

In general, whatever the direction of the equation, we should try to work out how this life event cuts across or gels with the tasks with which a child of this age and developmental stage would be struggling anyway. How can an adolescent follow the drive towards independence in the face of a serious illness like cancer, when the demands of hospital treatment may isolate him from social interactions, when the illness itself and the technology of treatment may undermine his sense of self-mastery, when disfigurement may ruin his bodily image, and when metabolic imbalance and lack of schooling may compromise his intellectual ability to make decisions? Small wonder that parents and paediatricians alike may treat him as a child.

Such life events may not be all bad. Some are joyous in themselves, or turn out to be 'happy accidents' that have hugely beneficial effects on child and family life. Even major losses are opportunities for learning about the world and readjusting family relationships, roles and expectations in a positive way, however painful that may feel at the time. And young children and adolescents have been known to face up to illness with a spiritual maturity that is a lesson to the adults around them.

The family

Most child and adolescent development, as we have seen, is set within the context of family life. If that statement had been made just a few decades ago, we would have had a good idea of what it implied – two young parents bringing up their children with grandparents somewhere close by. But there are now many different sorts of family, none better than the rest but different in circumstances, structure and needs.

The difference between the haves and have-nots in society is greater than it has ever been. One in 3 children in the country where I live and work, Wales, is brought up in material poverty; in some towns families are into their third generation without employment. But there are other forms of deprivation too. In professional families, with both parents working flat out to pay the mortgage and huge academic pressures on the children to succeed, caring relationships may be stretched to the limit.

Old family structures may have disappeared. Children may no longer receive the training in parenting skills that they used to get by helping to look after younger brothers and sisters in large families. Parents have to be more mobile in the search for work and have often moved far away from their origins and the grandparents, aunts and uncles who might have helped out.

There are increasing numbers of parents who have remained single by choice or have separated from former partners. Those partners may struggle to keep contact with their children, sometimes amicably but often in an atmosphere of continuing hostility. Some remain estranged from their children and the single parent is left to shoulder the everyday burdens of childrearing alone.

In so-called 'reconstructed' families, step-parents must build a relationship with the children of their partner's former marriage, with all the jealousies that may cause. Foster parents give what security they can to children who have been rescued from family trauma and who may test out their new parents to see if they are just the same as the rest. Parents who adopt children may worry that their adolescent's natural wish to find out about her family of origin will undermine the relationships they have so carefully nurtured.

Many adults, pursuing their careers first, now choose to have babies later in life. This means that they will be facing up to the demands of adolescents in relative old age, just when they might once have expected to be free of parental commitments. Teenage mothers, whether they anticipated it or not, will be charged with the responsibilities of looking after a baby when they might still have been enjoying their own adolescence.

In all of this, you can see that families are made up of common building blocks – the relationships between family members (how they get on with each other); the roles founded on those relationships (who does what in the family); and the family rules (how they do it) that are handed down from one generation to another. But we need to work out what these are like in this particular child's family, and to do so as objectively as possible when the family we are looking at may be very different from our own family and the ideas of normality we may have as a result.

Thus family relationships are held together like a spider's web, criss-crossing with each other and each strand dependent on the rest. It is not possible to alter one relationship in a family – a mother's relationship with her son or a father's with his daughter – without all the rest being altered in some way too. And family solidarity may be built on negative feelings just as much as on positive ones. Many are the couples who have been bound together by mutual hostility – and pity the poor children trapped somewhere in between, their behaviour and the need 'to do something about him' being part of the glue.

Traditional family roles may have been shaken up where, for example, it is the mother who is the breadwinner and the father who stays at home to take the children to school and look after the house, either by mutual consent or because of unemployment or disability. The family rule-book may be applied equally to how the family settle everyday arguments and to how they deal with major catastrophes. The way the children are handled, whether they are protected from any part in the matter or whether they are allowed to share more openly in what is happening, may influence their whole approach to adversity in later life.

Such rules may become so entrenched in family life that they acquire almost mythical status, and woe betide anyone who tries to break them! This may be comforting when the rules are positive – where boundaries are clear, where parents back each other up, where children are rewarded for good behaviour as much as punished for bad, where families communicate freely to settle their differences but allow each other private space when needed, and above all where the relationships, roles and rules are flexible enough to change over time as the children grow up within them.

What is required of two young people living together is very different from what is required of parents with their first baby; what is required of parents bringing up young children is very different from what is required of those dealing with adolescents growing into adulthood; and different again from watching, as grandparents, while their children produce their own families in turn. Same couple, different responsibilities. Where relationships, roles and rules are too rigid to accommodate these changes, disasters may occur. And they are likely to recur in one generation after another if the myths go unchallenged.

Having said that, most families cope with developmental transitions surprisingly well, despite the difficulties of parenting and the lack of training we get for it. Skirmishes around the 'terrible twos' and adolescence, which we have looked at above, are quite normal in families. Children should emerge from them with their self-esteem enhanced and parents with respect for their achievements. Both will go on to the next stage of life with renewed confidence. But it is possible for parents to care too little or too much about what their children are doing.

If they care too little, then their neglected children may find other ways of getting the sense of care and belonging they have been denied. Teenage girls may become pregnant in the belief (conscious or not) that caring for their own child may make up for not being cared for themselves. And at least they can achieve some sort of status by pushing a pram down the high street. Teenage boys may drift into a gang culture as a substitute for family support.

If they care too much, if they try to smother their developing children with concern for safety, dictating their friendships, refusing to allow sleepovers, demanding their noses be kept to the academic grindstone, voicing their disapproval of girlfriends and boyfriends, fighting pitched battles over every aspect of dress and teenage behaviour, then their children may choose more dangerous ways of establishing control over their own lives. Normal adolescent rebellion may turn into something much more pathological, like an eating disorder or running away.

Good-enough parents know instinctively where to draw the boundaries, how to stand back and allow their growing children to find things out for themselves within those boundaries, and how to survive the tantrums and turmoil as those children kick healthily against them – knowing that their parents will be there to pick up the pieces if it all goes wrong. And if those parents make an occasional mistake, as normal parents will do, there will be enough good will on all sides to carry them through. But this is complicated at the best of times. It becomes even more so, as we will see, where the child has a mental health disorder.

The social system

As well as their family of origin, children belong to a wider 'family' of culture, peer group, the community in which they live, its institutions such as schools, and the systems of health and social care that may be called upon to look after them. The dynamics within and between all these components may have a significant influence on their lives.

A closer look will be taken at this in later chapters; suffice it here to make just a few general points. Children are not born with culture, they are born into it – and all the rules of that culture they will take in with their mother's milk. Their culture will determine how they think and behave in a general sense, and what is possible in their lives in some very particular senses, like marriage. Though in some cultures there seems little room for adolescence as children pass straight into adulthood via one sort of initiation rite or another, the broad stages of child development may be common to most; but the particular way those stages are expressed will be different.

Parents within those cultures will know what this implies, but those working with the family from outside will need to be aware of the differences, respect them and accommodate them, lest they raise expectations about family roles that cannot be fulfilled. Even so, Asian girls, for example, may become trapped between traditional values at home and freer attitudes they come into contact with at school. Significant numbers have harmed themselves in their distress.

Peer-group relationships are enormously important in children's development. They are the context in which children first learn concepts like sharing, fairness and cooperative play. They are the forum for developing self-esteem in later childhood and early adolescence. And they are the yardstick by which adolescents will judge themselves. In other words, when things are going well they are a force for good. When things are going badly, they can be purgatory.

The unpopular child who is bullied and left out of playground games, the teenager who is shy and unable to find a boyfriend, may be crucified by their peer group and need a great deal of parental support. Parents may be tempted to play down a situation that might seem trivial to them but is crucial to their child. Tragedies have happened where a teenager of fragile self-esteem has lost a boyfriend and parents have met her distress with a dismissive comment: 'Cheer up, there are plenty more fish in the sea!'

Good-enough parents will encourage friendships from an early age and try not to be too judgemental about those they approve of and those they do not. Children who are secure in their self-esteem will find out for themselves, by trial and error, the sort of friends they wish to make and hold on to. Those who are more fragile, if not taken seriously or if overprotected, may be driven into any relationship, suitable or not. Yet again this is a difficult tightrope for parents to walk.

And this, of course, includes sexual relationships. Attitudes to sexuality are so bound up in family and cultural values, and there is so much tension between these and the expectations raised by TV, films, books, magazines, music and youth culture that it is difficult to say anything too firmly. It remains, however, the role of parents and other significant adults to educate children and adolescents about such relationships. They need to reassure children at times of potentially frightening sexual development, such as the onset of periods; they need to talk to them about the mechanics of sexual intercourse, contraception and sexually transmitted diseases; and they should remember that they may be the role model their children follow. It is no good expecting adolescents to be cautious about sexual relationships if their parents' marriage has broken up because of their infidelity.

Parents will need to be broadminded about their children's emerging sexuality in general, but this is easier said than done. Young children are naturally curious about their own bodies and those of others. They will want to explore their bodies in play or seek comfort by self-stimulation at times of anxiety. They should not be made to feel that this is 'dirty' by parents who are coy about their own bodies or teachers who throw up their hands in horror at the sight of a child masturbating in class. This is not necessarily a sign of background abuse.

The same parents should be aware of the growing need for sexual privacy in adolescence, when the locked bathroom door can easily become a battleground. The same is true of the school changing room and the hospital ward. There is no more miserable sight than the developing teenager trapped on a paediatric or an adult ward, surrounded by intrusive young children or dementing and disinhibited older patients.

Perhaps the most challenging issue of all is that of homosexuality. It is not the role of a therapist to be judgemental here, whatever parents may wish. It is the role of a therapist to help the adolescent who is unhappy in his homosexual feelings to work out whether he is fleeing from heterosexual relationships because of some past trauma, or from more satisfying homosexual relationships because of his own shame and the censure of adults around him. It is also the role of the therapist to offer reassurance that homosexual feelings may be a normal stage of development for everyone and a permanent state for some. But the tolerance of parents may be stretched to breaking point unless they receive help in understanding their child's feelings and coming to terms with them.

Schools are the hot-house in which peer-group relationships are fostered and flourish or founder. Missing out on school means missing out on social learning just as much as on academic opportunity. This is beginning to be recognized in a more holistic view of the teacher's role, though nobody would blame teachers for becoming confused by the repeated change in what is expected of them. They were once said to be central to all aspects of child development, then told they would be judged on exam results only. Now they are the champions of emotional-literacy programmes, just when appropriate skills have been stripped from their training.

Nevertheless, teachers are *in loco parentis* for much of the children's week and their influence may be just as strong as that of parents. They have a responsibility to use that influence to promote healthy relationships and to protect children from the bullying that can drive vulnerable young people to self-harm and suicide. To do so effectively, with all the heartache it may sometimes entail, teachers may need as much advice and support as the children and parents at home.

Finally, in this jigsaw of behavioural influences, there are wider responsibilities for the social 'family' to think about. For good or ill, how the various people involved in a child's life relate to each other may replicate and reinforce the relationships between parents and between the conflicting feelings inside the child herself.

Thus hospital teams that argue with each other, and with GPs, social workers and teachers outside, may take on the tensions that already exist between parents over their child's welfare and the child's own mixed hopes and fears about what is happening to her. Similarly, if they work more cooperatively and sensitively together, they may help to heal relationships between parents and traumatized feelings within the child.

Disorders and interventions

With all this as a background, how should we approach the disorders of childhood and adolescence, and how can they be helped? Again, this will be covered in detail in succeeding chapters. But here are ten questions to set the scene.

How common are mental health problems in children and adolescents?

To some extent this depends on how we define the problem. Let's say that there are 10 million under-eighteens in the UK (there are actually nearer 11 million, but that makes the maths more complicated). One fifth of these (2 million) will have mental health problems sufficient to interfere with their normal enjoyment of child and adolescent development. Of that number, half (1 million) will have a formal, clinical psychiatric illness by any system of classification. Even if we took the top 3 per cent of these as being the most disturbed of all – young people depressed to the point of suicide, anorexic to the point of bodily collapse, conduct disordered to the point of being a danger to themselves and others – that would be 30,000 at any one time.

These are strikingly large numbers and there is some evidence that there is a progression between the categories. Those with mental health problems may develop more diagnosable mental illness if left unhelped. Those with moderate mental illness may become more seriously disturbed if left untreated. Within the figures, some conditions are more common than others, and this brings us to the next question.

Are these problems getting more frequent?

Judging by the amount of publicity they receive and the load their referral creates for GPs and specialist clinics, you would be forgiven for thinking so. In fact, there is no clear evidence that the neurodevelopmental conditions like attention deficit hyperactivity disorder (ADHD) and those on the autistic spectrum, for example, have increased in recent years. We may be picking up those children who previously went undiagnosed, though some would say that the balance has shifted the other way and that we are now medicalizing behaviour that could be accounted for by the background in which some of them live.

What may be increasing is dis-ease in its widest sense – the sadness and anxiety that blights the lives of so many children and led UNICEF to declare that, of all the most developed nations, Britain was now the unhappiest place in which to be brought up. Some of that may slip over into a clinical depression and, as previously noted, it has been said that there are one or two depressed young people in every secondary-school class, many of them undetected and unhelped. Certainly rates of self-harm and suicide amongst young people are worryingly high. This is a matter for more accessible services and socio-political policy to address.

Why should we worry about children's problems?

Many of the difficulties we have been discussing might be resolved with some explanation of what they mean in terms of development and with advice about how to handle them. But frank developmental disorders and psychiatric illness, once established, are unlikely to go away and might get worse over time. We are beginning to recognize that ADHD and the autistic spectrum disorders are chronic conditions that persist into adult life. If complicated by behavioural difficulties, they can lead to all sorts of later problems, including criminal convictions. The learning disabilities may crucially interfere with educational achievement. Too many depressed young people take their own lives in lieu of receiving help.

Looking backwards, it seems that most adult psychiatric disorders have their roots in childhood and adolescence, and the burden on individuals and society by this stage is high. Depression and anxiety are now the greatest cause of time spent off work in the Western world. It makes sense to prevent this where possible by tackling them at source.

When should we intervene?

The sooner the better, but this means early detection. Not even the most laid-back parent would fail to spot a young child losing some of the capacities he once had and regressing to a more primitive developmental level. But many disorders begin quite insidiously with occasional problems that only those in closest contact with the child might pick up. Indeed, since some disorders are quantitatively different (in degree of abnormality) rather than qualitatively different (of a totally different kind), parents and schools may be tempted to make allowances rather than face the fact that a child needs specialist help.

Even with today's technology, the first alert will be sounded by everyday symptoms rather than by a brain scan. Parents worried about something that strikes them as odd in their child's behaviour should never be afraid to take those worries to their GP and beyond. Professionals should always take those worries seriously, even if nothing shows up as yet on more sophisticated investigation. Diagnosis remains a hands-on process, in every sense of the expression.

Is diagnosis always clear-cut?

Unfortunately not. This is partly due to the nature of the disorders themselves. It is well recognized that psychiatric disorders often co-exist.

Young people may be both anxious and depressed at the same time; adolescents with eating disorders may have an obsessional disorder that is wider than their preoccupation with food. And the same is true of developmental disorders too.

Many children with ADHD have social and communication difficulties that could be described as autistic traits; the more severely affected may have a full-blown autistic disorder. What's more, there are well-documented links between ADHD and motor difficulties, with over half of those with ADHD meeting criteria for developmental coordination disorder. On top of this, learning difficulties (with spelling, reading and maths) are common in children with ADHD and nearly two thirds of them have one or more psychiatric problems too. So rare is it to find ADHD without 'co-morbidity' (overlap with other disorders) that perhaps we should think about it as a cluster of problems and accept the fact that pure diagnosis is impossible.

At the top end of our age range, adult-like psychiatric illnesses such as schizophrenia and bipolar disorder may begin to emerge, though these are far less common. But the exact diagnosis may remain unclear for years. Often the disorder may be heralded by changes in mood or behaviour, or by simple oddness of personality, long before any psychotic episode. The adolescent may be handed on to adult services in an atmosphere of uncertainty that is difficult for everyone to deal with, not least the adolescent himself.

Why do so many people get involved?

From what we have just said, it will be clear that children and adolescents with problems are affected in many areas of their lives simultaneously. They may have multiple physical difficulties, each one of which may not seem serious in itself but which together may undermine self-esteem. They may have speech problems or learning difficulties. They may be emotionally distressed and disturbed in their behaviour. These problems may lead to tension at home, poor peer-group relationships and difficulties in school. There may be times when neither they nor the adults around them can cope.

So in order to help we need to take a holistic approach – looking at every aspect of the child's needs together. People from many different disciplines will assess the situation and add their expertise to the treatment package. These may include child and adolescent mental health workers (psychiatrists, psychologists and psychiatric nurses), community or hospital paediatricians, paediatric neurologists, educational psychologists, speech and language therapists, occupational therapists, physiotherapists, social workers, GPs and health visitors. This can be bewildering for children and parents at the centre of it all. The confusion will be lessened if roles are spelled out clearly and everybody works in cooperation with each other, rather than passing the family on as if it were a relay race.

What treatments will be needed?

This depends on the disorder involved and later chapters will describe these in detail. But it is rare for there to be one 'magic bullet' that will do the trick. Most disorders require a package of treatments that may involve medication as an adjunct, a back-up, to a behavioural programme linking home and school. Some problems may need more 'talking therapy' to help uncover the root of a child's difficulties, to address his distorted beliefs about himself and the world, and to support the family with the tensions placed on their relationships. Wherever possible, this will be carried out in the community, keeping the child in his normal environment. Just occasionally, an adolescent with an illness in a critical state may need to be treated more safely and effectively in a specialized in-patient unit.

The very mention of medication is a reminder that treatments are not without controversy. Vital though they may sometimes be, medications such as antidepressants have to be used very cautiously for children and adolescents, in whom side-effects are easily underestimated and efficacy overplayed. We should always remember that the child's brain is a developing organ and the potential benefits of medication have to be weighed against the uncertainties of how the brain may be affected over the years.

In all cases, a single form of help like medication has to be set in the context of the whole treatment package, including sorting out the practical problems that the child's disorder may have caused. At best, the combination of medication such as Ritalin (methylphenidate) in ADHD, a behavioural programme and practical help may allow the normal processes of development to have a better chance at home and in school, at a critical stage in a child's life.

What are the implications for services?

As we have seen, the problem may not be that too few services are involved, but too many – often at different times, tackling particular crises then withdrawing again until the next crisis occurs. No one seems to hold in their care the whole trajectory of a vulnerable child's needs, from fallopian tube to adulthood. For example, we know that the transition from primary to secondary school is likely to be particularly difficult for a child on the autistic spectrum (see Chapter 11). Such a child may find it impossible to place himself in someone else's shoes, see the world from their point of view and make compromises between his own and their wishes – the task for all adolescents in secondary education. The essence of continuing care would be to anticipate such difficulties, build on the child's strengths to deal with them, intervene when that is not enough, and inform and support the parents and teachers involved. Short-term aims within a long-term plan.

It is difficult to see how this could be achieved without services for children and adolescents becoming joint in every sense – jointly commissioned and financed, jointly assessing the profile of vulnerable children in their area, and jointly implementing care from their pooled resources. There are examples of such joint working already in the UK, often (ironically) where resources are thinnest and creativity under enlightened leadership has become a necessity.

Have I caused my child's problems?

Past writers have implicated parents in their children's problems on at least four levels – predisposing them to problems; precipitating the problems; prolonging the problems; and participating in the consequences of the problems. All this has heaped guilt on the heads of parents who may already be distressed. So what is the truth?

It would be foolish to deny that parents may pass on a genetic vulnerability to a particular disorder. Twin studies and adoption studies have shown that there is a strong hereditary link in disorders as different as ADHD and depression, and the hunt is on to identify the genes involved. It would also be foolish to deny that disturbed relationships in a family could create an atmosphere in which such vulnerability comes to the surface. In extreme cases, parental abuse can cause a disorder afresh. It is also possible for family life to become so organized around the disorder that it is difficult for everyone to get back to normality when the child has recovered. Indeed, warring parents might be diverted from their own difficulties by having to concentrate on a sick child. Subconsciously at least, they might then have a vested interest in that illness persisting.

But this is a very long way from saying that most childhood disorders are caused by the parents in some sense. Except in those rare cases of abuse from which the child needs rescue, the parents are often equal victims of the disorder and the disruption of family life that may ensue. They will need help and support too, so that their child can draw upon their strengths. In this way, the parents become part of the solution, not part of the problem.

What level of help might be needed?

There are three broad levels of intervention possible, in proportion to the seriousness of the disorder. Take, for example, problems with eating.

Many young children develop food fads that are a normal part of growing up. Parents need little more than reassurance that this is so. Indeed, to focus on them too closely might encourage the behaviour.

Some pre-pubescent girls begin selective eating, such as avoiding certain foods, which is potentially more serious. Their general development may still be on track, but help in the form of advice and support may be needed to avoid this slipping (as it may do in 50 per cent of them) into a full-blown eating disorder.

The eating disorders themselves (anorexia and bulimia; see Chapter 15) are psychiatric illnesses that are classically associated with adolescence but are occurring at earlier ages these days and may persist into adulthood. Anorexia involves a complicated interaction between cognitive distortion (thinking that you are fatter than you are), eating behaviour (selective and restricted food intake), and the physical consequences (including starvation and extreme emaciation) that may in turn affect cognition and so on, in a vicious circle. The outcome is potentially fatal, and child and family need referral for specialist help.

However, would it not make sense if we were able to prevent some of these disorders occurring in the first place, rather than 'fire-fighting' once they are established? In the case of eating disorders, this might involve social measures to prevent adolescents being bombarded with images of slimness; but in other situations we can be much more specific than this.

We know that women who misuse substances during pregnancy (smoke heavily, take cannabis regularly, are addicted to opiates or drink to excess) risk harming their babies in a number of ways. The baby may be born prematurely and underweight. The proper care of the baby may be undermined by the mother's lifestyle. And in extreme cases, the baby may be born with an opiate addiction of its own, from which it will need to be carefully withdrawn, or with a more permanent condition such as foetal alcohol syndrome. Helping the mother to reduce her substance misuse, at least during pregnancy, may spare her baby the consequences – therapy *in utero*!

Clinical scenarios

Now let's put some flesh on the bones of this discussion. Here are half a dozen typical scenarios with an explanation of what issues are important and what type of intervention might be needed in each case.

Gareth is a four-year-old boy who has invaded his parents' bed. It started when he woke with a nightmare and they took him into their bed to comfort him; now it seems to happen every night. If he is put back into his own bed, he screams until one of the parents gets up, climbs into Gareth's bed with him or brings him back into theirs. Everyone is giving the parents advice. Some say Gareth will grow out of it by himself; some say his parents will have to be cruel to be kind.

Commentary. This is a very common problem, but a difficult one none the less. It is not good for a growing child to be dominating his parents' private life in this way, though we might want to be sure that he is not being 'used' to protect one parent against the sexual advances of the other! The parents will first need to agree that they will stick together to resolve the situation. They must be prepared to put up with it getting even more stressful for a while when Gareth tests them out – and he will.

Both parents should talk to Gareth together. They should tell him that they will keep him in his own bed when he screams to come into theirs and that they will return him if he slips in of his own accord. They should carry it out firmly, no matter what Gareth throws at them, taking it in turns to deal with the situation. They should be reassured that no four-year-old is likely to keep it up for longer than a week or so, but they may not get much sleep in the meantime.

Everyone will need a reward when it's all over. For the parents, part of this will be the realization that they have successfully tackled something that is a common feature of childhood development, is not a sign of any abnormality, but often becomes a problem for those of lesser resolve.

Rhian, aged five, is referred to the child psychiatrist at the request of her parents. Her two-year-old brother has been in hospital for many weeks with meningitis and its complications. Her mother has spent most of her time at the hospital bedside. Her father, struggling to stay in work and support his wife and son, has had little time for Rhian. There have been increasing rows at home between Rhian and a rather strict paternal grandmother who has been brought in to help out. Things came to a head when Rhian was punished for smashing up some of her brother's toys and shouting, 'I wish he would hurry up and die so that Mummy can come home!'

Commentary. It is just such a situation, where everyone is trying to contain their anxiety, that is likely to be blown apart by a five-year-old's honesty of emotion. Rhian might well be feeling jealous of a little brother anyway and is understandably angry that his illness has taken her mother away from her. She may not even know what 'dying' means, but if it would get everything back to normal, what more natural than to wish for it to happen? In fact, if her brother did die, Rhian would probably feel, at this age of magical thinking, that she had caused it – and would be as devastated as everyone else.

Perhaps it is time for someone to be honest with Rhian. She could be taken to see her brother in hospital and have the situation explained to her in language that she might understand. A way might be found for her to contribute to his care and to give her some special reward for doing so. Children are often made more curious than upset by visits to hospital, but the adults will need a lot of reassurance to allow this to happen.

Darren is eight years old and causing problems at home and in school because of his disruptive behaviour. His mother is struggling to bring up three children on her own on very little money and in poor living conditions. She has virtually lost control of Darren, who spends most evenings out late, hanging out with older boys. At school, Darren is often taken out of class because he fidgets, wanders about or interrupts the teachers and other pupils. He has been banned from all school trips because the bus driver says he is dangerous. He ruined everybody's day on the last trip because the teachers had to spend their time looking for him. He has been referred to the educational psychologist at the request of the school because 'he must be hyperactive . . . will you put him on that Ritalin, please?'

Commentary. On first impression, Darren does fulfil the triad of overactive, disorganized behaviour, short attention span and impetuosity that is typical of a child with ADHD. And his behaviour does seem consistent across every context in which he lives – home, school and community. Unless he is helped to change his behaviour, relationships at home will reach breaking point, he may well be excluded from mainstream education, and he is likely to get into trouble with the police with other boys.

However, before making a diagnosis of ADHD we would have to be very sure that Darren's behaviour is not simply a reaction to his living situation. If he is found to have the disorder, medication should be only an adjunct to a behavioural programme. Darren's mother and teachers, who are at their wits' end with him, will need a lot of support to switch to a positive approach, and both programme and medication will need regular monitoring over the years.

Tom is a twelve-year-old with Asperger's syndrome, a disorder on the autistic spectrum that means he has difficulty understanding some relatively simple things unless they are spelled out to him in detail, even though he has a high IQ. He has few friends because he is demanding, bossy and unable to see the world from anyone else's point of view. He often gets into fights when he feels he has been unfairly treated and his end-of-term reports betray his teachers' increasing exasperation. Help is sought after he is banned from the swimming pool for hitting a young girl who splashed him. Tom says this wasn't fair because it was her who had broken the rules by diving in.

Commentary. The move up to secondary school, coinciding as it does with the demands of adolescence, is always difficult for someone on the autistic spectrum, whatever their intelligence. Unless teachers are made aware of the problems that Tom is likely to have with some kinds of work, they will be disappointed by his performance. Reports will be just a description of Asperger's syndrome itself.

Fairness is very important to someone like Tom and it is no surprise that he should lash out when he feels he is a victim. But it is little use trying to appeal to a moral code in which boys don't hit girls. Tom just would not be able to appreciate it. Better, perhaps, to point out that he gets into trouble when he does it, that it is a nicer life when he isn't in trouble, and it is therefore better for him if he controls his temper – even if he feels she deserved it!

Sharon is a fifteen-year-old schoolgirl who has gone to her GP because she wants to be put on the contraceptive pill. She has an active sex life and doesn't trust boys to use condoms. Her mother dropped out of school when she became pregnant with Sharon and when she was not much older than Sharon herself. Sharon is bright, wants to go to college and is determined 'not to make the same mistake as my mother'. She asks the GP not to tell her mother because she is a Catholic and would be sure to object. The GP is worried about the legal and ethical implications of not telling the parent of someone under age.

Commentary. This is the sort of problem that keeps doctors awake at night. Legally, it is covered by the very similar and notorious Gillick case in which a mother took action against a GP's employers. The GP had put her daughter on the pill on the grounds that it was better to risk the wrath of Mrs Gillick than to have her daughter's life ruined by a teenage pregnancy. The House of Lords, the ultimate court of appeal, found narrowly in favour of the GP. A 'minor' (a child under sixteen) is able to opt into (though not out of) treatment against the parents' wishes, or without their knowledge, provided that the child is able to understand what she is doing and its consequences – and that efforts are made to involve the parents as soon as possible.

Sharon would certainly satisfy these criteria, but this doesn't lessen the anxiety for the GP. Lurking under all this, of course, is another legal and ethical issue. If Sharon is having sex at fifteen, the man involved is committing a crime. But in a consensual situation in which Sharon is likely to deny it, there is unlikely to be enough evidence to bring about a charge. The GP should make sure that Sharon knows about the dangers of sexually transmitted diseases.

Annette has had increasing amounts of time off school with headaches and stomachaches that have been investigated by her GP and paediatricians without any organic cause being discovered. At sixteen, Annette's once promising academic work is falling off rapidly and she won't now get the sort of GCSE results everyone expected. Relationships at home are strained because of financial pressures. Annette's mother is being treated for clinical depression and spends a lot of time in bed. Her father is drinking heavily and often loses his temper. Annette spends much of her own life looking after her younger brother and sisters, cooking for them and making sure they get to school on time.

Commentary. Annette's aches and pains could be interpreted in two ways. Children (and some adults for that matter) have a knack of converting emotional distress into physical symptoms that are no less real because they don't show up on blood tests or X-rays. And Annette is certainly an adolescent under stress. What's more, her aches and pains give her an opportunity to do something about her stress. By keeping her off school, they allow her to get between her warring parents, to protect her mother from her increasingly violent father, and to take over her mother's role in looking after her siblings. In other words, Annette is caught in the classic trap of the young carer, and the services, if they are not careful, will collude in it.

It is right for adolescents to have a role in looking after problems at home, but not at the expense of their own lives. Annette needs to be relieved of the burden of her anxieties by the appropriate services becoming involved with her parents' problems, freeing her to get back to school and her social life. She will also need a proper psychological assessment to make sure she is not herself clinically depressed. She has a heavy genetic loading from her mother, and children often show their depression in somatic (bodily) symptoms rather than classic mood disturbance.

A question of risk

Finally in this introduction to child development, we come to the vexed question of risk and the attitude our society has to childhood itself. As we have seen, many childhood problems resolve themselves with a little advice and reassurance; others require more prolonged treatment but are none the less curable. A minority are chronic conditions that render the child vulnerable at key points in life, especially those transitions from childhood to adolescence and adolescence to adulthood. To that extent, such children could be said to be 'at risk' of things going wrong. Since we can predict the difficulties they will have, it makes sense to plan for them in advance, by talking to teachers about how they might be handled in class, for example.

A small but important group of children is placed at risk, not because of any disorder of their own, but because of the poor quality of their parenting – neglect, emotional, physical or sexual abuse, or occasionally all four combined. The long-term consequences of such abuse are so dire that the abused child may himself become an abuser in turn, so that a history of abuse may run through several generations of the same family. There are legal structures and protocols for rescuing children where necessary, though tragedies still occur where the warning signs go unheeded.

Having said all this, risk is also a vital part of growing up. Children and adolescents must naturally take risks as they explore the physical world and its emotional relationships. The good-enough parent will encourage them to do so, whilst steering them away from the greatest dangers and being on hand to help out if it all comes crashing down around their ears. Parents who overprotect their children may cause just as much harm as those who neglect them. Sheltered from all experience of risk, such children may be unable to cope when they meet it outside the family home. Others may rebel in dangerous ways against the web their parents weave around them.

In other words, an optimum amount of risk is a healthy part of growing up. And yet we live in a society where adolescents are either pilloried for their reactions to the conditions we expect them to live in, or are so hedged about with red tape and regulations that they are in danger of becoming battery-chicken children – a society that exploits an idealized image of children and neglects their real needs. Perhaps we should be asking ourselves whether we really like children and adolescents, for their own sake. Which brings us back to the point where we began.

Dr Mike Shooter

FURTHER READING

There are countless books on growing up and more are added to the pile every year. Readers should browse around and see what suits them best. In the meantime, here are a few that caught Dr Shooter's eye.

Bee, Helen, and Boyd, Denise, *The Developing Child*, Pearson Education Inc., 2007.

Byron, Tanya, *Your Toddler Month by Month*, Dorling Kindersley, 2008.

Cohen, David, *The Father's Book*, John Wiley and Sons Ltd, 2006.

Hayman, Suzie, *Stepfamilies*, Simon and Schuster UK Ltd, 2005.

Highe, Jackie, *The Modern Grandparents' Guide*, Piatkus Books, 2008.

Livingstone, Tessa, *Child of Our Time: Early Learning*, Bantam Press, 2008.

Mann, Sandi, Seager, Paul, and Wineberg, Jenny, *Surviving the Terrible Teens*, White Ladder Press, 2008.

Morris, Rachel, *The Single Parent's Handbook*, Pearson Education Ltd, 2007.

2 The Brain and Brain Development

THE BRAIN IS PERHAPS the most complex organ in our bodies. It is made up of 100 billion microscopic nerve cells (*neurones*) and several times as many supporting (*glial*) cells which act a bit like bubble-wrap protecting the neurones.

The neurones and their supporting glial cells are grouped together in the brain according to their job. There are different ways of dividing up the brain to make it easier to understand; one way is to think of it as an onion.

The outer layer is the *cortex*, and most of the 100 billion neurones are found within a few millimetres of its surface. The cortex is itself divided into *lobes*, as can be seen in the diagram on page 50. Each lobe has particular jobs. For example, the *occipital lobe* at the back of the brain processes what we see and the *temporal lobe* processes what we hear and is involved with memory. Our *parietal lobes* take in information from our bodies about any physical sensations we may experience through touch. Our *frontal lobes* are what make us most different from other animals; among other roles they are involved with thinking, planning, concentrating, problem-solving and making judgements – the so-called 'executive functions'.

The middle brain layer, the *limbic system*, is involved in regulating our feelings and emotions and is also needed to remember things.

The innermost layer is the *central core* and this looks after all the functions necessary for pure survival, like eating and drinking, breathing and sleeping.

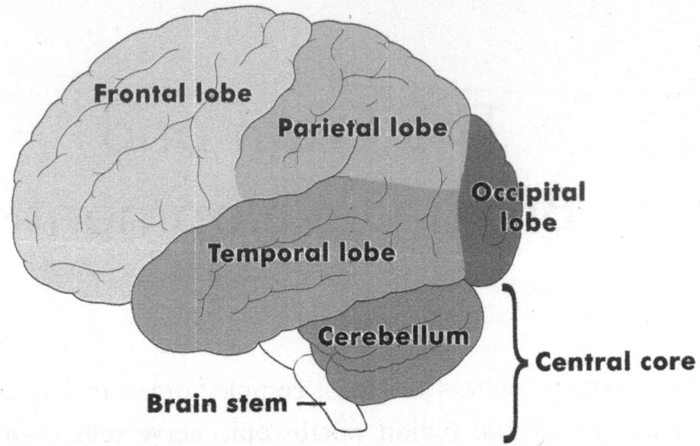

The brain clearly has a huge job to do and it does it by being linked with the rest of the body, getting information about what's going on both within the body and in the outside world (via our five senses) and then sending messages to the body to tell us what to do.

Brain development

By the time a mother-to-be knows she is pregnant, her developing baby's brain is already starting to take shape. By birth, the 100 billion neurones mentioned above are pretty much already in place. The protective glial cells don't just serve as bubble-wrap, they act as 'trailblazers', showing the neurones in the developing baby's brain where to go. We don't know whether each neurone 'knows' what it is meant to be when it is formed, and therefore travels to the right place in the brain, or whether it specializes in a certain job because of where it ends up. It may be a bit of both.

Once they've got to where they need to go, each neurone makes connections and links with other similar or related neurones so that they can start communicating with each other (at areas called *synapses*) and functioning as a group. These groups of neurones then in turn make more and more links with other neurones in different areas of the brain.

Connections don't just develop within the brain; they also form to connect the brain with the body via the spinal cord and neurones in the body (*peripheral nerves*).

Interestingly, all developing babies' brains are 'female'. It is only when baby boys' testes start producing testosterone (when the mother is somewhere between eight and twenty-four weeks pregnant) that the boy brains become 'masculinized'.

Although developing babies are protected to an extent by being contained within their mothers' wombs, the growing brain is known to be particularly affected by the mother's health and well-being. Exposure to some infections, drug and alcohol use, and even severe stress in the mother, have been shown in some cases to cause problems in the baby's developing brain.

Brain development is not by any stretch completed at birth, despite virtually all the 100 billion neurones being in place. A newborn baby's brain will roughly double in weight by the time he is six months old, and will be at 90 per cent of adult weight at six years old. Some of this extra weight comes from a huge expansion in the number of glial cells, but most of it is explained by the increasingly complicated connections the neurones make with each other.

While the central core (page 49) has to be functioning as soon as a baby is born to ensure survival, the cortex (page 49) develops over time as a result of the baby experiencing the environment around him via his senses. We know that for different functions the developing brain has specific 'critical periods' in which most of the development has to occur for the brain to be able to function to its best level. There are, for example, critical periods in the development of our ability to see properly (within the first year) and pick up language (the first few years). We know from some animal studies that if the environment is lacking in, say, things to see, then the baby's ability to process what it sees at a later date will be affected. At the same time, we know that young children can easily pick up more than one language if they have heard them from an early age.

These critical periods are times when the brain shows what is called 'plasticity'. This is a huge ability to make extra connections between neurones, or to lose those which are unused or 'redundant', and then to develop in particular ways, depending on what it has experienced from its environment. Children's brains are generally more 'plastic' than adults', as they continue to grow throughout childhood, but at these critical periods they show plasticity even more.

A further critical period where the brain shows plasticity is that of adolescence. The hormonal changes at puberty provoke several changes in the body and the brain. Of particular importance at this age is the young person's social and emotional development. Here, a warm and stimulating emotional environment is likely to support healthy development, whereas a deprived, abusive or toxic environment (for example, through drugs) may be more damaging.

A critical period therefore presents an opportunity for optimum development of which a young person can take advantage, given the right environment. The flip side of this is that it's also a time when the brain will be most vulnerable to damage caused by a negative environment.

Dr Mona Freeman

INFORMATION

REFERENCES

Blakemore, S.-J., and Choudhury, S., 'Development of the adolescent brain: implications for executive function and social cognition', *Journal of Child Psychology and Psychiatry*, 47, 2006; 296–312.

Dubin, M., *How the Brain Works*, Blackwell Science, 2002.

Rose, S., *The 21st Century Brain: Explaining, Mending and Manipulating the Mind*, Vintage, 2006.

Smith, E., Nolen-Hoeksema, S., and Fredrickson, B., *Atkinson and Hilgard's Introduction to Psychology* (14th edn), Wadsworth Publishing Co. Inc., 2003.

3 Coping with Problems

SADLY, WE KNOW THAT BOTH around the world and closer to home there are children who have to cope with a lot of hardship and difficulty. It may be a huge event affecting entire populations, such as war or a natural disaster like an earthquake. Such events bring with them traumatic experiences, bereavement, the loss of a home, village or indeed even country and culture if people are forced to flee and become refugees.

It may also be an event affecting just the young person or her immediate family, such as having to cope with a physical illness, an ill parent, the loss of a parent through death or divorce, having parents who fight and argue a lot, or being bullied or abused.

All these experiences would be difficult and challenging for anyone. Yet we know that some children show often remarkable abilities to manage and cope when bad things happen. We call these children 'resilient'.

Some children by their very nature or temperament will be more resilient than others. This is not something that can be changed, but may explain why children within the same family may have very different responses and abilities to cope with the same traumatic event, like a parental divorce, for example. Other children may have to cope with their own illnesses, such as asthma or diabetes, which will put a strain on a child's resources for managing additional problems.

Still, it is sometimes possible for children to become more resilient. There are a few different things that we know can help.

Children often gain a lot of confidence and improve their self-esteem if they can find an activity in which they are talented; this may be a sport, music, or something they do at school. It may be that joining an after-school club that includes this activity can have a huge positive effect.

We also know that children are often helped through a difficult situation if they have someone outside their immediate family to talk to and confide in. This will probably mean friends, but we often find that a resilient young person has a close grandparent, aunt or uncle, teacher or mentor to whom they can turn.

Most of the difficult events and experiences with which children have to cope will involve or affect their immediate family as well. It is important that a family can still spend time doing things they enjoy and that are fun, so that family life isn't completely overshadowed by the problem or difficulty.

None of these things will take the difficulty away, but they may make it easier for the child to cope with it. In turn, learning how to cope better when bad things happen will provide the child with ideas of how to cope as she grows older and suffers difficulties, losses and setbacks, which, as we all know, are an inevitable part of life.

Dr Mona Freeman

REFERENCES

Goodman, R., and Scott, S., *Child Psychiatry* (2nd edn), Blackwell, 2005.

Rutter, M., and Taylor, E. (eds), *Child and Adolescent Psychiatry* (4th edn), Blackwell, 2002.

Part Two

Parenting

4 Parenting and Families

THIS SECTION IS ABOUT PARENTING. It is impossible to think about the role and tasks of parents and care-givers without also considering families. In the multicultural society in which we live, families come in all shapes and sizes. Many children grow up in reconstituted families and benefit from the richness that comes from having a large extended family. In fact, the 'traditional' two-parent, two-children family is a modern phenomenon. Extended families, reconstituted families and orphaned children were the norm before the twentieth century.

When writing about parenting and families it can be difficult to get the language right, and we hope that this chapter does not appear to be judgemental and is inclusive. It is important to recognize that difference and diversity are good things and that there is certainly not a correct model of parenting. As parents, we are well aware that bringing up children is a difficult task and that it is easy to blame us when things go wrong.

Family is an important source of support for parents – if not physical support, then the emotional support that comes from the extended family. Grandparents, uncles and aunts may not live in the same house or street, but children still feel very connected to them and there are many ways to communicate across long distances.

Within this section we will refer to 'parents', although we recognize that other people may take on the role of primary care-giver.

Government policies

Through government policies, and as a society, we strive to ensure that children are brought up in families. Research has shown that families are best placed to care for children. Sadly, there will always be a few children who are not able to benefit from a secure and happy family life. Alternative ways of caring for these children then have to be found.

The government programme *Every Child Matters* sets out five outcomes which every child, whatever their background, should be able to achieve:

- to be healthy
- to stay safe
- to enjoy and achieve
- to make a positive contribution
- to achieve economic well-being

Parents and care-givers cannot do all this on their own, but they do have a vital role in helping their children to achieve these goals.

It is recognized how important it is for children to have a good start in life – research has shown that support in the early years is essential to delivering the outcomes set out above. The government has therefore developed services in England to provide this support through the initiative Sure Start, which brings together early education, childcare, health and family support and provides a wide range of different programmes. Further information about your local Sure Start can be found through your local authority, as what they provide varies from area to area. Similar schemes are being delivered in other parts of the UK. Children Centres and Extended Schools are also being developed to increase the provision beyond the early years.

There are many organizations that can offer help and advice – some of these are listed on pp. 95–96.

Becoming a parent

The early interaction between parents and children establishes the foundation upon which their relationship develops. This section therefore considers in some depth the early parenting tasks.

Becoming a parent means that life will change dramatically. It means taking on responsibility for another human being, whose needs have to be put first. This life-changing event will stir up all sorts of strong emotions that can take people by surprise. Our own experience of being parented will have a strong influence on how we ourselves act as parents, and how our children parent in their turn. The relationship we have with our parents becomes a blueprint for how we form intimate and other relationships, including friendships and work relationships.

Although we think of parents as being biologically related mothers and fathers, parenting can take many different forms. Becoming step-parents, foster parents or adoptive parents are other ways in which people take on the parenting role. Grandparents may take a share in the upbringing of their grandchildren, and the importance of the support that grandparents can provide should not be underestimated. Other family members can find themselves caring for a relative's child. Although the traditional family has changed over time, there have always been alternative ways that children have been cared for because of life events such as death and separation. The law recognizes these different arrangements through legal orders such as residence orders, special guardianship and kinship carers. These are explained in detail on pp. 84–88.

A NEW BABY IN THE FAMILY!

Pat and Tony had been together for two years when Pat found out she was pregnant. She wasn't sure she was ready for a baby, but Tony was over the moon. He had two children from a previous relationship and did not see them very often. Pat, however, had just been made a supervisor at work and had been looking forward to the new challenge.

When baby Amy was born, Pat felt the centre of attention. Amy was beautiful and, apart from a couple of weepy days after the birth, everything was great. But Amy wouldn't sleep, Tony worked long hours and Pat found the long days at home difficult. Tony felt left out and began to resent the amount of time Pat spent with Amy.

Slowly Pat began to adapt to motherhood. Her mother realized she needed a bit of time to herself and would look after Amy so that Pat could meet her friends. Tony recognized he needed to give Pat more support and help more with Amy. Pat really appreciated this and they began to feel that they were working together in looking after Amy. This brought them closer together as a couple.

The health visitor introduced Pat to a mother and toddler group where she made new friends. After six months she went back to work part-time and, although she missed Amy, she felt that the balance of work and family life was right for her.

The birth of a baby is celebrated as a happy event, a cause of celebration for family and friends. However, some parents find that the turmoil it creates can lead to depression, isolation and the loss of important work relationships. The emotions they feel for their infant can be overwhelming. A new baby also needs a great deal of physical care which can be very demanding.

Impact on the family

The birth of a baby to an established couple or family requires relationships to be renegotiated. A first baby will mean that a couple have to rework their relationship from just meeting each other's needs as a partnership, into a partnership that includes the joint parenting tasks. This is a huge emotional shift and is far more demanding than we recognize. New parents will need support.

If parents already have children, then they will find themselves torn between meeting the needs of the new baby (who can in this situation sometimes get relatively neglected!) and those of their toddler, who is likely to protest loudly at the appearance of a rival for Mum and Dad's attention.

Grandparents are an important source of help and support at this time.

Maternal preoccupation

It is normal for a mother to become preoccupied with her baby's welfare. These are common questions that a new mother will ask herself:

- Will I love my baby?
- Will my baby love me?
- Is my baby feeding OK?
- Is she putting on weight?
- What if she won't sleep?
- What if I can't comfort her?
- Can I meet my baby's needs?
- What if I can't cope?

The mother's absorption with her baby's welfare is necessary so that the baby will have her needs met and be kept safe.

The role of the father

The baby's father can feel left out. If the mother is taking a large share of the day-to-day care – what is the role of the father? Daniel Stern, writing in the 1960s, discusses this in his books. He describes the communication between mother and baby as a 'dance' with a definite rhythm. He considers the role of the father to be a supportive one, which 'holds' the mother–baby relationship so that the mother can devote her attention to her baby. Many modern fathers may object to this portrayal of their role, and certainly a lot of young fathers wish to take on a greater share of the care of their children.

FATHERING

Paul is very excited at the prospect of becoming a new father. He has been with his partner Jane for ten years, and they both work and share the household chores. However, he feels anxious about how things will change once the baby is born. He and Jane have always worked together as equal partners in their relationship. He does not want that to change. He expects Jane to carry on working after the baby is born and he wants to be involved with caring for the baby.

He has talked with his close friend Rashid about what being a father means to him. They have discussed how things have changed over two or three generations for both of them – even though they come from cultures where family life is very different.

Rashid's father expects to be in charge of the whole family and has high expectations of all his children, including how they behave. Rashid is not sure that when he becomes a father he will be able to do things the way his own father has done. Paul comes from a family where his father worked long hours and his mother gave up work to look after the children.

Neither of them is sure about how a father is supposed to behave in today's modern world.

When parenting is discussed or written about, the focus is usually placed on the mother. Robin Skynner describes the father as a 'lifeline' in the early days, but suggests he then needs to 'reclaim' the mother as the child grows.

In a more egalitarian model of fathering, fathers might not see themselves as being in competition with the infant for their partner's attention. Families are able to adapt and change according to social trends, and fathering is determined by the prevailing social context. The role of the father has moved from distant breadwinner and disciplinarian, to provider of fun and role model for sons, and finally to co-parent. However, mothers are normally fully committed to their babies after birth, and a father who wishes to care for his baby may find himself in competition with his partner. There is evidence that the father's relationship with his child is mediated through the mother, so it will very much depend on his relationship with her.

What is 'responsible fathering'? There has been an attempt to define this in the USA. Considerations of what would constitute a responsible father include:

- being able to support his child both emotionally and financially
- sharing the care of the child with the mother

These responsibilities can be difficult to maintain if the father is no longer living with the mother. Many fathers who separate from their children's mother lose contact with the children. The psychological benefits of having a father present in a child's life can be lost if there is conflict between the parents. Making the right decision, in the best interest of the children, about whether or not to maintain contact, can be an agonizing choice for fathers. These issues are further explored in the section on stepfamilies, as many fathers find themselves parenting children who are not their own. This brings its own set of relationship complexities for a father to navigate.

The good-enough parent

Children thrive on unconditional and positive emotions. Critical or negative emotional responses can lead to feelings of insecurity. Babies and small children develop secure attachments best when parents meet both their physical and emotional needs in a timely and predictable way. If a baby cries, the parents will be at hand to comfort, feed, change, settle or provide whatever they think the baby needs. However, it is not possible to get this right all the time. There are no such things as perfect parents!

In fact, parents who were perfect would not be very good parents at all because their baby would not learn to deal with frustration and would not be motivated to do things for herself. When Donald Winnicott describes the 'good-enough parent' what he means is that parents need to practise sensitive parenting. This is when, as their baby grows and develops, parents are sensitive to whether she should have her needs met immediately, or whether she can wait and manage herself. For example, when a baby stirs in her sleep and begins to wake and cry, if the parent comforts her before she has a chance to settle back to sleep, then she will not learn to do this by herself.

The term 'good enough' is sometimes used to mean adequate, but it is more than this. All children need some adversity in their lives in order to learn how to cope with it. That is not to say that we should put them at risk of danger – absolutely not! However, we do need to allow children the freedom to experiment and learn by themselves. There is much discussion about children not having enough freedom and being wrapped in cottonwool. It is our job as parents to help them manage any independence we give them, and this is just as true for infants and toddlers as it is for teenagers.

The other mechanism by which parents understand their baby's emotion is through the process of identification. Every parent knows what it is like to feel your baby's distress – if your child is hurting, you hurt. However, if this happens too much, it is impossible for you as a parent to keep in check your child's anxiety and help her manage her feelings. Very small children are unable to regulate their feelings and parents have to stay calm and in charge of their own feelings in order to help their children manage theirs.

How babies communicate

The relationship between parent and child is a very special one. In order to think about parenting, it is important to consider what each partner (baby and parent) in the relationship brings, and how the relationship between them develops.

We tend to think of babies as being passive, blank slates, so it may come as a surprise to you to learn that they are programmed to be social beings. Next time you are with a mother and her baby, observe how each of them behaves. What will you notice? You will see the parent gaze at her child, start cooing and exaggerating her facial expressions, and her speech will change. Parent and child begin to perform what has been described as a form of synchronized dance.

The sorts of behaviours that occur when adults and babies interact are:

- long gazes – for example, gazes during feeding
- an exaggerated way of speaking, with a high pitch and falsetto range

Here is an example from Daniel Stern of a parent talking to her baby. The timing of the 'conversation' is important:

'Aren't you cute?' (*1.42 seconds*)
pause (*0.60 seconds*)
imagined response from the infant (*0.43 seconds*)
pause (*0.60 seconds*)
'Yes, you are.'

- exaggerated facial expressions
- mock frowns
- exaggerated smiles
- mock surprise

Watch how the baby responds. Often they will laugh, waggle their limbs and vocalize with babbling. They are having a conversation!

Why are these behaviours important? They are the way that babies learn to share feelings and discover how relationships work.

By the end of their first year, infants are able to do more than simply respond in this way. They are able to work out how other people are feeling and also how they might behave. This allows them to make judgements about the intentions of others.

How parents respond to their babies

What is amazing is that any adult will communicate with a baby in this way. I have sat in a doctor's waiting room and seen a baby of about five months engage with, and entertain, the whole waiting room. So this behaviour is not exclusively reserved for parents – babies are very social beings!

We all know that babies and children need love, but why? Love is part of a special relationship that connects two people together in a strong emotional relationship.

Professionals use a number of terms when discussing the relationship between infants and their parents:

- bonding
- attachment
- attunement
- basic trust

Bonding is something that occurs very soon after birth and refers to the mother's behaviour with her infant. This was described by two paediatricians, Marshall Klaus and John Kennell, who, in the seventies, observed that mothers would gaze at their infants, hold them and touch them in very specific ways immediately after the birth. Their work was extremely important, in that it changed the way that mothers and babies were treated in maternity units. Instead of babies being removed from their mothers to sleep in nurseries, as had been the practice, they were kept in the same room, so-called 'rooming in'. Most people these days would consider it very strange if a newborn baby were removed to a nursery and cared for by nurses.

Attachment is a set of behaviours that allows children to use a parent – or other important care-giver – as a secure base from which they can explore. But again, it is much more significant than this, as it has important implications for how the child grows up to manage relationships, how she copes with difficult situations and how safe she feels to explore and develop.

Attunement – the ability of parents to 'tune' into their baby's communication – is essential in ensuring that the baby is given what she needs. This is another way in which babies learn about emotions and relationships. When care-givers are sensitive to a baby, they make judgements about how the baby is feeling. They then reflect this back to the baby by recognizing what the baby is communicating. In turn, the baby becomes aware that she has communicated to another person what she is feeling. This allows her to learn about the feelings of others, as well as recognizing her own.

Basic trust is developed if a baby's emotional and physical needs are met in a timely and predictable way. Through this, she learns to judge whether a person is trustworthy or not. If a child grows up as someone who cannot trust other people, and views them with suspicion, then she will find it difficult to manage intimate relationships.

For a parent, these processes are all about getting to know your baby, being able to think about what she needs and share what she feels. These are the ways that the relationship between parent and child builds and develops. There are many things that can interfere with this process and one of the most common is postnatal depression. We will discuss later how this may affect the mother–infant relationship.

What if I don't love my baby?

Motherhood has been idealized by our culture. There are huge expectations from society that a mother will have strong positive feelings about her baby, and if this doesn't happen then she can find herself unsupported, isolated, feeling guilty and desperate. Even normal maternal indifference towards a baby is not talked about openly. However, it is a fact that not all mothers experience the expected 'rush of love'; love can grow more slowly. In addition, the loss of freedom and identity that follows the birth of a baby can be difficult to come to terms with.

Some mothers do find it difficult to love their babies. This can be to do with postnatal depression (see p. 77), the baby's difficult temperament, the baby being born prematurely, a disability, a difficult relationship with their own mother, abuse, a difficult relationship with their partner – sadly, not all babies are wanted.

The support and understanding that are provided by the baby's father, family and friends are crucial, and the role of the health visitor important. Sure Start, mentioned earlier, can also provide a place where mothers can talk about their feelings without being judged.

How to manage difficult behaviour

Ann was becoming more and more desperate. Four-year-old Liam just wouldn't do anything she asked. She had tried everything – bribing him, telling him off, and threatening him. She had managed to avoid smacking but was worried she might really lose her temper. The more she threatened and shouted, the worse he got.

Her friend suggested she went along to a parenting group. Ann was not convinced this would help, but she decided to give it a go. Through the group, she realized that she was giving Liam lots of attention when he behaved badly but very little positive attention when he was good. She recognized how all the threats and negative attention were impacting her relationship with her son, which meant that there was little positive interaction.

She learned to play with Liam, giving him positive attention – which he lapped up. She stopped criticizing him, ignoring his bad behaviour instead. Ignoring was hard, but it did seem to work. When he had a really bad outburst she used 'time out', finding that this meant she could stay calm and manage the situation better.

Things weren't perfect, but she felt back in control and able to have fun with Liam again.

As a society we have strong cultural attitudes towards children's behaviour. It is almost as though we start from the assumption that children behave badly. We therefore tend to punish bad behaviour and ignore children when they behave well. We know ourselves that we are more likely to do a good job for our boss when we are praised and appreciated, so why should it be different for children? Children will want to please the adults who are important to them, so children are more likely to behave well in a good relationship. We, as adults, have an important job to do in modelling good behaviour for children – so if children's experience of adult behaviour is that they are rude, fight and swear, then they will copy this. Often our society behaves in one way but expects children to behave in another.

Children – and young people – respond best to praise and positive responses from adults. So how can you get your child to do what you want them to do? A simple rule is to praise good behaviour and ignore bad behaviour. Of course it is not as simple as that. Some bad behaviour cannot be ignored because the child is either putting himself or others at risk, or being very destructive. There are strategies that can be used to manage these situations.

Parenting skills can be taught and there are several parent-management programmes on offer in which parents can take part. Most parenting-skills groups teach how to use positive 'child-centred' behaviours and how to avoid so many 'child-directive' behaviours. Once parents have mastered the positive skills, they are taught to give clear commands and to use 'time out' for bad behaviour. Many parents find that if they use a positive approach with their children, such as giving praise and attention for good behaviour, then they rarely have to use time out or other sanctions. There is also evidence that the strategies that are taught on parenting programmes also enable parents to get on better with their children and so help build a positive relationship.

This chapter does not have the scope to cover all aspects of good parenting skills, but described below are 'child-centred' behaviours and 'child-directive' behaviours. These are important as they give a guide to the sort of parental behaviours that contribute to gaining compliance from a child and to those that will tend to provoke an oppositional response.

Child-centred behaviours

Descriptive commenting is a way of letting a child know that he is being given attention. It is like giving a running commentary on what the child is doing. This is something we all do with small babies but stop when children get older. As well as describing what he is doing, comments on how you think he is feeling are also good. For example, 'I can see you really love playing with your cars. You are very good at making them race together.'

Give praise. Praise is a very powerful reinforcer of behaviour. The trick with small children is to use 'contingent' praise – that is, immediately after the child has done something good. In this way the child comes to understand that the behaviour is related to the praise. Labelling the behaviour is also a good way of doing this. For example, 'Well done for eating your apple. You are a good boy.' Praise should always be given when a child does something they have been asked to do.

Smiles are very important in any human interaction. They reinforce good behaviour and show a child that his behaviour is approved of. Sometimes, however, adults laugh or smile when a child does something naughty because it is funny. This will confuse the child and encourage repetition of what will quickly become unwanted behaviour.

Imitation is another way of demonstrating positive attention.

Positive touches. Children love hugs and cuddles. They are a very good way of confirming that a parent approves of the way the child is behaving. Even better is a hug with a positive statement which labels the behaviour: 'I love it when you tidy your toys away so nicely.'

Ignoring. Parents are often very bad at ignoring, but it is a very powerful parental action because its effect is to extinguish unwanted behaviour, which will disappear if not reinforced. There is very little behaviour that cannot be ignored when dealing with small children. A decision to ignore or not should be made ahead of the behaviour and then stuck to. The important thing is to be consistent and persist with ignoring, even though it is difficult to keep up, especially if the child escalates the behaviour to get attention. The ignoring should be stopped as soon as the child complies. If the behaviour cannot be ignored, then other strategies should be used, such as time out.

Ask to play. In order to encourage children's creativity and to keep them engaged, it is important not to take over their play. Let them take the lead. One simple strategy is to ask them what they would like you to do.

Child-directive behaviours

Commands should be used sparingly. There are good and bad ways of giving commands. A command should be clear. The child's name should be used and once given – and this is the tricky part – it is important to ensure that the child complies, otherwise she will learn that she does not have to comply when a command is issued.

'No' should be avoided if possible. The desired behaviour should be requested instead. So rather than saying, 'No, don't jump on the furniture', it would be better to say, 'I want you to sit down quietly.' It may be helpful to add a consequence: 'If you don't sit quietly then I will switch off the television.'

Teaching is not bad in itself, but too much can spoil a child's enjoyment and creativity, and interfere with positive interaction. Correcting a child all the time can be experienced as criticism.

Questions, if too many are asked, can have the same effect as teaching.

Criticisms lead to negative interaction between parent and child and make it more likely that a child will be uncooperative.

Negative touches. These are usually part of a pattern of coercive behaviours, such as pushing or poking, between parent and child and are inevitably counter-productive. The cooperation of the child is lost and the impact on the parent–child relationship can be damaged. Certainly persistent physical punishment will have a negative impact on the child's emotional development. Patterns of coercive behaviour on the part of both parent and child need to be addressed and professional help may be needed.

The role of discipline

None of the above is to say that discipline is not important, but what is its place?

As children grow they need consistency and predictability. Small children may become very frustrated – we all know about the 'terrible twos'. They wish to have more autonomy, but are too young to make sound judgements about their needs. Parents act as containers – of distress, frustration and anxiety – and guide and manage their children's difficult emotions.

Time out is a useful technique for managing unwanted behaviour. The term is shorthand for 'time out from positive attention'. It is an extreme form of ignoring. The rule of thumb is that it should last for a minute for each year of a child's age. It is important to get good support from someone who knows how to use this technique. A parent-management group will provide support and teach this skill.

Sanctions are a good way of setting clear boundaries for a child. A sanction is when a rule is given – this needs to be communicated clearly in advance – followed up by the consequence if the rule is broken. For example, 'The rule is that you tidy your toys before bedtime. If you do not tidy your toys then you won't be able to play on the computer tomorrow when you come home from school.' It needs to be very specific and followed through. If a sanction is not enforced, the child learns that he can respond by having a tantrum so that the parent will give in.

Temperament

We all recognize that some children are easy and compliant, while others are harder to cope with, even as babies. In the 1970s, two researchers called Stella Chess and Alexander Thomas investigated the significant differences in the behaviour of infants, which they attributed to temperament. Some babies are naturally placid, sleep and feed in a regular fashion and are more adaptable. Others are irritable, less predictable and more wakeful. These behaviours do not appear to persist after one year, but temperament is still an important factor in determining how children behave.

Parental difficulty in meeting the needs of their babies or toddlers

Factors in the baby

- disability
- prematurity
- temperament

Factors in the parents

- mental illness/postnatal depression
- drug and alcohol misuse
- parents' own experience of being parented
- relationship difficulties between the parents
- learning difficulties

Other factors

- difficult birth
- unplanned pregnancy
- other stresses or life events

Postnatal depression

Jenny was over the moon when Sarah was born. David, her husband, was great. He took over the cooking and cleaning, which meant she could concentrate on Sarah. But when David went back to work after two weeks' paternity leave, he began to come home to find Jenny in tears, the baby crying and the house in a mess. Jenny wasn't sleeping and seemed to bc anxious all the time. Their health visitor, Sally, did a questionnaire which showed that Jenny was depressed. Sally arranged to visit on a weekly basis, so Jenny was able to talk about her fears and worries. She realized that she missed her mother, who had died suddenly when she was only twenty. She thought she had got over losing her, but realized that having Sarah brought back her loss. Being able to talk to Sally was a big help. Jenny's mood slowly improved and she found she was able to get back on top of things. She began to enjoy her time with Sarah and being together with Sarah and David as a family.

Mental illness can be the reason behind a parent finding it difficult to look after their child. Parental mental illness can take many forms and can affect children in different ways. When thinking about early childhood, it is important to consider one of the commonest mental health problems – postnatal depression.

The symptoms of postnatal depression usually become evident after the first two weeks following the birth. 'Baby blues' are the weepiness that often occurs in the first few days after birth and are caused by the massive hormonal changes that birth precipitates. They usually resolve after a few days. Postnatal depression is much more persistent and presents with the following symptoms:

- sleep disturbance
- social withdrawal
- anxiety
- excessive guilt
- hopelessness
- impaired concentration
- depressed mood

Women may try to hide their depression because they feel ashamed that they are not happy after the birth of their baby. But the arrival of a new baby creates a great deal of stress and a new mother will need support and understanding if she is experiencing negative emotions.

Because of its impact on both mother and child, it is very important that postnatal depression is identified early and treated quickly. In order to help identification, health visitors use a screening tool known as the Edinburgh Postnatal Depression Scale (EPDS).

How does the mother's depression impact on the baby?

As we have seen, Daniel Stern described the sophisticated communication between mother and baby as a dance. Researchers have investigated the impact of postnatal depression on babies by using the same method as Stern – that is, filming babies and their mothers and looking at the films frame by frame to allow examination of the communication between them. They discovered that in women suffering from postnatal depression the pattern of communication changes, with some mothers understimulating their infants and others overstimulating them. Lynn Morris, in her research, found that babies suffered long-term effects from their mother's depression, which included:

- higher rates of behavioural disorders
- poorer physical health
- a higher rate of insecure attachment
- depressive symptoms
- poorer cognitive performance – particularly boys
- more speech and language difficulties

Another researcher found that three-year-olds whose mothers were depressed had poorer reading skills at the age of eight.

It is therefore important that mothers are treated promptly. If a mother scores highly on the EPDS then she is offered 'listening visits' by her health visitor. This has been shown to be very effective. If the mother's mood does not improve, then it may be necessary to consider other talking therapies or, if necessary, medication.

Modern family life and parenting

There are a number of trends that affect family life in the UK.

- Fewer people are marrying. The number of unmarried adults rose in 2006 and there was a further fall of 4 per cent in the number of weddings.
- Fewer people are divorcing. The divorce rate in 2006 fell for a second consecutive year.
- Nearly a quarter of children (24 per cent) in the UK were living in lone-parent families in 2006 – more than three times the proportion in 1972.
- One third of lone mothers in the UK in 2001 were aged under thirty-five.
- The number of children born outside marriage increased from 8 per cent in 1970 to 41 per cent in 2003.
- The number of stepfamilies is increasing. In 2001, 10 per cent of all families with dependent children in the UK were stepfamilies.
- 17 per cent of men born in 1970 are stepfathers, while 6 per cent of children born in 2001 have no contact with their fathers.
- Births to teenage mothers are particularly likely to take place outside marriage. In 2000 almost 9 in 10 live births to women aged under twenty in England and Wales occurred outside marriage.

Divorce and separation

Parental divorce and separation will undoubtedly have an impact on children's well-being. It is not just an event, but a process that is ongoing for children. Research from the Joseph Rowntree Foundation has found that most children wish their parents had not separated and would like them to get back together. However, the immediate distress that children experience at the time of separation does fade with time.

Divorce and separation are linked to poor outcomes for children, so it is important to consider what factors might improve this, both in the shorter and longer term.

Good communication between parents will help the children to come to terms with what has happened. Having an understanding about why the separation has come about will allay fears that it is 'somehow my fault that Mum/Dad has left'. Talking to them about how contact arrangements will work will reassure them that they will not lose their parent. Other members of the extended family can also be lost when parents separate, so contact arrangements should include grandparents and other family members.

Many of the long-term poor outcomes for children are linked with financial hardship following family breakdown.

Reconstituted families (stepfamilies)

Families do not set out to be stepfamilies, so families that come together in this situation – sometimes known as 'reconstituted families' – do so after loss or family breakdown. Younger children are usually able to adapt more easily to being part of a stepfamily because they have less investment in previous relationships or family configurations. A shared family history helps children know who they are – in other words develop a sense of their identity. A reconstituted family does not have that sense of a shared history – important people may be missing – and so may have to work hard to develop a shared history for the new family.

It may be difficult for step-parents to have the same feelings for their stepchildren as they would for children born to them. They can be left feeling guilty and with unrealistic expectations of how the relationship with their stepchild should be. Sometimes mothers find it hard to allow a new partner to take on the 'dad' role, especially when discipline is an issue. It is helpful if parents can be clear about roles and responsibilities and if they all (parents and step-parents) work together to lessen conflict.

Many stepfamilies manage to function very well. Children can find it very rewarding to have four loving parents and a large extended family that cares for them. There is always someone to go to with a problem who is likely to listen.

Teenage parents

The government has a strategy to tackle the high rates of teenage pregnancy, which is linked to poorer outcomes for children. Children born to teenage mothers have 60 per cent higher rates of infant mortality and are at increased risk of low birth weight. Poor emotional health and well-being are experienced by teenage mothers and they have poorer economic well-being.

The Teenage Pregnancy Strategy's target is to:

- halve the under-eighteen conception rate by 2010, and establish a firm downward trend in the under-sixteen rate
- increase the proportion of teenage parents in education, training or employment to 60 per cent by 2010, to reduce their risk of long-term social exclusion

Working mothers

No one ever talks about 'working fathers'. This reveals the societal attitudes that still exist about mothers who work outside the home.

Many working mothers feel guilty about leaving their child in child-care, although some are lucky enough to have members of their extended family to provide care.

The research about whether or not childcare (as opposed to being cared for by a parent – male or female – at home) damages children is confusing. The age of the child is important, as is the quality of the care. Research suggests that good childcare leads to improved play, sociability, creativity, ability to solve social conflicts, self-control, language and learning.

There is some evidence that very young children who are cared for in day nurseries show an increased tendency to be aggressive towards other children. More recently, research has suggested poorer educational outcomes for children with working mothers. However, research from America suggests that the outcomes are also strongly linked to family and parental characteristics.

Certainly children can also benefit from the improved financial circumstances that a working mother can bring. Poor outcomes for children are associated with poverty and socio-economic deprivation.

What the research means for individual families and children is difficult to assess because there are so many different factors involved. Each family will need to decide what is best for them, but it is likely that mothers will continue to feel guilty while society expects them to be the main care-givers for children. Improved flexible working arrangements and fathers taking more responsibility for sharing in the care will go some way towards making it easier for mothers to feel less guilty about working.

Alternative care

Government policy is that all children deserve to grow up as part of a loving family who can help them flourish during childhood and beyond. The majority of children in this country are safe and secure in a family unit that loves and values them. The adults are committed to them and guide them through childhood to adulthood. But where this is not an option, Children's Social Care may need to step in – and sometimes it is necessary for children to live away from their family. Most of these children, cared for by the state, eventually return home (almost 1 in 3 returns within eight weeks).

For children who cannot go back home quickly, decisions need to be made as soon as possible about where they will live. Sometimes when parents cannot care for their children, they may have made their own arrangements for them to be cared for by other adults – leaving them with extended family members or friends. Otherwise, there are many different ways in which Children's Social Care can provide substitute parenting outside the birth family.

- **Friends and family.** The child may be placed with family or friends. This can be done without an Order if it is a close relative (for example, grandparent, sibling, uncle, aunt) and falls within the definition set out in Section 105 of the Children Act 1989. This may happen if, for example, the birth parents die or if very young parents request that the grandparents raise their child. In such cases, Children's Social Care Services and court orders are generally not required if there are no concerns about the child's welfare and no disputes between the adults. The child's position may be secured by a Residence Order, which is made by the court and gives the substitute parent parental responsibility shared with the birth parent(s).

- **Children's Social Care Services** exist in each local council in the UK, though in slightly different forms in Scotland and Northern Ireland. They provide services to safeguard, care for and support children, young people and their families. The services provided by Children's Social Care adhere to specific legislation which includes the Children Act 1989, the Children Act 2004, and the Department for Children, Schools and Families' *Every Child Matters: Change for Children* agenda. England, Wales, Scotland and Northern Ireland also have their own Children and Young People Commissioners. Their role is to promote the views, interests and rights of children and young people and, with the exception of England's commissioner, to safeguard children's rights. Other countries have similar services though their structures, legislation and child-care practice may differ.

- **'Looked after' children**. Sometimes Children's Social Care Services need to act in the best interests of the child or young person and provide them with care away from their family if there is a safeguarding aspect. This is known as the child being 'looked after'. The child is provided with accommodation, and is usually placed with approved foster carers, though sometimes different forms of residential care are needed. Approved foster carers will have been assessed and trained under statutory fostering regulations. A child may become 'looked after' as a result of a voluntary agreement with the holders of parental responsibility for the child (usually the parents) or, alternatively, under a Care Order made by the family courts. Under a voluntary agreement, those who hold parental responsibility retain it all. With a Care Order, responsibility is shared with the local council in the form of the Children's Social Care Service.

- **Special Guardianship Orders** are made by the court, and allow a child or young person to live permanently with a non-parent, giving parental responsibility to that person. They are intended to provide a permanent nurturing home for children who cannot return to their birth parent(s), but want to maintain links with their birth family. The legislation was introduced with the anticipation that Special Guardianship Orders might be used where foster carers are providing a long-term home to a child, and both they and the child want to secure the child within their family. Special Guardianship gives the foster carers parental responsibility and the Care Order or voluntary agreement to accommodate the child. It ends when the carers are no longer foster carers for the child, but substitute parents. This helps to remove the stigma of 'being in care' and of being 'different'.

- **The difference between Residence Orders and Special Guardianship Orders** is that a Special Guardian does not have to exercise parental responsibility jointly with others who may also hold it. They can exercise parental responsibility to the exclusion of all others who also have it (for example, birth parents), apart from another Special Guardian (for example, if the child is placed with a couple, both adults being Special Guardians). However, the holder of a Residence Order exercises parental responsibility jointly with the other people who have it (for example, birth parents), and decisions, such as choice of secondary school, are made jointly.

- **Special Guardians**, however, do not have total parental responsibility as is the case with adoption. For example, Special Guardians cannot change a child's name or live abroad for more than three months – in such cases, the court would make a decision after considering the different parties' views and wishes, including the child's.

- **Adoption** is a way of providing a new family for children when their own parents cannot raise them. Adoption is a legal procedure with the Order being made by a court. The birth parents lose all their legal ties and parental responsibilities for the child, and these are transferred to the adopters so that the child becomes a full member of the new adoptive family.

- **Adoption Orders** are irrevocable and lifelong, unlike both Residence Orders and Special Guardianship Orders, which can both be varied or discharged by the court. A Special Guardianship Order expires when the young person reaches eighteen. Residence Orders expire at sixteen, but these can be extended to the age of eighteen if it is in the young person's best interests.

- **Private fostering.** This is very different from the care of children provided by local councils when the child is 'looked after' and placed with approved foster carers. It is a private arrangement between the parent and carer, who is known as a private foster carer. It occurs when a child under the age of sixteen (or under eighteen if disabled) is placed by his parents for more than twenty-eight days in the care of an adult who is not the child's guardian, does not hold parental responsibility for the child and is not a close relative (a grandparent, sibling, aunt or uncle).

Private fostering can occur for many reasons, for example when children come from abroad to live with distant relatives or unrelated family friends in order that they may access educational or health facilities, or when children live with family friends after arguments at home. It is estimated that around 10,000 children in England are privately fostered.

Whilst Children's Social Care Services are not involved in making these private arrangements, they do have a responsibility to protect privately fostered children and there are legal rules governing such placements. Private foster carers have to tell their local Children's Social Care Service if they are planning to care for a child through such an arrangement. If they are already caring for a child in a private fostering arrangement, they need to notify the council as soon as they learn about the regulations. The local Children's Social Care Service has a duty to assess the situation and decide whether it is a suitable and safe environment for the child, and then to visit regularly to monitor the child's welfare.

Further details about private fostering can be obtained by contacting your local Children's Social Care Service (details can be found in local libraries, council offices or Citizens Advice Bureaux) or on the website given at the end of the chapter.

When caring for and parenting a child or young person who has been removed from their birth family, for any reason – for example, bereavement, parental illness, neglect or abuse issues – it is important to understand the impact of these events upon the child, how he might be coping with them and his understanding of what has happened. This is no easy task and requires patience, observational skills, stamina, humour and an ability to see events through the eyes of that child. Often children in neglectful and abusive situations will have adapted their behaviour to try to protect and care for themselves. For example, an overly ingratiating child will try to please the adults and will tell tales in order to show themself in a good light. Often such behaviours have developed when there has been volatile, unpredictable parenting and the children have sought to protect themselves by trying to appease their previous parent.

The substitute parenting task therefore involves 'parenting plus', as often you are doing a double task of parenting: helping the child to relinquish and 'unlearn' the now redundant behaviours that were responsive to the abusive/neglectful parenting, and then learn about and trust in more sensitive and appropriate parenting.

Permanency in substitute families

Since the early 1990s there have been several changes in childcare policy and practice which have impacted upon the character of adoption, especially since 2000, with a governmental drive to increase the number of children adopted from within the public care system. The number of relinquished local babies available for adoption has decreased over recent decades as the stigma of single parenthood has declined and public policy has enabled single parenthood. Another development has been the placement of older children from public care and children with special needs, as well as a number of inter-country adoptions. As a result, adoption has become more diverse, although 'stranger' adoption of a baby has never in practice been 'straightforward', as all those involved in the adoption triangle – i.e. birth parent(s), adoptee and adoptive parent(s) – will know.

For example, with inter-country adoption, although children may be placed as infants, the lengthy processes involved, because of the need to protect them and ensure that they are being placed with approved prospective adopters, mean that they may be twelve months old or more by the time they are placed in their new home. These children will have had previous parenting experiences, quite commonly in residential/institutional care or in a type of foster care. Culturally, not only language but also parenting/childrearing practices may be different, and levels of stimulation and possibly personal contact may have been limited in the residential or foster care. All these factors will have had some degree of impact upon the developing infant and will require sensitive, adaptive approaches from the 'new' adoptive parent or foster carer.

Adoption and fostering in the twenty-first century place the needs of the child as paramount, whereas in the earlier decades of the twentieth century – before an understanding of child development and the impact of maltreatment – children and babies were largely seen as blank canvases upon which the early experiences in their formative months had little impact.

These children will all have experienced some form of parenting before being placed with their permanent family. It is often how they have been parented that has caused the concerns for their welfare and impacted upon their development. The adoption of older children from public care, who will typically have experienced abuse, is now a significant part of the UK adoption profile. Child maltreatment frequently results in these children displaying behavioural, emotional and relationship difficulties (see Chapter 9). They also have the added developmental tasks of understanding and integrating their identity – 'Who am I?' As they move from one family to another and as they grow, the need to understand and integrate the reasons for not being able to live within their birth family and their feelings becomes a significant developmental task.

Adoptive parents of children from the care system and foster carers often have the double task of helping the children to 'unlearn' the behaviours which they had developed to cope with their abusive/neglectful/inconsistent/unpredictable first parenting and which are now inappropriate. Then they need to learn to respond to and trust more sensitively attuned and responsive protective parents. This is a difficult task. Parenting by adoption/fostering is in many ways more 'public' than parenting by birth – especially when it involves older children, sibling groups, and those with behavioural and emotional difficulties.

Adoptive parents may have previously undergone years of trying for their own children, often involving medical intervention, and will then have had to undergo the assessment and approval process before eventually being matched with their child. To the uninformed observer, a five-year-old child is expected to behave like any five-year-old who has been raised in a caring, stable home and, if unsettled at first, should settle soon, drawing a line under his past experiences. The possible longer-term impact of abuse and loss is not understood; nor is the fact that the adopters, like any first-time parents of a newborn baby, are still adjusting to the task of parenting – of moving from a unit of one or two to units of two, three, four or even five overnight. They have only a five-minute experience of their five-year-old child – a child who comes up and running with a range of behaviours, likes, dislikes and personality.

Sensitive substitute parenting

For all children, whatever their background, there is no such thing as perfect parenting. Sensitive parenting is about responding to a particular child's specific needs in a way that is effective for that child. In essence, it's warm, firm, with appropriate rules and boundaries, and encouraging.

It is important to try to understand the perception or view of the world that a child has formed through his experiences of maltreatment, neglect or loss of birth family. What the child believes and expects about the world, relationships and parent figures comes from his earlier experiences and attachment relationships. These beliefs and expectations are known as the 'internal working model' and will shape how a child behaves and perceives situations.

'My care-giver/parent was always very angry towards me and I found them frightening. Therefore all care-givers/parents will be like that. Therefore I must always take control of stressful situations myself.'

A better understanding of the child's internal working model will help in the process of building and providing a secure base for the child. It can also help us understand why some strategies are more effective than others in managing that child's behaviour. Sensitive parenting does not mean that the child's inappropriate behaviour should be excused or ignored on the grounds that he doesn't know any different, or because the behaviour has become a learned 'habit'. The child is a social being and needs to be helped to live socially so that he can make friends, adjust to school and to changing social situations. Equally, what may work effectively for one child may awaken negative memories for another – for example, a neglected child being sent to the bedroom.

Explanations have to be given, with consequences where appropriate, for why certain behaviours are not correct, and frequent labelled praise is needed to reinforce newly learned behaviours. It takes time to relinquish previous protective behaviours that worked in earlier parenting settings and to trust that the new parent figures will be different – that they will give attention and care without the child constantly having to whine, shout or tantrum in order to ensure some needs are met. Previous parents might have been physically present but not emotionally or cognitively responsive, possibly on account of a drug or substance abuse. How will a child know you are different if he has had limited positive parenting experiences? How does he learn to trust that you will continue to be responsive? How will he know initially that, when you are ill with a cold and have to rest, it is not about ignoring his needs – as a result of which he might regress to earlier learned behaviours of demanding attention in his insecurity? At such times the foster/adoptive parent, faced by such seemingly insensitive, self-centred behaviour from their child, needs to pause and consider what this behaviour is about and what it is communicating. A tall order when you are perhaps feeling under the weather.

In essence adoptive/foster parents need to be 'psychological detectives' – trying to look through the child's window into his world and trying to think past his behaviour to the meaning behind it.

Interpreting the child's behaviour

Behaviour is communication. Is it:

- a learned response from the past, which was shaped by the child's previous environment?
- a conscious act to test your limits?
- an unconscious code of the child's unmet needs?
- a biochemical/neurological trigger over which the child has no control (e.g. ADHD, autism)?

Behaviour is frequently a coded message. The task is to read the code and attempt to meet the needs that the behaviour is expressing. Ask yourself the following two questions:

At what developmental age would this behaviour be appropriate? Then respond to the child as if he were at that developmental age, but with strategies appropriate to his chronological age (so that he does not feel humiliated). Remember you are filling in the gaps in his social learning about appropriate behaviours, which should have occurred at an earlier age. Clear, careful explanations are needed as to why that behaviour is not correct, does not work or makes the situation worse, and then consider together what might work and why. Sometimes in certain situations the problem-solving needs to occur later, when the child is calmer and the situation safer.

One may think that if an adoptive parent/foster carer acts in this way, then the child will never grow up. But if the adoptive parent/foster carer does *not* act in this way, the child *can* never grow up.

How might the child be perceiving and misperceiving the actions of others – both children and adults? What might the child be feeling? Children from neglectful, abusive backgrounds might not have the ability to recognize, understand and give voice to feelings. Children from normalized, stable, sensitive-parenting families have from birth had their feelings repeatedly identified and reflected back to them – 'What a patient boy waiting for his milk'; 'Oh, that's a sad face – what a pity you've dropped your sweet.'

Such reflective and descriptive commentary can continue whatever the age of the child, helping them identify and learn what certain feelings are and how they feel – for example, 'I can see you have struggled to finish that jigsaw – you seemed angry but stayed calm and worked it out. Well done for managing your angry feelings.'

A stable, safe and predictable environment, coupled with parental responsiveness and sensitivity to the child's physical, intellectual and emotional needs, will work to provide a secure base and healthier relationships. Inappropriate relationships and behaviours have been learned within unhealthy relationships and in turn need to be re-learned and corrected within healthier, containing and caring relationships.

Definitions

Fostering by approved foster carers. Foster carers are adults who have been approved and trained by local authorities' Children's Social Care Services, or by independent or voluntary fostering agencies. The government stipulates statutory assessment criteria and the foster services, whether local authority, voluntary or independent, are all inspected by Ofsted.

Foster carers do not have parental responsibility for the child – this either remains with the birth parent(s) if the child came into voluntary care, or is shared between the birth parent(s) and Children's Social Care as a result of a court having made a Care Order.

Adoption by approved adoptive parent(s). Adopters are adults who have been approved by adoption agencies. Adoptive agencies can be part of the local authority Children's Social Care, a voluntary agency or an independent agency. They are all inspected on a three-yearly basis by Ofsted.

Dr Margaret Bamforth and Dr Clare O'Donnell

INFORMATION

REFERENCES

Chess, S., and Thomas, A., *Temperament in Clinical Practice*, Guilford, NY, 1986.

Department of Education and Skills, *Every Child Matters*, HMSO, 2004. *www.everychildmatters.gov.uk*

Every Child Matters, 'Special Guardianship'. *www.everychildmatters.gov.uk/socialcare/childrenincare/guardianship*

Every Child Matters, 'Teenage Pregnancy Strategy'. *www.everychildmatters.gov.uk/health/teenagepregnancy/about*

Joseph Rowntree Foundation, *Divorce and Separation: the Outcomes for Children*: *www.jrf.org.uk/knowledge/findings/foundations/spr6108.asp*

Klaus, M. H., and Kennell, J. H., *Maternal – Infant Bonding: the Impact of Early Separation or Loss on Family Development*, Mosby, 1976.

Murray, L., 'The Impact of Postnatal Depression on Infant Development', *Journal of Child Psychology and Psychiatry*, 33 (3),1992; 543–61.

Skynner, R., and Cleese, J., *Families and How to Survive Them*, Oxford University Press, 1984.

Stern, D., *The Interpersonal World of the Infant: a View from Psychoanalysis and Developmental Psychology*, Basic Books, 2000.

Stern, D., *The First Relationship: Infant and Mother*, Harvard University Press, 2002.

Sure Start: government programme to deliver the best start in life for every child: *www.surestart.gov.uk*

Winnicott, D. W., *Playing and Reality*, Tavistock Publications, 1982.

Winnicott, D. W., *The Child, the Family and the Outside World (Classics in Child Development)*, (2nd edn), Da Capo Press, 1993.

SUPPORT ORGANIZATIONS

BBC website: *www.bbc.co.uk/parenting*

British Association for Adoption and Fostering: leading UK charity working for children separated from their birth families: *www.baaf.org.uk*

Children's Society: leading children's charity committed to making childhood better for all children in the UK. Tel: 0845 300 1128. *www.childrenssociety.org.uk*

Contact a Family: UK charity for families with disabled children. Helpline: 0808 808 3555. *www.cafamily.org.uk*

Fathers Direct: society that gives all children a strong and positive relationship with their father and any father-figures. Tel: 0845 634 1328. *www.fatherhoodinstitute.org*

Gingerbread: the leading national charity working to help the UK's 1.9 million lone parents and their children. Lone Parent Helpline: 0800 018 5026. *www.oneparentfamilies.org.uk*

National Youth Agency: supports those involved in young people's personal and social development. *www.nya.org.uk*

NCH Action for Children: supports and speaks out for the most vulnerable children and young people in the UK. *www.nch.org.uk*

Parenting UK: the national organization for people who work with parents. Our aim is to promote best practice in all parenting services. Tel: 020 7284 8370. *www.parentinguk.org*

Parentline Plus: national charity that works for, and with, parents. Helpline: 0808 800 2222. *www.parentlineplus.org.uk*

Parents at Work: campaigning charity that helps children, working parents and carers and their employers benefit from a better balance between home and work. Helpline: 0800 013 0313. *www.workingfamilies.org.uk*

WEBSITES OUTSIDE THE UK

Australia

Raising children network – the Australian parenting website: *http://raisingchildren.net.au*

Canada

Canadian Parents – Canada's parenting community: *www.canadianparents.com*

New Zealand

Parent to Parent – Matua ki te Matua: *www.parent2parent.org.nz/start.htm*

5 Parenting Skills in Adolescence

'When I was a boy of fourteen, my father was so ignorant I could hardly stand to have the old man around. But when I got to be twenty-one, I was astonished at how much the old man had learned in seven years.'

Mark Twain

THERE ARE MORE THAN 24 million parents in the UK – grandparents, step-parents, brothers and sisters acting as carers, foster carers, as well as mums and dads. Many of us worry about how we will cope with teenage children, even though most of them are thoughtful and considerate. Recent studies show that most teenagers like their parents – and even get on well with them.

Today there is a great deal of pressure on young people to grow up quickly, possibly too quickly. Parents (in the West, at least) tend to spend less time with their children than in the past. Adolescents spend more time on their own, are more independent, but perhaps don't have the emotional security that their parents had. Economic and cultural pressures encourage parents to spend more time at work and less with their children.

Parenting needs common sense, pragmatism, a sense of humour and, sometimes, good luck. But not all of us are 'naturals' and some of us struggle, particularly with teenagers. Most families get through under their own steam, but some need extra help.

What is adolescence?

Parents often ask, 'Why has my lovely son/daughter turned into this bolshy teenager?'

Adolescence begins when a young person starts puberty – around eleven years of age in girls and thirteen years in boys, although some may not start until their mid-teens. The body, emotions and thinking all change. The physical changes happen fairly quickly, but the changes in thinking and feeling can take years. Psychologically, teenagers are adjusting to their new physical maturity. Socially, they are working out how they fit in with the demands and expectations of others.

The brain goes through huge changes, particularly the frontal lobes, which control our most sophisticated thinking. These changes take years and enable an individual to work out the risk attached to various situations, as well as any possible rewards from them. But early in their teens, adolescents are more often swayed by their new feelings or the need to be accepted by their friends, rather than by a cool weighing up of risk and benefit. The adolescent mind is a work in progress, slowly becoming more self-aware and more in control. Adult guidance and structure are still needed, but less and less as the young person gets older.

Emotional awareness develops. Teenagers may feel guilty about feeling angry, or shame for feeling frightened, although adults will often not notice these emotional overtones. Adolescents are going through this at a time when they will, to some extent, be distancing themselves from their parents – and anybody else who has supported and guided them in childhood.

They start to use moral principles in controlling their emotions and behaviour. Boys see this in terms of having to obey rules. Girls tend to value personal relationships. However, as with adults, just because a young person knows what is morally right or wrong, it does not necessarily mean they will do the right thing.

The sense of identity also develops. In early adolescence (12–18 years), people need to find a group to which they can belong and by which they feel accepted. In late adolescence (19-22 years), people become more interested in developing their own individual identity, separate from the group.

What is normal adolescent behaviour?

Normal Adolescence

Zak is fourteen years old and lives with his mum and younger brother, Charlie, who is eight years old. Zak and his mum have recently started having arguments about the state of his room and how much time he spends with his friends. Zak feels his mum is 'always on my back' and 'treats me like a child'. His mum feels Zak is rude, sulky and defiant. At school, Zak achieves well and he has a good group of friends.

Adolescents' battles to become independent from their families can be upsetting for some parents, but they are normal. If adolescents have a secure relationship with their parents and feel certain that they are loved, they can confidently explore the world from the safe base that is their home. They will usually then stray only so far – in the way that small children will run away, but not too far – from the parents who are doggedly trying to protect them.

That said, independence involves developing thoughts and opinions that may be different from those of the parents – and this can lead to disagreements and arguments. Adolescents will confront or defy their parents at times. This can feel threatening, especially if the young person is now physically bigger than the parent. Adolescents will challenge rules, but they don't usually want to jeopardize their relationship with their parents. They may swing unpredictably from total confidence to the realization that they still need support and reassurance from their parents.

As part of this distancing process, adolescents spend less time with their families and more with friends. It is normal that, even when at home, hours can be spent away from the family and talking to friends on the phone, by text or on the internet.

This developing sense of identity can also involve experimenting with clothes, hair or make-up, piercings or tattoos – trying out different looks before finding one they are comfortable with. Part of this, particularly in girls, can include the desire to lose weight – normal as long as they continue to eat healthily.

Teenagers may also try out how it feels to be part of different social groups. This can make parents anxious, but talking about their new friends can be reassuring.

Adolescents commonly want to experiment and take risks, for example riding a motorbike, drinking alcohol, smoking and taking drugs. This can be difficult for parents and there may come a point at which they need to intervene, as they still need to ensure their child's safety and well-being. Some negotiation may be needed to agree a set of rules that ensures the teenager's safety while not cramping his style too much.

Common topics

A parent must be prepared to talk openly and honestly about anything that young people raise. Hopefully, home is a place where people can talk freely and there are no subjects that are 'off limits'. Research has shown that adolescents who feel able to talk to their parents have, among others, lower rates of teenage pregnancy, depression and drug or alcohol abuse. However, even if a parent wants to talk about something, it is generally wise to let the adolescent raise the topic. One's anxiety as a parent can make us try to force conversations that a teenager does not want to have at that time. If issues can be raised and discussed at the young person's pace, he is less likely to feel that he is being treated 'like a child'.

Sex. This can be an embarrassing topic of conversation. Information and knowledge are important, but not enough on their own to change sexual behaviour. Rather than improving sexual health, sex education can sometimes make it worse. However, teenagers are more likely to delay sex if their parents say that it is important to behave responsibly. It may be reassuring to know that research shows that two thirds of teenagers have still not had sex by the age of sixteen.

Drugs and alcohol. Use is increasing in children and adolescents, so is a common concern. But two thirds of fifteen-year-olds have never tried drugs. Those from secure backgrounds who do experiment will not normally become regular substance users. It is rare too for adolescents to develop problems with gambling. Parents should do some research about alcohol, drugs and gambling so that they can have a sensible and open discussion.

Bullying. About 1 in 20 secondary-school children is bullied. A sudden reluctance to go to school or a decline in grades can be a sign of this. Schools are sometimes not aware of the subtleties of adolescent behaviour and can deny bullying, or even blame the child who is being bullied. If a teenager says this is happening, he should be believed, even if this can sometimes lead to disagreement with the school.

Bereavement. Adolescents start to understand their own mortality and can have a normal fear of death. If older family members die, it is important to talk to them about the death and be honest about sharing feelings. Generally, adolescents should be allowed to attend family funerals. Like adults, they may find the support of extended families and friends comforting at this time, especially if their own grief is acknowledged. Young people's grief may not be obvious but it will be no less genuine or deep.

Separation and divorce. These are often felt by a child as a bereavement. Parents need to tell their children what is happening without going into too much detail. Don't use children as agony aunts or emotional crutches. They will also feel the loss less if they can keep in regular touch with their other parent.

What is not normal adolescent behaviour?

ABNORMAL ADOLESCENCE

Luke is fifteen years old, is an only child and lives with his parents. He has come home drunk a few times in the last six months and once had to be brought home by the police, although no charges were made. Luke's parents have received a couple of phone calls because he has left school without permission. He has been seen walking around town with the same group of boys with whom he goes out drinking. Luke is due to sit his GCSEs shortly and may be stressed about this. His parents have tried talking to him, but he gets angry and storms off.

Major changes, such as the arrival of a new baby, the separation or divorce of parents, a house move or bereavement, may be more difficult to deal with during adolescence. If a young person is struggling to achieve a sense of who she is and where she fits into the world anyway, she may react badly when that world changes radically around her. Behaviour that was already difficult can become more extreme and may move from being normal teenage behaviour to something she needs extra help with.

The general rule is that if behaviour is having a marked, negative impact on the young person or the people around her, it is no longer normal behaviour. Help is needed if:

- the behaviour seems more extreme than that of other teenagers the parent knows
- the undesirable behaviour lasts a long time
- the young person becomes unwell, physically or mentally
- the behaviour presents a risk of harm – or causes actual harm
- the behaviour stops them from going to school or socializing with friends

While adolescents do experiment, most of them take few risks, stay safe and actually grow up in a very similar way to their parents. However, it is not normal if they:

- put themselves or others at risk from regular, unprotected sex
- use alcohol or drugs to a degree that it affects their health or well-being
- regularly miss school without permission
- offend regularly or seriously and so are known to the police

Although a certain level of stress is normal and healthy, it is not right for an adolescent to be under so much stress that she becomes unhappy or unwell. Exam stress is good, but not if it is causing sleeplessness, tearfulness or feelings of low self-esteem.

It is not normal for a young person to become so preoccupied with appearance that it affects her health. Excessive dieting, excessive exercise, making herself vomit, abusing laxatives or wanting cosmetic surgery are all signs that a young person needs help.

Mental health problems in adolescence

As we saw in the chapter on Growing Up (see page 32), about one fifth of adolescents will have mental health problems sufficient to interfere with their normal enjoyment of child and adolescent development. About half (10%) of these will have a formal, clinical psychiatric illness and will need to be seen by a professional. These conditions are covered in greater detail in later chapters.

How do I help my child?

HELPING ADOLESCENTS

Louise is sixteen years old and lives with her parents and her older brother, Connor. Louise has been seeing her boyfriend, who is seventeen, for six months. Her parents have met him and are happy for her to date him, but have strict rules about curfew. Normally a happy and confident girl, Louise has recently become somewhat withdrawn and distracted. When she was helping her mum cook tea, her mum asked if everything was OK. Louise told her mum that she was thinking about sleeping with her boyfriend but was confused and nervous. She and her mum were then able to talk about this.

Young people who get on well with their parents are more likely to develop good social and emotional skills. How people get on with each other is much more important than how much money they have or how educated they are. The same things matter all through a child's growing up – warmth, stability and consistency.

Communication

Family communications run at least three ways – from the child to the parents, from the parents to the child and between the parents. Even if separated, parents need to stay in touch and keep talking.

Adolescents can find so much about their world confusing and need to be able to depend on their parents to be consistent and reliable. So it is particularly unhelpful if one parent keeps secrets or sides with the child against the other parent. Parents need to make sure they are giving the same messages and working together as a team.

Parents should:

- Listen as well as talk. Adolescents have a strong sense of personal privacy. If you try to make your son or daughter talk about something, they will see this as an intrusion and just clam up.
- Involve your children when discussing issues that concern them.
- Be completely honest – teenagers know their parents well and will see through lies (even white lies) very quickly.
- Not interrupt – adolescents may take a while to make their point, so allow them to finish before offering an opinion or advice.
- Watch your language – if you try to 'get alongside' your child by using teenage slang or catchphrases it will sound quite false. In time, a teenager may allow her parent to use certain words!
- Be clear and to the point – comments should be relevant to the discussion. Advice given out of context will often be forgotten or ignored.
- Try not to get upset when discussing behaviour you don't approve of.

- Guidance or rules may need to be set out, but if you are over-critical or judgemental, the message won't get through.
- Own up when you don't have an answer – and then find somewhere (or someone) that does. If you do this with your child it can bring you closer.
- When giving advice, try not to nag – work out how many times you can mention something before you become really irritating.
- Lighten up sometimes – it shouldn't all be serious. Having a laugh together can deepen trust, make it easier to talk about difficult things and help you to spend more time together.

Control – limits and consequences

Setting limits (rules) and deciding on consequences (punishments) are as important during adolescence as they are with younger children. Of course, the limits for adolescents and toddlers are very different. Parents must decide together what is and is not acceptable.

There are some fundamentals – showing respect, being polite and not stealing, for example. But there are also negotiables – curfew, bedtime and levels of responsibility, such as looking after their room and their money.

Families from different backgrounds will have different views on what is right. Boundaries often work best when discussed together, so all the family should decide what is to be expected. This will depend on the age of the individual, as will the consequences if rules are broken. As teenagers mature, they will need fewer and fewer obvious rules.

Parents should:

- Remain calm and in control, even though this can be difficult in the heat of the moment.
- Walk the talk – if you want to be taken seriously, you must practise what you preach.
- Agree sanctions/punishments in advance. These need to be clear, appropriate to the age, and proportionate (a minor

misbehaviour should not attract a major punishment).

- Use sanctions/punishments immediately after any rule-breaking.
- Use sanctions/punishments consistently – they don't work if used only some of the time.
- Not use physical punishments. Young people who are hit at home are more likely to have emotional problems and to be violent themselves.
- Reward good behaviour – this can be more effective than just punishing bad behaviour. Rewards should be agreed upon together – they won't work if they are not something the adolescent wants.
- Talk to other parents about what is acceptable behaviour, or what are appropriate consequences. Young people will certainly know what other teenagers are allowed to do and will try to use this information when negotiating. Parents can only make sense of this if they know what other parents are doing.

Handling anger

Try to:

- talk about the issue as soon as possible
- stay calm and don't over-react
- talk quietly and non-confrontationally – it is hard for an adolescent to be the only angry person in a room
- pick your battles, letting small issues pass by to save energy for the really important ones
- be prepared to walk away and talk later – but explain why you are doing this

Staying friends with your child

The keys are to:

- Be there – if you are not available to your children, you cannot expect to have a productive relationship with them.

- Show affection – tell them that you love them, give them a hug (although perhaps not in front of their friends!).
- Respect their views. Listen to them and acknowledge their views, even if you disagree strongly with them.
- Respect their space – for example, make sure that you knock on the bedroom door.
- Know that you can't do everything. It is important for adolescents to have role models as they grow. If they have no same-sex parent, adolescents may seek out a teacher or a member of their extended family.
- Balance carefully the need to protect and teach them with the need to let them find their own way in the world. Adolescents can then experiment and take safe risks knowing they can return for guidance and support.
- Be prepared for your teenager sometimes to behave in a very mature way, sometimes in a more childlike way. If they need a bit more looking after, for example when feeling ill, nervous or upset, they can become sulky as they struggle to ask for the help they need.

What if this is not enough?

Even if communication is good, sensible limits are set, punishments are consistent and respect is shown, life is never perfect. Some teenagers have such serious problems – such as aggression and violence – that help is needed. A visit to the GP can provide advice to start with, and then referral on to Child and Adolescent Mental Health Services (CAMHS) if further help is needed.

Parenting programmes

Parenting programmes are available, such as the American Strengthening Families Program. This involves attending sessions, both separately and as families, and working on a range of topics. Young people who have attended the programme have proved to have lower rates of substance abuse and fewer problems in school. Parents who attended were better at skills like setting limits, and had a more positive relationship with their child.

Parenting and the law

'Parental responsibility' has been a legal term in England and Wales since 2003, in Scotland since 2006 and in Northern Ireland since 2002. It applies to all parents named on the child's birth certificate, unless the child is adopted or under the care of the local authority. It describes the rights, duties, powers, responsibilities and authority that most parents have in respect of their children. For example, it includes the responsibility to provide a home for the child, to provide education, the duty of protecting the child and the right to give consent to medical treatment and to choose a child's religion.

Reassurance and hope

Parenting adolescents can be difficult and challenging at times – but young people are resilient, and it is OK not to know all the answers all the time. It is also OK to admit that you do not know. Adolescents will have more respect for parents who are honest than for those who pretend they know everything. This kind of honesty can also help to foster a more genuine, sharing adult relationship for the future when the parent/child boundaries are less defined.

Although adolescence can be difficult at times, it is satisfying to see your children move on to the next stage of their lives – as mature and confident young adults.

Dr Zoe Gilder and Dr Paul McArdle

SUPPORT ORGANIZATIONS

Parentline Plus: national charity that works for, and with, parents. Helpline: 0808 800 2222. *www.parentline.org.uk*

Raising kids: offers support, information and friendship to everyone who is raising children, whatever their circumstances or income. Tel: 020 8222 3923. *www.raisingkids.co.uk*

Trust for the Study of Adolescence: registered UK charity and applied research and training organization. Produces and sells materials, books and audiotapes for parents of teenagers. Tel: 01273 693311. *www.tsa.uk.com*

Young Minds: national charity committed to improving the mental health and emotional well-being of all children and young people. Tel: 0808 802 5544 (parents' information service) or 0207 336 8445 (general). *www.youngminds.org.uk*

Talk to Frank: free, confidential drugs information and advice for young people and parents. Helpline: 0800 776600. *www.talktofrank.com*

PADA (Parents Against Drug Abuse): national organization that delivers support and services to the families of substance users across the country. Helpline: 0845 702 3867. *www.pada.org.uk*

beat: formerly the Eating Disorders Association, a charity that provides information, advice and support around eating disorders. Helpline: 08456 341414. *www.b-eat.co.uk*

ParentsCentre: information and support for parents on how to help with a child's learning, including advice on choosing a school and finding childcare. *www.parentscentre.gov.uk*

WEBSITES OUTSIDE THE UK

Australia

Parent Link: *www.parentlink.act.gov.au/index*

Canada

Troubled Teens Behaviors: helping families deal with teen, adolescent and child problem behavior. *www.balmoralfarm.ns.ca*

New Zealand
New Zealand Ministry of Health – Manatū Hauora:
www.moh.govt.nz/moh.nsf

FURTHER READING

Surviving Adolescence – a toolkit for parents, Royal College of Psychiatrists' factsheet from the *Mental Health and Growing Up* series, *www.rcpsych.ac.uk, 2004.*

Part Three

School

6 Choosing a School and Problems at School

For many children, school is their first real encounter with the outside world. At school a child has to perform in a way that he has never had to at home, to separate from parents, meet social and academic challenges, and make friends. For the majority of children and young people school is a positive experience, although there may be stressors from time to time.

Choosing a school

The first challenge for many parents is choosing a school. It may be a relatively simple decision, or there may be several schools nearby, with varying reputations. The one you prefer may be oversubscribed. When choosing a school it can help to remember that most children and young people are resilient and will settle into their new environment easily. Also, although the quality of the education offered is important, the most crucial factor in determining how well a child does academically is the level of support from their family. There may not be an ideal school that ticks all the right boxes, so choosing one may involve a series of 'informed' trade-offs.

The quality of leadership by staff in a school and the range of children it takes are probably the most important factors that determine academic performance.

How to apply for a school place or enrol your child

England and Wales

First and most important, you need to apply to the schools of your choice by the closing date for applications. Even if your child's nursery or primary school is linked to the school you want him to go to, he won't be considered for a place unless you apply.

Local authorities coordinate the admissions process for all types of state school in England and Wales. You can obtain a copy of your local authority's application form either online or on paper direct from the local authority.

For state primary schools in England you will be asked to put down one or two choices. For state secondary schools in England you can apply to up to three different schools. There is a strict deadline for submission of the application form and not getting it in on time may jeopardize your child's chance of getting a place at your preferred school.

For primary schools the deadline for applications is usually the autumn term a year before the child is due to start school. That means applying when your child is three or four years old. For secondary schools it is the November or December before your child is due to change schools, when your child is in Year 6. So you need to start planning well in advance.

Scotland

Scottish councils are divided into school catchment areas and children living in a particular catchment area usually go to that school (i.e. the council designates a particular school). Children have to start school by the August after their fifth birthday or, if their birthday falls between August and February of the following year, they can start school before the age of five. Parents may request that their child starts school earlier by contacting the education authority, although this is unusual. Children transfer to secondary school the year they reach twelve.

Parents do not need to apply for a place at the designated primary school, although they do need to enrol their child several months in advance. A similar system of catchment-area or designated schools operates at secondary school, although the procedures for enrolment can vary from one council to another. It is best to find out from either the school or the council directly, well in advance.

Although most children and young people attend their local catchment-area school, parents and young people can choose a different school by making a placing request to the local council. If there is a place in the school they have requested, the council is obliged to offer this. However, it does not have to expand the school to offer extra places if it is full.

Northern Ireland

In Northern Ireland the first year of compulsory schooling is the year after the child's fourth birthday, with the child's age on 1 July being the date that determines school entry. There is a need to enrol children in primary school, although virtually all children are given a place in the first-choice school because most schools are undersubscribed. Details of the enrolment procedures can be obtained from the relevant Education and Library Board, although these five area Boards are to be amalgamated into a single Education and Skills Authority with effect from January 2010.

Northern Ireland no longer operates an 11-plus exam system (the Transfer Procedure Test). Post-primary transfer in September 2010 will operate on the basis of Transfer 2010 guidance produced by the Department of Education, which recommends the use of non-academic admissions criteria. However, a number of grammar schools are intending to operate independently-administered entrance tests, details of which can be obtained from individual schools.

Independent schools

Independent schools (i.e. those not funded or maintained by the state) operate their own admissions procedures. Details can be obtained direct from the school. As with state schools, it is wise to do this well in advance. In some areas this can mean applying eighteen months or more before your child would be due to start.

How to choose a school

Filling in the application form is often the easiest part. Deciding which schools to choose can be much harder.

From September 2008 all local authorities in England and Wales will provide Choice Advisers whose job is to provide independent advice to parents, particularly those who for whatever reason might find the transfer process from primary to secondary school difficult. However, many parents will still want to do their own research. Advisors can only advise; the final decision is still yours as a parent.

Choosing involves thinking about what kind of school would best suit your child and family circumstances, as well as finding out about the schools themselves. While it is not often possible for children to be meaningfully involved in choosing a primary school, it is usually a good idea to involve older children in deciding which secondary school they attend.

If, as is the case for most parents, you intend to send your child to a state school, the local authority is the best place to start. They can provide you with a list of schools in your area.

If you opt for an independent school you can find out about those in your area, but unlike state schools there is no coordinating body equivalent to the local authority. The Independent Schools Council has a useful website and has recently developed a school search facility which is accessible via their website: www.isc.co.uk.

Each year, local authorities in England and Wales produce a

prospectus booklet, usually known as the *Information for Parents* booklet, which has details on a number of important areas, including :

- the application process and deadlines
- the number of pupils in each school
- how places will be allocated if the school is oversubscribed (the admissions criteria)

These booklets can be obtained free of charge from your local authority or via your local library. In Scotland and Northern Ireland, you should contact the local authority for details of schools in your area.

Once you have identified possible schools, you can begin to do your research.

In England and Wales each year the Department for Children, Schools and Families (DCSF) publishes information on the attainments of pupils in each state school. These so-called 'league tables' provide some indication of how well a school is performing. The league tables tend to reflect the mix of pupils entering the school rather than just the quality of teaching.

Four such tables are published each year:

- Key Stage 2 tables (the results of the Key Stage 2 tests that all children in state primary schools sit at age 10–11)
- Key Stage 3 tables (the results of the tests in English, Maths and Science that all children sit at age 12–13).
- Key Stage 4 tables (the school's GCSE results or equivalent)
- Post-16 tables (the school's or college's results for general and vocational AS- and A-levels, as well as a variety of other qualifications)

For primary schools, look at the Key Stage 2 tables. Francis Gilbert, author of *The New School Rules*, recommends looking carefully at the results for English and Maths, and especially at whether a primary school is scoring below 50 per cent at Level 4 in English, as this could mean that a critical mass of pupils is struggling with literacy. For secondary schools, parents will want to look at the percentage of pupils obtaining grades A*–C in English and Maths, and again less than 50 per cent may be cause for concern. It is also worth looking at the percentage of pupils gaining five or more A*–C passes at GCSE – you can compare this to the national average as well as to the results for other schools in your area.

In England and Wales, the school's Ofsted report is a more detailed and a more useful indicator of what the school is actually like than the league tables. Ofsted inspects all state schools every three years and gathers a wide range of evidence, including observation of lessons, input from parents, discussions with pupils and staff, as well as examples of pupils' work and performance data. The report comments on a wide range of areas and outlines what the school could do to improve. Schools are expected to act on these recommendations and many publish their plan in their annual report. Ofsted reports are available online on www.ofsted.gov.uk.

In Northern Ireland, school attainments and inspections are published for individual schools. Parents can discuss their choice of secondary school with the primary-school principal.

The system for monitoring school performance, including school inspections, in Scotland is also under review.

Independent schools that are registered with the Independent Schools Council (ISC) are inspected by the Independent Schools Inspectorate every six years. These inspections are similar to Ofsted inspections and reports are available either from the school itself or direct from the ISC.

As well as reading about the school, it is also a good idea to see it for yourself. Some schools have set open days when the parents of potential pupils, and the children themselves, can visit. Others will organize individual visits if parents request these. It's a good idea to decide in advance what it is you want to learn from the visit. Many adults, having been out of school for years, are unfamiliar with the current education system. It is surprisingly easy to feel like a child again when you are suddenly faced with a headteacher!

On the school visit use your eyes and ears.

- Is the school welcoming?
- Do staff and pupils seem happy?
- Are you encouraged to see the whole school?
- Check the library. Is it well used and does it have a wide range of books?
- Check the walls and noticeboards. Is pupils' work on display? Does the work on display appear to be recent? Does it appear to reflect a range of ability, or is it more of a showpiece of more outstanding work?
- Check the classrooms. Are children busy? Is there a hum of activity or just noise?
- What are the sports and IT facilities like?
- What is the school's policy on bullying?
- What is the behaviour code/policy?
- What is the staff turnover?
- What is the homework policy?
- What pastoral care is available?
- How can parents become involved in their child's education?
- What after-school clubs or extra-curricular activities are available?
- Check the school gate and the playground.

This isn't a comprehensive list and there may be other things that you would add that are important for you and your child.

Having done your research you should be ready to draw up a short-list. When doing this you need to take into account the admission criteria. There is little point choosing a school if your child does not fit the admission criteria, although these can be subject to challenge.

It is important to remember that the school with the best academic reputation may not be the best one for your child. For example, if your child is shy and finds it difficult to make friends, he may be better off going to the same school as most of his friends, even if this doesn't have the best reputation academically. You may need to take into account family circumstances – for example, if you are separated and your child spends time with both of you, you may need to choose a school that is geographically between you. Increasingly, schools are also offering extended services such as pre- and after-school clubs/childcare; again, this may influence the choice you make.

Making the best decision for your child can sometimes mean making compromises and – particularly for secondary schools when a compromise solution is needed – it is important to involve your child in the decision if possible.

Starting primary school

When they start school, most children have already had some experience of a pre-school or nursery setting. Although they are very young, it is important to remember that they may have already faced and survived some big challenges: the first time someone else looked after them or the first time they stayed at nursery, for example. But whatever their previous experience, starting school is a big event.

For many children, school hours bring a new routine to their day. Some will be away from home for longer than they are used to. Children who have had a close relationship with a childminder or nanny whom they now no longer see may take time to adjust to the separation. They may also have to get used to such things as different mealtimes and new expectations about table manners, asking to go to the toilet and dressing independently.

It is normal for children's behaviour to regress a little when they start school. They may become more babyish or demanding at home.

Most children will need a little more of your attention at this time and it is important to help them feel secure.

There are things you can do to help your child settle in to school. Whenever possible, try to visit the school with your child before his first day. Try to arrange to show him around his new classroom and meet his teacher. Show him the toilets, playground and hall and where he can leave his things. Find out about the daily routine from the teacher and let your child know what to expect.

- Ask the teacher how she settles the children and how she deals with misbehaviour.
- If anyone else your child knows is also starting at the school, try to arrange for them to play together before they start.
- Anticipate things your child might find difficult – such as tying laces – and either practise these or find an alternative solution (Velcro shoes are good!).
- If the school has an evening for new parents, go along and take note of all the items your child will need on his first day.
- Talk to your child about starting school. Read him stories or watch children's TV programmes about starting school; play at being at school.
- Tell your child positive stories about your own experiences of school. You could let him know that most children feel a bit worried or shy at first but it soon passes.
- About a week or so before school starts, begin to introduce a term-time routine, moving your child's bedtime to one suitable for school nights and introducing more regular eating habits with meals at set times.
- Involve your child in getting ready for his first day. The evening before term starts, you and your child can get ready for school together.

- Remember that your child will pick up on your feelings, so if you approach his first day with confidence there is a better chance that he'll be fine.
- The first few times you say goodbye at school may be very emotional for you. But try to send your child off with a smile. Remind him that you'll be there to collect him later. Children may be upset at being left, but it is important to remember that most adapt very quickly – even those who appear very distressed – and that Reception-class teachers are very used to helping children settle in.
- If you are worried about your child settling in, talk to the class teacher about it. Teachers can often reassure you and help you think how to help your child get used to being left at school.
- Make sure you're a little early to collect your child at the end of the first few days – even a few minutes late can seem like for ever to a waiting child. You will want to know how he has been, but young children don't tend to respond to questions such as 'How was school?' Most will talk in their own time, so avoid pressing them but give them the opportunity to talk. Children are often tired and hungry at the end of the school day, so a snack and some quiet time are often what they need.

Starting secondary school

Secondary school marks quite a change in most children's experience of school. They move from a close connection with one teacher all year to more impersonal relationships with a larger number of subject teachers. Instead of lessons being brought to them, they have to organize themselves to get to the right place, with the right equipment, at the right time. Having been the most mature and high-status pupils in their primary school, they suddenly find themselves being the 'babies' in a much larger system. There may be an increased focus upon grades and

performance, and more homework. Although all this can sound quite daunting, it is important to remember that for most children this change occurs at a time when developmentally they are ready to start making more decisions and to be more independent. Although it can be initially unsettling (for parents as well as for children), most children manage the transition well, even if they are a little anxious at the start.

There are things you can do to ease the transition.

- Visiting the school before your child is due to start is helpful. Secondary schools have open days for Year 6 pupils as well as for parents. Finding out about the rules and routines of the new school is crucial; very often it's the small things – such as knowing whether you are allowed to go to the toilet during lessons, or where you can leave your things – that make the difference. Your child may be able to help construct a list of 'things they want to know'.

- Parents often feel uncertain about how to relate to secondary schools. It's a good idea to ask the head of year or form tutor about how best to do this.

- It is important to have an idea of what is expected of your child academically – this doesn't mean a detailed knowledge of the subjects he will be taught, but more an idea of the range of subjects and what is required in terms of homework. Try to make sure he has a quiet place to study and work out a homework routine with him. It's important to let your child develop his own routine, so don't interfere too much in the beginning unless you can see he is struggling or the work isn't getting done.
- If your child is going to a different school to his friends, you could let the form tutor know about this in advance so that, for example, in assigning seating positions in class, she can ensure your child has someone to sit next to. You could also find out who else is going to the school, maybe by approaching other parents at the open days, and try to set up an introduction for your child.
- Make sure he understands road-safety issues, how to contact you, how to use school transport. You can practise these things in advance.
- Talk to your child about what to expect. Try to be positive about the change, but at the same time let him know that it is normal to be a bit worried. You can use stories about yourself, or other people he knows, or his favourite characters, starting school.
- In the first few weeks try to make sure a parent is there in the morning to see him off and in the evenings when he comes home. Make yourself available to talk. You know your own child and can work out whether you should prompt him to tell you about school or whether it is best to wait for him to talk.

It can be tiring in the beginning. Some children revert to more babyish or immature behaviour at home; you shouldn't worry too much about this – it is usually only temporary.

Childcare

Childcare may become less of a problem once children start school, but for many parents there is still a need for some childcare to bridge the gap between school and work, and to cover school holidays. You may decide to use family or friends, or to continue with the childcare you used previously, sticking with the same childminder or nanny. There are, however, additional resources now that your child has started school.

After-school clubs are places for children to go after the school day has finished, usually from around 3.30 to 6 p.m. The club may be in your child's school, in another local school, or in different premises altogether. Children can engage in fun, relaxing activities supervised by playworkers. Sometimes playworkers will escort children from the school to the club.

The advantages of an after-school club are that, if they operate for more than two hours a day and take under-eights, they will be registered. Even if they are not registered, they may be quality-assured. Your child will be guaranteed a place if he goes to the attached school and you can opt for part-time places. Some children, however, prefer to relax in a quieter, less busy environment or to see their own friends after school.

Breakfast clubs are places where children can be dropped off before school and enjoy breakfast together. They can be in a school dining area, school hall, community centre or a classroom.

Holiday playschemes operate in the school holidays and offer groups of children a range of organized activities, from art and crafts to outings. They are usually open between 8.30 a.m. and 6 p.m. Some larger employers run holiday playschemes for employees' children.

Learning problems

Every parent wants to know that their child is happy and doing well at school. Unfortunately, sometimes things don't go so smoothly and this section addresses common problems children may experience at school.

Occasionally children may struggle with schoolwork. A child who 'finds learning significantly more difficult than most children of the same age' is said to have learning difficulties. Some problems are confined to particular areas of learning, such as reading, spelling and writing (these include dyslexia and dyspraxia), or numeracy (dyscalculia) – so-called specific learning difficulties (see pp. 144, 145 and 146). In other cases children may have more wide-ranging learning difficulties, with problems in most areas, which if severe enough are referred to as global learning disabilities.

In addition, a child's education may be affected by a range of factors, such as:

- a physical disability
- a problem with sight, hearing or speech
- a long-term medical problem
- social, emotional or behavioural problems
- mental health problems
- being particularly gifted
- having English as an additional language (though this in itself may not constitute a Special Educational Need)

Some potential learning problems will have been identified by you or your child's health visitor, GP or paediatrician before starting school. These could include delays in motor milestones, speech and language delay, a general learning disability, and neurodevelopmental disorders such as autism, or attention deficit hyperactivity disorder (ADHD). Others may become apparent only after starting school. Up to 2 children out of 10 will have learning difficulties at some time during their education. (See Chapters 7 and 11.)

Special Educational Needs (SEN) is a legal term used to describe a learning difficulty that calls for special educational provision to be made for that child (Special Educational Needs Code of Practice, 2001, England and Wales). Similar laws apply in Scotland, Northern Ireland and the Republic of Ireland, although the terminology may be different. The code aims to guide the identification, assessment and provision for Special Educational Needs at the earliest opportunity.

Relation of learning difficulties to mental health

A child who is doing badly at school compared to his classmates may develop a low opinion of himself, have behavioural problems, or have difficulty concentrating and find classes 'boring'. In addition to being a potential cause of emotional and behavioural problems in children, learning difficulties often co-occur with behavioural problems and disorders such as ADHD, or autistic spectrum disorders.

Sometimes a child's behaviour will present a more obvious problem at school than learning difficulties, so it is important to consider various underlying causes of difficult behaviour and treat them accordingly.

What can you do if you are concerned?

If you have a child below school age who you feel has a learning difficulty, speak to your doctor or health visitor. They will be able to arrange specialist assessment if necessary.

If your child is of school age, the first step would be to arrange a meeting with his teacher or year tutor to discuss your concerns. It is often helpful to make a note of your worries in writing prior to the meeting. You may wish to involve the Special Educational Needs Coordinator (SENCO) – Special Educational Needs Organiser (SENDO) in Ireland – at this stage. You could also request your child's school records from the headteacher to check on progress.

You will need to know whether the school think that your child has any difficulty and ask them to explain his Key Stage tests (SATs), or other national tests, results. If your child's scores are below average for the level expected for his age, or are not improving with subsequent testing, this may mean that he has a learning difficulty. Find out whether he has had any further assessment, been set any targets or is already getting extra help.

What help could be offered?

If there are concerns, the school may offer extra help through 'differentiation', which means using different ways of teaching to suit your child's learning style and pace. If this is not enough, then they can offer help through the model recommended in the code of practice called School Action or School Action Plus (Early Years Action and Early Years Action Plus in pre-school). The school will draw in information on your child's needs and consult you and your child regarding what help is to be offered. A written document called an Individual Education Plan (IEP) will be drawn up, outlining specific targets, the type of help that will be offered and a specific review date. School Action Plus involves additional assessment by external specialists, such as specialist teachers, an educational psychologist or a health professional, which is used to make recommendations for the IEP.

If the school still has significant concerns about your child's learning despite these measures, they can ask the local educational authority (LEA) to carry out a statutory assessment of Special Educational Needs, which takes several months. You can request that this assessment be done even if your child's school do not agree, though it will be up to the LEA to decide whether to carry out an assessment. If the assessment shows that your child needs more or different help to what is offered on School Action Plus, then they will be given a Statement of Special Educational Needs (SEN), which is a legal document outlining what support will be available and which school your child should attend. Your views will be taken into account.

Special schools

Most children who have a learning difficulty attend mainstream school and today there is an emphasis on integrating children with learning problems into mainstream education. This can mean providing extra support, a modified curriculum, or sometimes children may attend some lessons in a special unit within the school. Some children – particularly those who have a global learning disability or complex physical or sensory impairments – may be better catered for in a special school. Children who have severe emotional and behavioural problems may attend a special school for children with such difficulties – Emotional and Behavioural Difficulties (EBD) schools – or pupil referral units (PRUs).

The laws on Special Educational Needs provision are broadly similar between England, Wales, Northern Ireland and the Republic of Ireland. However, Scotland uses different terminology (Additional Support Needs rather than Special Educational Needs, and the Coordinated Support Plan (CSP) instead of Statement of SEN). Please see the resource section at the end of the chapter for links to the relevant documents.

Problems with school attendance

School refusal

A child who does not go to school due to fears or worries is said to have 'school refusal', also known as 'school phobia'. School refusal often occurs at school transition times (ages five, ten or eleven, and sometimes at thirteen or fourteen) and may start after a break from school, such as after an illness or when returning from a holiday. The child may complain of physical symptoms such as stomach aches or headaches (for which no underlying physical cause is found) as school approaches, but be free of symptoms at other times. When attending school is insisted on, he may become more clingy, show signs of anxiety or have tantrums.

School refusal may be triggered by problems in school, such as bullying, difficulty in making friends, problems with a teacher or learning difficulties. Alternatively, the child may fear being separated from his parents or worry about a parent's health. School refusal is associated with other anxiety disorders such as separation anxiety, and in teenagers may be associated with agoraphobia, social phobia and depression (see Chapter 10).

If your child is showing signs of school refusal, you can help by listening carefully to his worries about school or home and considering yourself any factors at home or school that may be contributing to his difficulties. If he has physical symptoms, your GP can help to reassure you and your child by excluding any underlying physical cause.

Help is aimed at getting your child back in school as soon as possible. He will find it more difficult to face it the longer he avoids it. It is crucial that you work in partnership with the school in setting goals for his return. You may need to take small steps to get your child gradually used to the school environment. This may include accompanying him to school initially to ensure that he goes. An Educational Welfare Officer or Home–School Liaison Officer may be able to help. Child and Adolescent Mental Health Services can help by assessing and treating depression and anxiety, and by supporting parents in their effort to keep consistent boundaries during treatment, when a child may have increased levels of distress. For some older children who have been out of school for a long time, there may be alternative 'halfway' educational provision, such as a pupil referral unit. Home tuition is an option for young people where other measures have not been successful, though this can have the disadvantages of lack of opportunities to socialize with peers and a limited curriculum.

Truancy

Children who truant are not normally scared to go to school and may skip all or part of school, often without their parents' knowledge. Truancy is associated with antisocial behaviours such as breaking the law, lying or stealing. Such children may have learning difficulties and not see the point of attending school, or they may have problems at home. Some parents allow their children to stay at home to avoid them wandering the streets. Others believe that school is harmful to their children.

Children who repeatedly miss school risk learning setbacks and lose out on future opportunities. If the problem is tackled early, it may be more easily solved. As a parent, you are legally obliged to ensure that your child attends school regularly. First, listen to your child to try to understand how he sees the problem. Then discuss it with the school, an Educational Welfare Officer or a Parent Partnership Officer and agree a plan to work together on ensuring improved attendance. Parent Support Advisers (PSAs) can sometimes offer support to parents in this situation.

Exam stress

Exams can be a stressful experience for young people and their families. Here are some ways that you can help your child.

- Find out in advance exactly what is expected of pupils, when the exams are and what coursework needs to be handed in. Your child's school may have recommended specific revision techniques or courses.
- Early on, help him get into a routine of doing homework at a set time, such as before dinner, so that he can continue this when planning and doing revision.
- Reduce distraction by finding your child a quiet place to work. Help him devise a revision timetable and encourage him to work on the subjects that he finds difficult.
- During revision, encourage your child to take breaks and to eat regularly. Offer healthy snacks and remind him to drink enough fluids, but limit caffeine-containing drinks like cola, energy drinks or coffee. Some young people prefer to study at night, though this should not be at the expense of sleep, which

risks impairing performance on the day. Exercise can help to maintain a calm and alert mind. Try not to nag or criticize. Instead, be positive and encouraging.

- Failure at exams can feel devastating for a young person, so reassure your child that there will be more opportunities in the future and he can only do his best. Plan a reward for him for after he has handed in a big piece of coursework or sat an exam, however he feels it went.

Bullying

Bullying, defined as the use of aggression with the intention of hurting another person, is, sadly, a common occurrence in both primary and secondary schools. Bullying can be physical, such as hitting, pushing or blocking a child's way; verbal, such as name-calling or threats; or emotional, such as excluding a child, 'sending them to Coventry' or spreading rumours.

Bullies target those who appear different or vulnerable and will use these differences as a means to exert power and control over another person. Children may be vulnerable as a result of difficulties at home, such as parents separating, bereavement or domestic violence, which may mean either they behave differently or they are less able to deal with bullying when it occurs. Children with physical or learning difficulties may be targeted more frequently.

Though bullying commonly takes place in the playground, class-room or changing room, with increasing use of technology it can also occur via mobile-phone calls and text messages, or over the internet (see 'Cyberbullying' below).

Bullying is a miserable experience for the child or young person concerned and is an important contributing factor to mental health problems in young people, particularly depression, self-harm and suicidal threats or attempts (see Chapter 18).

A child or young person who is being bullied may find it hard to tell you or her teacher for fear that it will make the bullying worse; out of embarrassment or fear that she will be told off; or in the belief that the bullying is her fault or that she won't be believed. It is therefore important to recognize possible signs of bullying and ask your child directly.

Signs of bullying include:

- school refusal or truancy
- fall in performance of schoolwork
- upset after using the internet or receiving mobile-phone calls or text messages (cyberbullying)
- unexplained cuts, scratches or bruises
- repeated 'loss' of dinner money or possessions, or torn clothes
- aggression towards siblings
- signs of anxiety and depression, including difficulty sleeping, bad dreams, loss of appetite
- self-harm or suicide threats
- other emotional or behavioural changes

What you can do about bullying

If you are worried that your child is being bullied, you could ask her directly. Alternatively, if you are unsure, the following questions may be helpful.

- What did you do at school/at lunchtime today?
- Is there anyone at school that you don't like and why?
- Are you looking forward to going to school tomorrow?
- Is there anyone that you would like to invite home?

Above all, listen carefully to your child. Reassure her that you believe her, that she is doing the right thing in confiding in you and that you will work with her teachers to stop the bullying.

Some children will insist that you do not talk to the school and that they will sort out the problem themselves, sometimes through fear that the bullying will get worse. However, you cannot promise that you will keep the bullying a secret. In some instances, you will need to speak to your child's school against her wishes in order to put a stop to the bullying.

Keep a written record of all incidents. It is worth finding out the school's approach to bullying. By law, all UK state schools must have an anti-bullying policy or programme, although approaches may vary considerably. UK anti-bullying charity Kidscape recommends a whole school 'telling' approach which puts emphasis on everyone at the school, particularly bystanders or 'accessories' to bullying, taking responsibility and reporting bullying. This can be accompanied by raising awareness of bullying in pupils' own projects and in the Personal Social Health Education and Citizenship (PSHE) curriculum. Other approaches include training older pupils as peer mentors to support victims of bullying, and a 'no-blame approach', through which a teacher leads a group, including the bully and the victim, to discuss the bullying and its effect on the victim. There should be sanctions for the bullies, as well as help for them to change their behaviour and receive support, as children who bully also have an increased risk of mental health problems.

Your school may be able to offer help from the school counsellor or doctor. They or your GP can make a referral to your local Child and Adolescent Mental Health Services if your child has become depressed, is self-harming or expresses suicidal threats or behaviour, or has school refusal.

Cyberbullying

Cyberbullying involves use of technology, commonly the internet and mobile phones, in bullying. This may take the form of sending unpleasant text messages, video-messaging, posting private photos on websites, or writing unkind comments about someone – sometimes by using someone else's name or account on social networking sites. Cyberbullying presents new challenges because of the difficulty of controlling the spread of harmful messages and images, the wide audience involved, and also the distance between bully and victim, which can reduce the sense of responsibility and empathy towards the victim. What starts out as a joke easily gets out of hand and the bully may not be aware of the consequences of his or her actions. Bystanders or 'accessories' to bullies are particularly common in this form of bullying, further adding to the initial problem by commenting on and forwarding messages and images.

What can you do to help?

Become familiar with the sites that your child uses and know how to use safety features on software and services on the internet. Check what protections your child's internet or mobile-phone provider can offer. Keep internet use confined to a public space at home – a living room rather than a bedroom – and notice if your child seems upset or withdrawn after using the internet (or after receiving phone calls or texts) – it may be a sign that she is being bullied. The Department for Children, Schools and Families recommends teaching your child the seven-point anti-cyberbullying code (Cyberbullying – A Whole-School Community Issue, Childnet International, 2007, p. 5).

What can you do if your child is a bully?

It can be upsetting and embarrassing to discover that your child is being a bully, but it's important not to get angry with her.

As a start, try to talk to her calmly in order to find out why she is making other children unhappy. Try to understand why she is behaving in this way. Do other people, including family members, use aggression or bullying tactics to get what they want? If this is the case, try to discourage their behaviour too. It's possible that your child's behaviour is a result of some other problem, such as stress, anxiety, being jealous of a brother or sister, or being frustrated at school.

You need to let your child know that you find her behaviour unacceptable and you want it to stop. This may involve dealing with other difficult behaviour as well. Using sanctions for undesirable behaviours, such as reducing or stopping pocket money, limiting when she can see her friends, or extra chores, is useful. In addition, it is important to reward positive behaviour, particularly if you notice your child being kind or helpful. This doesn't necessarily mean material rewards. Showing you are pleased and proud is very effective.

Try to help your child develop other ways of coping with anger, such as counting to ten or walking away from the situation. Ensuring you are available to talk and also to help your child work out how she can repair the situation are important for her as well as for the victim of the bullying.

Speak to the school to see what you, and your child, can do to help stop the bullying. If your child is part of a group that is involved in a bullying gang, try to get them to develop new interests and friends. For example, you could encourage them to join an after-school club or a local sports team.

Gang culture

Tragic violent deaths among teenagers have led to understandable public concern over the problems of violent gang culture in schools, although many of those young people killed have not been involved in gangs themselves. When we talk about 'gang culture' we do not mean the more harmless friendship groups, but groups in which membership is associated with violence.

There are debates about how best to tackle gang culture, but most point to a need for coordinated approaches across agencies such as schools, the police, youth offending services, as well as local communities themselves. In addition to policing and dealing with the criminal behaviour itself, a key issue is tackling the 'glamour' associated with gang membership and ensuring that young people at risk of being drawn into gangs are offered positive things to do. Joined-up policies are needed on issues such as transport and school exclusion. The evidence suggests that it is on the journeys to and from school that children and young people are most likely to get caught up in gang activity.

There is much that parents and families can do to prevent or reduce the risk of their child becoming involved in gang activity:

- show a positive interest in your child's life
- be proud of him when he does well
- have clear limits regarding behaviour and try to stick to them
- know where your child is and what he is doing
- encourage him to become involved in positive activities outside school
- as a family provide positive adult role models

The government has recently produced a useful booklet for parents on the issue of young people and gangs. For further discussion, see Chapter 19.

How to interact with school if there is a problem

It is important to seek help early if you or your child thinks there is a problem at school. First talk to your child to try to understand her views on what is going wrong. Document any incidents and correspondence, including dates and times, relating to the problem. Then arrange a meeting with school. The first contact would be your child's class teacher in primary school. For a child in secondary school policies vary, but your child's form tutor, head of year or headteacher may be appropriate contacts. If the issue is about SEN, it would be best to involve the SENCO. If your complaint is about a teacher, and it cannot be resolved informally, then it should be dealt with by another member of staff. By law, all schools in England and Wales have a school complaints procedure of which you can ask for a copy. The Advisory Centre for Education (ACE) produces booklets that explain your legal rights and advise you on managing meetings and related matters.

Dr Margaret Murphy and Dr Indra Singam

INFORMATION

SUPPORT ORGANIZATIONS

Advisory Centre for Education: national charity providing independent advice for parents and carers of children aged five–sixteen in state-funded education. Tel: 0808 800 5793. *www.ace-ed.org.uk*

Parentzone: local resources for families. *www.parentzone.com*

Independent Schools Council: *www.isc.co.uk*

The Royal College of Psychiatrists: useful information on mental health problems for parents, teachers and young people. *www.rcpsych.ac.uk*

NHS National Library for Health, Mental Health Specialist Library: *www.library.nhs.uk/mentalHealth*

The Scottish Government: Education and Training. *www.scotland.gov.uk/Topics/Education*

Department of Education (Northern Ireland): *www.deni.gov.uk*

Department of Education and Science (Republic of Ireland): *www.education.ie*

National Association for Special Educational Needs (NASEN): information and advice on learning problems. Tel: 01827 311500. *www.nasen.org.uk*

Scotland: Enquire – The Scottish Advice Service for Additional Support for Learning. Tel: 0845 123 2303. *www.enquire.org.uk*

Republic of Ireland: The National Council for Special Education. Tel: 046 948 6400. *www.ncse.ie*

Kidscape: charity established specifically to prevent bullying and child sexual abuse. Helpline: 08451 205 204. *www.kidscape.org.uk/info/index.asp*

BullyingUK: *www.bullying.co.uk*

Digizen website: provides advice on understanding, preventing and responding to cyberbullying. *www.digizen.org/cyberbullying*

Advice on what you can do to help prevent your child getting involved in a gang: *www.direct.gov.uk/en/Parents/Yourchildshealthandsafety/WorriedAbout/DG_171325*

WEBSITES OUTSIDE THE UK

Australia
Raising children network: the Australian parenting website. *http://raisingchildren.net.au*

Canada
Ontario Ministry of Training, College and Universities: *www.edu.gov.on.ca/eng/tcu*

New Zealand
New Zealand Government: *http://newzealand.govt.nz*

FURTHER READING

Francis Gilbert, *The New School Rules: a Parent's Guide to Getting the Best Education for Your Child*, Portrait, 2007.

7 Children with Special Educational Needs

THERE IS A GROUP of conditions that affect a child's development. Although these various difficulties affect children in different ways, there are some common factors between them and children may sometimes have a combination of developmental problems.

Learning disabilities

Understanding learning disabilities

Learning disability used to be known as mental handicap or mental retardation. A child with a general learning disability finds it more difficult to learn, understand and do things compared to other children of the same age. The degree of disability can vary greatly. Some children will never learn to speak, and even when they grow up will need help with looking after themselves – for example, feeding, dressing or going to the toilet. On the other hand, the disability may be mild and some children and young people with milder learning disabilities attend mainstream school with support. Those with more severe learning disabilities often require special schooling (see pp. 127–31 for information on special schooling and obtaining extra help in school).

Learning disability and mental health

A general learning disability is not a mental illness. Unlike mental illness, from which people normally recover, it is a lifelong condition. However, children with learning disabilities who have other problems such as epilepsy are more likely to develop mental-health problems than other children.

What causes learning disability?

In half of all cases no cause is found, but some disorders are inherited genetically, sometimes as part of a genetic syndrome such as Down's Syndrome. They can also be caused by infection or brain trauma before, during or after birth.

What can be done to help?

Early on, the health visitor and GP should be able to recognize developmental delay and will refer the child to the Child Development Team, who may identify underlying conditions which may be treatable. Progress is likely to continue, though slowly.

Adolescence and young adulthood can be particularly difficult times for people with learning problems when sexuality and contraception need to be thought through and addressed. Later, issues around independent living can be particularly problematic, as resources can be limited. The good news is that specific services for children and young people with learning disabilities are being developed across the UK, so access to help should improve (see Chapter 21).

Treatment of associated conditions is particularly important for anyone with special needs, and regular monitoring of health and learning should be carried out as a matter of routine to prevent any problems.

Carers' needs are also very important, and for children who need intensive care and supervision, respite facilities, support and benefits will be important to help families cope.

Learning difficulties

General learning disability is different from specific learning difficulty. A child with a specific learning difficulty is as able as any other child, except in one or two areas of their learning. For instance, they may find it difficult to recognize letters, or to cope with numbers or reading. There are many different types of specific learning disability, including dyslexia, dyspraxia and dyscalculia (see below).

Dyslexia

What is it like?

Difficulty with reading – including problems with reading speed, accuracy or comprehension – despite adequate intelligence and teaching is referred to as dyslexia. Often, it is associated with clumsiness, poor right/left orientation, delayed speech development in early childhood, and a family history of developmental reading, speech or language disorders (there is a strong genetic component). Often there is an associated difficulty in spelling, and people can remain poor spellers as adults despite being very intelligent (I know many doctors like this!). There may also be poor visual memory, poor auditory (hearing) memory or both, which can make it difficult for a child to learn to read and spell; difficulties with sequencing; reversal of letters (beyond developmental norms); and difficulty distinguishing sounds and shapes on a page. As a consequence, reading and spelling take a lot longer to master, which can be very frustrating for an otherwise intelligent child.

Dyslexia can affect up to 12 per cent of the population and has a strong association with behavioural difficulties, especially in boys.

Diagnosing dyslexia

A diagnosis of dyslexia will be based on the following evidence:

- reading achievement (measured by standardized tests of reading accuracy or comprehension) is substantially below that

expected given the child's age and measured intelligence.
- the reading difficulties are more severe than would simply be explained by any associated sensory deficit, such as visual or hearing problems.
- the problems must significantly interfere with academic achievement or activities of daily living that require reading skills.

What can be done to help?

If you suspect a child has this disorder, you can ask for the educational psychologist to do psychometric testing to identify it and, if necessary, your child will receive extra help in school. If the child is bright but under-achieving, this may be the underlying problem, and close liaison between home and school always helps.

Extra support at home and at school – extra time in exams, access to teaching aids, such as the use of computers with spell checks, or of dictaphones (for older children) – can all be extremely helpful to the dyslexic child.

Parents can help by supporting their child with homework, checking she understands what she has to do and helping her get organized. Positive encouragement and praise, especially when things progress slowly, are always helpful, and criticism must be avoided.

Dyscalculia

What is it like?

This is a specific difficulty with maths work. It can be extremely specific, as in the unusual case of a university professor of mathematics who to this day cannot learn and remember his times tables, but clearly is very bright and good at maths!

What can be done to help?

The approaches used to help this disorder are similar to those for dyslexia – see above.

Dyspraxia (Developmental Coordination Disorder (DCD)/Clumsiness)

What is it like?

Typical difficulties experienced by children with DCD

Identified by parents	**Identified by school**
❖ dressing	❖ writing
❖ eating/spilling	❖ using scissors
❖ doing activities under time pressure	❖ puzzle activities
	❖ changing for physical education
❖ riding a bike	❖ ball skills
❖ being accident-prone	❖ running

DCD is one of the most common developmental disorders, affecting up to 10 per cent of schoolchildren (it affects 5–6 boys to every 1 girl). It refers to both fine and gross motor coordination problems. Fine motor coordination problems may lead to difficulties in such things as tying shoelaces and handwriting. Gross motor coordination problems can include difficulty with team sports, such as not knowing where to run in football, and being accident-prone and spilling drinks. The child may get his clothes on back to front, get muddled about the sequence of things, be disorganized and often lose things. He may find it difficult to cope with more than one or two instructions at a time, and may have a poor understanding of interpersonal space, getting too close to people ('in their face') without realizing it. The child is often slow with his work, gets discouraged and tires easily, especially with handwriting tasks – and particularly so if after putting in a huge effort he is told to stop being lazy, speed up and write more tidily!

Copying from the board is very difficult, because the child loses his place on the page and the board, and has to start over each time he moves his eyes from board to paper. There may also be added subtle visual problems as well.

What can be done to help?

- A key issue is to raise self-esteem and facilitate activities that the child would seek to avoid, without loss of face but with praise and encouragement. Practice of key targeted difficulties – e.g. football practice – is undertaken with individuals of similar ability, rather than avoided completely.
- Teachers can make a huge difference by allowing extra time (this is usually permitted in public exams, too), allowing the child to work on ready-copied sheets rather than copying from the board, praising what can be done rather than criticizing what can't, and allowing the use of a computer with support.
- For some children, suitable tools should be provided to help with difficult tasks – e.g. adapted scissors (long-looped or left-handed), use of a slanted worktop and easy-grip pens and pencils to help handwriting, and use of a computer instead of handwriting, with support materials for learning to touch-type and to help with organization.
- Complex tasks can be broken down into smaller steps with breaks in between.
- Sports such as swimming, riding, cycling, canoeing, walking, badminton and martial arts can improve strength, confidence and stamina, especially if the non-competitive aspects are reinforced.
- Hobbies like cookery, photography, gardening and drama can be alternative sources of self-esteem to more traditional activities like football (especially for boys, where not being part of the football crowd can lead to a social void in some communities).

- As always, a close proactive parent–school partnership is helpful.
- Professionals such as occupational therapists and physiotherapists can develop specific motor programmes that the child, supported by parents and teachers, can practise to improve targetted skills. Psychologists can develop cognitive behavioural approaches to enable the child, working with parents and teachers, to raise their self-esteem.
- Associated conditions need to be identified and treated in their own right. In particular, eye-testing may also reveal subtle problems that can be corrected.

Dr Dinah Jayson

INFORMATION

SUPPORT ORGANIZATIONS

Mencap: the voice of learning disability. *www.mencap.org.uk*

The British Dyslexia Association: *www.bdadyslexia.org.uk*

The Dyscalculia Centre: *www.dyscalculia.me.uk*

Dyspraxia and Developmental Coordination Disorder (DCD): *www.dyscovery.co.uk*

WEBSITES OUTSIDE THE UK

Australia
www.dyslexia-australia.net

Canada
www.dyslexia-canada.com

New Zealand
www.dyslexia-nz.com

Part Four

Emotional Health

8 Emotional Health and Well-being

WHAT IS 'EMOTIONAL HEALTH AND WELL-BEING'? The term appears straightforward enough at first sight. However, there is no single definition. This and other similar terms are used in a number of ways. People can be forgiven for feeling confused about their meaning, particularly when they are used in relation to children and young people.

For some people the language of health has negative connotations to do with illness and leads to inappropriate medicalization. This is seen as potentially disadvantageous for children and young people. However, in line with the World Health Organization's definition, 'health' should be seen as a broad and positive concept, not limited simply to the absence of illness. For the sake of simplicity, we will use the single term 'emotional well-being'.

Sometimes the word 'emotional' is used with the word 'social', as in 'emotional and social well-being'. The terms 'mental' or 'psychological well-being' are also in frequent use. The latter two encompass more than emotional well-being and refer to all functions of the mind, not just those to do with emotions or feelings.

Many of the terms overlap in their meaning. Some people, including professionals working with children, use them differently, depending upon the context or on their particular beliefs or opinions. 'Emotional well-being' is sometimes used loosely as a catch-all phrase, perhaps to avoid using the term 'mental'. However, in this chapter it is simply used to refer to the person's state of emotional well-being or 'feeling good'.

How is emotional well-being related to mental health?

It is generally recognized that emotional well-being is an important aspect of mental health. However, it is only one aspect of mental health and should not be used as a substitute term. There are a number of definitions of 'mental health' – and these vary across cultures – but there is broad agreement on its essential components. In 1995, the NHS Health Advisory Service Thematic Review on Child and Adolescent Mental Health Services in the UK set out a view of the main components of mental health:

- the ability to develop psychologically, emotionally, intellectually and spiritually
- the ability to initiate, develop and sustain mutually satisfying personal relationships
- the ability to become aware of others and to empathize with them
- the ability to use psychological distress as a developmental process, so that it does not hinder or impair further development

It was recognized that, when applied to children and young people, the stage of development needs to be taken into account. Young Minds, the national charity specifically focused on children's mental health, similarly stated that, in addition to emotional well-being, 'happiness, integrity, creativity; and the capacity to cope with stress and difficulty' are all components of positive mental health in children and young people. Despite these broad definitions, the term 'mental health' still has connotations of mental illness. Colloquial use of the word 'mental', particularly by children and young people, can mean crazy, mad or insane, and because of this there are many who would prefer to avoid using the term 'mental health' completely. However, this may do a disservice to those who do have mental health problems, which, when severe and persistent, may have lifelong consequences. The stigma of mental illness, which is largely based on lack of knowledge and on misunderstanding, will not be lessened by disguising it within softer language.

Positive and negative emotional well-being

The intensity of emotional well-being inevitably varies. A child who is happy or joyful is unlikely to be so at the same level all the time. Similarly, feelings of contentment, a more neutral state of being, will change according to circumstances. Day-to-day disappointments, as well as more serious stressful events, cannot be completely avoided.

Fear, sadness and anger are all examples of emotions that will have a negative effect on emotional well-being. It is to be expected that for most children and young people these feelings will neither go on for too long, nor interfere in the long term with their development or learning. It is important that a child is able to 'bounce back' from adverse experiences that affect emotional well-being.

If negative emotional well-being persists in a child, it may herald the beginning of a serious mental health problem that may require additional help. This raises the debate about the nature of the relationship between emotional well-being and mental ill-health. Are they at opposite ends of a spectrum, or are they separate but related concepts?

A child grieving after the death of someone close will experience negative emotional well-being and may feel depressed and angry, but such feelings are usual and can be seen as normal reactions to loss. In such circumstances, it would be wrong to consider this child to be unwell or suffering from a mental health problem. In contrast, a young person suffering from the manic phase of bipolar disorder – also referred to as manic-depressive illness – may have a high degree of positive emotional well-being but none the less be mentally unwell. The debate about the relationship of these terms continues.

How to recognize positive emotional well-being

Children or young people who have positive emotional well-being are more likely to:

- like and respect themselves and have high self-esteem
- be able to accept and enjoy success
- know what experiences give them pleasure
- not be too hard on themselves when facing failure
- be optimistic
- be able to name emotions and express their feelings clearly
- be able to bounce back from disappointment
- not let negative feelings overwhelm them or react impulsively
- understand the feelings of others

Differences in 'emotional style'

No two children are the same and normal differences in emotional well-being can be described as differences in emotional style. We have different expectations of children according to their age and how well they are developing. Temper tantrums are an example of difficulty in managing emotions. They are to be expected from toddlers but less so from older children. Being able to differentiate and describe feelings is something that is acquired over time, so we do not expect a young child to be as articulate as an older child. The willingness to talk about feelings also varies. Teenagers can sometimes be reluctant to share their feelings with parents, even if they were able to do so at a younger age.

Children who have grown up in similar circumstances, as may be the case with siblings, can be very different in terms of their sensitivity to stresses and the way they express and manage their feelings. Some of these differences may be explained by inherited factors that determine their temperament and will be evident from infancy. However, there will be multiple influences throughout childhood that will affect both directly and indirectly a child's emotional well-being. We shouldn't be too quick to stereotype the behaviour of boys and girls; however, they do tend to differ in the way they experience, express and manage feelings.

Some of these differences are innate and some develop in response to societal and family influences. Different family and cultural traditions, such as the acceptability of being open about feelings or how best to cope with a problem, will also have an impact upon a child's development and need to be taken into account.

Some aspects of emotional style that may differ in children and young people are:

- their preferred way of expressing feelings – e.g. in pictures, words or play
- their willingness to talk about or express feelings
- their response to being praised
- their means of coping with distress
- their sensitivity to criticism
- their sensitivity to the feelings of others
- their need for support and guidance

Emotional literacy and emotional intelligence

Given the importance of emotional well-being, there has been a considerable amount of work to find ways in which it can be promoted. Within educational settings, the terms 'emotional literacy' and 'emotional intelligence' are most often used.

'Emotional literacy' is seen as an integral part of emotional and social well-being and is partly concerned with the learning and practice of emotional competencies. It is defined as the ability to understand ourselves and other people, and in particular to be aware of, understand and competently use information about our own and other people's emotional states. It includes the ability to understand, express and manage our own emotions; to respond to the emotions of others in ways that are helpful; and the ability to understand social situations and build relationships.

'Emotional intelligence' is similar to 'emotional literacy', but is a term more commonly used in the USA.

There is now a programme of work in schools in England to help children develop emotional well-being, as this is seen as important for their overall learning. Called SEAL (the Social and Emotional Aspects of Learning), it addresses five broad aspects of learning and has both personal and interpersonal components:

- self-awareness
- managing awareness
- motivation
- empathy
- social skills

The expression and management of emotions

While there are cultural differences, the ability to express feelings or to communicate an emotional state is seen as positive, protective and a skill to be encouraged if emotional well-being is to be achieved. Difficulty in doing so is seen as negative. It is the ability to express emotion appropriately that matters, not necessarily the way it is expressed.

The context is also important. It is easy to see that there are some situations where a free and uncontrolled expression of emotion can be unwise or even harmful. Likewise, those who have difficulty expressing emotions and appear to keep their feelings locked away or 'bottled up' may react badly when under stress. Some children and young people see this as the best way to cope with a problem, and the positive value of keeping a 'stiff upper lip' is still prevalent among many adults.

So the management of emotions is an additional skill that is both desirable and something that children need to learn if they are both to have good social relationships and to avoid being seen as troubled or troublesome.

But what of negative emotion? The ability to put into words and to communicate negative feelings is also seen as a strength, provided that the feelings are managed properly. Does the expression of understandable feelings of sadness at a loss, or of anger or fear when attacked, imply an abnormal state of negative well-being? Clearly this is not the case, unless those feelings continue, are intense and begin to interfere with day-to-day living. So a child or young person can, on balance, be said to be able to achieve emotional well-being even if there are times of understandable stress and distress that cause temporary periods of negative emotional well-being.

Helping children with negative emotional well-being and emotional problems

There is increasing awareness of the vulnerability of children and young people to mental health problems, and the impact that a negative sense of emotional well-being can have on children's learning in school and on their mental health.

At the more severe end of the spectrum, some 10 per cent of children in the UK have a mental health disorder (defined by a recognizable collection of symptoms and behaviours, and associated with significant distress and interference with day-to-day functioning). Of these, about 4 per cent have an emotional disorder such as anxiety or depression. A greater number have milder problems that do not meet the stricter criteria for a mental disorder.

While these problems will not always lead to more persistent and serious disorders, they may none the less affect a child's life and interfere with learning, relationships with family and friends, and social activities. It makes sense, therefore, to consider ways in which emotional well-being can be improved, particularly in children and young people who are seen to be at greater risk.

The various factors associated with greater risk are well understood and include parental mental illness, physical ill-health, social deprivation and family breakdown. Traditionally, the approach has tended to focus on directly addressing the problems and the relevant risk factors, and intervening to reduce them. However, the fact that children and young people facing the same risks, even in the same family, are affected in different ways and to different degrees has led to an interest in the concept of 'resilience', or the factors that protect children. It is doubtful that a focus on increasing resilience alone is sufficient to prevent children developing mental health problems, including emotional disorders, and most effective strategies involve both enhancing a child's resilience and addressing emerging problems.

Here are some ways in which you can help a child with negative emotional well-being:

- Encourage and praise positive thinking, feeling and behaviour when it occurs.
- Help her learn how to express and manage difficult feelings through your own example.
- Take opportunities to help her understand different feelings and emotions through pictures and conversations.
- Help her to talk about her feelings or express them in other ways, such as drawing and painting.
- Look for moments in which she can most comfortably express her feelings.

- Look for opportunities to engage her in pleasurable and rewarding experiences.
- Create an environment of safety and stability that provides support.

What help is available?

There is an increasing number of projects and programmes designed to enhance positive emotional skills in children. They aim to enhance resilience and contribute to a child's self-esteem – both valuable assets in obtaining a balance of positive emotional well-being.

FRIENDS, an effective programme developed in Australia, has been used in the UK and participants have been shown to have decreased anxiety levels and increased self-esteem when examined three months after completing the programme. Another programme sets out to increase resilience in young people by focusing on positive peer relations, enhanced self-efficacy, creativity and coherence – this last being defined as the ability to make meaningful and beneficial connections between different aspects of their past, present and future lives.

Both approaches focus on the development of positive personal attributes rather than tackling symptoms and problems directly. While the results of these programmes are encouraging, there is some way to go before being certain that enhancing resilience alone is sufficient to prevent emotional problems in children and young people.

*Dr Bob Jezzard**

* I am indebted to Katherine Weare, who, in a number of discussions in the past, has helped me better understand the promotion of emotional well-being and the research evidence that underpins it. I fear that this short chapter does not do justice to her contribution in the field – see guidance for further reading.

INFORMATION

REFERENCES

World Health Organization, *The World Health Report 2001. Mental Health: New Understanding, New Hope*, WHO, 2001. *http://who.int/whr/2001/en*

Young Minds, *Mental Health in Your School: a Guide for Teachers and Others Working in Schools*, Jessica Kingsley, 1996.

Green, H., et al., *Mental Health of Children and Young People in Great Britain, 2004*, Office for National Statistics, Palgrave Macmillan, 2005.

Stallard, P., et al., 'The FRIENDS Emotional Health Programme: Initial Findings from a School-based Project', *Child and Adolescent Mental Health*, 12, 2007; 32–7.

SUPPORT ORGANIZATIONS

Young Minds: national charity committed to improving the mental health and emotional well-being of all children and young people. Tel: 0800 018 2138 (parents' information service) or 0207 336 8445 (general). *www.youngminds.org.uk*

FURTHER READING

For a more detailed and comprehensive exploration of emotional well-being, its meaning and promotion, as well as practical steps that can be taken to enhance it, see:

Dwivedi, Kedar N., and Harper, Peter B. (eds), *Promoting the Emotional Well-being of Children and Adolescents and Preventing Their Mental Ill Health: a Handbook*, Jessica Kingsley, 2004.

Weare, Katherine, *Promoting Mental, Emotional and Social Health – a Whole School Approach*, Routledge, London, 2000.

Part Five

Serious Disorders: Context, Causes and Effects

9 Abuse, Neglect and Domestic Violence

Saul – the boy who wouldn't go to school

Saul, aged eight, lived with his mother, father, ten-year-old sister and five-year-old brother. Saul had not been to school for seven months. His parents had been together on and off for ten years. Each described the other as physically and verbally abusive, but neither parent could end the relationship. They were also somewhat chaotic and inconsistent with their children.

Saul was very anxious about his mother and younger brother. He would often check on his mother to see what sort of mood she was in. Sometimes he was her comforter, but she also blamed him for rows between his parents. The ongoing marital strife meant that the parents were unable to set boundaries for the children and could not instil predictable bedtimes or get them to school on time. Anyway, Saul preferred to stay at home, believing this would stop his parents fighting. From Saul's school, a link worker tried very hard to work with him and his parents on strategies to encourage him back to school. It transpired that Saul's mother managed to sabotage this work.

The education authorities started putting pressure on Saul's parents, threatening court action because of his non-attendance at school. The school link worker also referred the family to their local Child and Adolescent Mental Health Service (CAMHS, see pp. 108 and 132). In the initial meeting Saul's mother seemed at a loss as to why her son was not going to school. Saul appeared withdrawn, sullen and said very little. At the end of the appointment, as the next one was being arranged, he said to his mother that if it wasn't for her and his dad always fighting, he would be able to get to school and wouldn't need to come back to the clinic.

As time went on, it became clear that Saul's mother suffered extreme mood swings and would require help in her own right. To get Saul back into education, he began attending a pupil referral unit (see p. 131) and there he told a teacher that his mother had hit his older sister with a belt. It was then that Children's Social Care Services (CSCS – previously called Social Services) became involved with the family.

Eventually Saul became subject to child protection plans (see p. 172) because of emotional abuse and risk of physical abuse and similar plans were drawn up for his brother and sister. Saul was also found to have learning difficulties, in particular speech and language problems (see Chapter 7). During this process of intervention by professionals, Saul's parents did finally separate and it was decided that the father should have care of the children. Saul's father received support from his own family, CSCS (a family support worker) and local CAMHS. The family social worker also arranged for him to attend a parenting group.

Saul is still getting help for his poor self-esteem and low mood. He has a special mentor who takes him out for recreational activities in the week. In school he receives special help via a Statement of Special Educational Needs. Along with his siblings, he is being helped by CAMHS workers to process the stressful experiences to which they have been subjected by living with an unstable mother and in an abusive atmosphere of extreme marital conflict.

What is child abuse?

We can probably all think of some personal childhood experiences when we thought we were treated unkindly by our parents. Looking after children can be extremely stressful at times and parents can be pushed to their limits, doing or saying things that they later regret. For those of us who are parents, we may know only too well that we are capable of losing our tempers, shouting at or sometimes even smacking our children. When does this kind of behaviour become abusive? In answer to this question, one has to consider the severity, duration and nature of the abuse, and its ability to have lasting negative effects.

The extent of the problem

Unfortunately, the abuse or maltreatment of children occurs throughout the world and in all sectors of society. It is more common than we might care to think. The maltreatment of children can be extremely shocking and upsetting to confront. It is difficult to believe quite how cruel adults can be to children, which means we can sometimes fail to spot abuse when it is happening. This was one of the factors in the tragic and well-known case of Victoria Climbié. Despite the inquiry and the new legislation which followed Victoria's death, we have been confronted by the distressing death of Baby P and are trying to understand how this abuse was missed.

As parenting practices vary so widely worldwide, it is a matter of debate as to which cultural and religious practices are considered abusive. For example, female circumcision is the norm in some countries, whereas sending a very young child off to boarding school and the physical chastisement of children is normal in others. Although the physical punishment of children by parents is not illegal in England, it is in some countries (Sweden, for example). There are different types of abuse, including physical, sexual, and emotional abuse and neglect (see definitions below). Children growing up with domestic violence are also victims of abuse as a result of living in stressful and disturbing households.

It is important to identify children who are being abused because it can be profoundly damaging. Nowadays we are better at recognizing how abuse can lead to a variety of physical, emotional and behavioural problems (see below), which can be lifelong. In some cases, child abuse leads to fatalities.

Definitions of abuse

There are four categories:

Physical abuse includes hitting, shaking or non-accidental injury to a child, causing, for example, fractures, head injuries, bruises or burns. Included in this category is poor physical growth, due not to any medical cause but to adverse parenting. Physical harm may also be caused when a carer (usually the mother) makes a child ill on purpose and then seeks medical help for him. While it is difficult to believe this happens, sadly we do encounter such cases.

Sexual abuse includes sexually interfering with or assaulting a child or adolescent, and involving children in sexual activities (including watching pornography) which they don't fully understand and to which they are unable to give informed consent.

Emotional abuse includes constantly criticizing, threatening or rejecting a child; having age-inappropriate expectations of a child; being so overprotective that one limits the child's social interactions; and causing a child to see or hear the ill-treatment of another (as in domestic violence). Emotional abuse is invariably present in all other types of abuse.

Neglect is persistent failure to look after a child and can include: not giving him enough to eat; not attending to his hygiene or physical needs; not playing or talking with him; and failing to keep him safe. Neglect can involve a parent being emotionally distant and unavailable.

Who abuses children?

In most cases of abuse, the care-giver and abuser are one and the same person, or the abuser is someone in the immediate family circle. In sexual abuse, 80 per cent of offences are committed by a known family member or acquaintance. Some parents may abuse or neglect their children without meaning to (if, for instance, the parent is unwell), and a significant number of parents who abuse have themselves suffered abuse as children. Some of the parents will have mental health problems, including personality difficulties or depression.

As regards factors that can trigger abuse, children are more often at risk of abuse if they have special needs (or a physical or learning problem), or a difficult, demanding temperament. Other factors putting a child at a greater risk of abuse include a parent being mentally ill, social isolation and – particularly in the case of physical abuse – poverty, overcrowding and the parent being in violent relationships with other adults.

What is domestic violence?

The term 'domestic violence' is used to describe incidents of threatening behaviour, violence or abuse (for example, sexual or psychological) inflicted on a man or woman by their partner.

What connects domestic violence to child abuse?

Even when parents deny that children know domestic violence is occurring, children have a knack of sensing when things are not right for their parents. They overhear distressing things and see evidence of violence on their parents (such as bruises or black eyes). It is estimated that where there is domestic violence, children witness about 75 per cent of the abusive incidents. Also, in 50 per cent of such families, the children themselves suffer violence. Sexual and emotional abuse is more likely to happen in these families.

What are the effects of abuse, neglect and domestic violence on children?

Children can turn negative experiences into positive actions in adulthood. However, this is often not the case. It is difficult to predict the exact effects of abuse and domestic violence on children, but we see impairments in a wide range of functions. There are the obvious direct effects of abuse, as in the case of physical injuries, but there is also the unseen damage done to the developing brain and mind. Some children seem more resilient than others to the maltreatment they have suffered.

General effects

When children are chronically upset or exposed to stressful events, they can develop an abnormal stress response. This means a child might be extremely stirred up initially, but then over time becomes emotionally cut off as he gets used to the stresses. Also, the growing brain is particularly sensitive to the effects of stress hormones (such as cortisol), so the brains of abused children can develop differently from those of other children. Research is enabling us to discover more about this complex interplay of environmental influences and brain development, and therefore helping us understand how abuse can cause more subtle impairments in children, for instance on their memory, learning or language development.

As well as producing effects on the brain, there is another important and related consequence of abuse. This is in the area of attachment (see p. 69). Sensitive care-giving is important in helping a child regulate his emotions and behaviours and become securely attached. Children who are maltreated show disordered attachments to their care-givers and these early patterns persist into adult life, affecting future relationships.

As mentioned, the physical consequences of various forms of child abuse and neglect can be seen – bruises, head injury, fractures, poor growth, infection and unwanted pregnancy. However, in other types of abuse there may be no observable evidence. An older child might tell a teacher, for instance, what is happening. But in some cases, particularly in sexual and physical abuse, the child might be reluctant to speak about it either because he wants to protect the abuser if they are a loved one, or because he wants to prevent the family from breaking up. Often children have been sworn to secrecy and threatened with punishment if they tell. The child may also believe that what has happened is all his fault. In emotional abuse, the child is unlikely to complain because he doesn't understand the damaging nature of the interactions, which he will consider normal. Also, the child may believe himself to be bad, unlovable or stupid.

Specific effects – signs to look out for

There may well be different signs to watch out for, depending on the age and sex of the child and the type of abuse.

Physically abused children may:

- become more cautious or wary of adults
- be inhibited in their play
- have temper tantrums
- be reluctant to change clothes (e.g. for sports) in front of others
- be more aggressive. Boys in particular are more likely to become bullies and, when older, have problems such as conduct disorder (see p. 293) and display delinquent or anti-social behaviours. Girls can become more aggressive too, but are more likely to become depressed and, if older, develop eating disorders or self-harm (see Chapters 15, 17 and 18).
- be unable to concentrate, leading to under-achievement at school
- find it difficult to make friends

Sexually abused children may:

- suddenly behave differently when the abuse starts
- show sexually inappropriate behaviour for their age – e.g. use sexual words or sexual play
- be seductive or flirtatious with adults
- start wetting the bed or soiling themselves
- have frequent urinary infections and/or genital soreness
- have problems sleeping, particularly in younger children
- withdraw into themselves, become secretive and feel guilty
- become promiscuous or take to prostitution
- develop an eating disorder such as anorexia or bulimia (see Chapter 15)
- harm themselves such as by cutting or overdosing (see Chapter 18)
- shy away from physical contact
- run away
- drink too much alcohol or start using drugs (see Chapter 14)

Emotionally abused or neglected children may:

- be slow in walking and talking
- have feeding and growth problems
- feel badly about themselves
- find it hard to make friends
- be over-friendly with strangers
- be unable to develop imaginative play
- be distracted at school

Where there is domestic violence:

- younger children may show great distress, becoming anxious, complaining of tummy aches, wetting the bed, throwing temper tantrums, behaving younger than they are
- children may develop sleep problems
- older children may become more aggressive and disobedient in a similar way to those exposed to physical abuse. Boys may start to use violence to resolve conflict; girls may become withdrawn and complain of vague physical symptoms
- older children may truant or start to use drugs and alcohol
- children may begin to self-harm (see Chapter 18)
- children may develop school problems – behavioural or academic

All abuse (especially sexual or physical) may cause symptoms of post-traumatic stress disorder (the child may have nightmares, flashbacks or be easily startled; see Chapter 24).

Longer-term effects

Abuse can impact on all areas of adult life, such as job prospects, relationships and parenthood. Girls who have seen their mothers hit by men may accept this as normal and choose partners who are similarly violent. Patterns of abuse can be repeated by abuse victims copying the parenting style of their own parents. Some can also develop long-term psychiatric disorders, such as depression, post-traumatic stress disorder and personality disorder.

What can be done to help?

We all have a responsibility to protect children, so we need to be able to act appropriately when we encounter abuse. Children are helped by having good paediatric and childcare services in their area. If you suspect a child is being abused, you may be able to help them talk about it. Your local Children's Social Care Department will have Child Protection Advisers who can offer more detailed advice.

Victims of domestic violence can be helped to seek assistance and get themselves and their children to a place of safety, such as a women's refuge.

The safeguarding of the child is paramount once you know a child is being abused. The Children Act 1989 placed child abuse within a legal framework. Social Care Services will need to be involved and Child Protection procedures will be followed. Decisions need to be made about whether the abuse has caused, or is likely to cause, significant harm to the child's health or development. Other professionals who know the child will be invited to a child protection conference in order to make plans, and conclusions will be reached about whether interventions to change family functioning or parenting style will help prevent further abuse. Court proceedings may take place if the child needs to be removed to alternative care (temporarily or longer term; see Chapter 4) in order to be kept safe.

Treatment available

Health education for parents needs to begin before children are born. In pregnancy a mother is warned about the dangers of drug and alcohol misuse, but can also be told how living with a violent partner can be dangerous for her children. It is also important to recognize and treat depression in mothers, both before and after giving birth.

There are voluntary and charitable organizations that provide help and information to children and victims of abuse and domestic violence (see Support Organizations, at the end of the chapter).

Many children need specialist treatment because of the abuse they have endured. The child and family might need input from the local CAMHS. Specialists may work with the whole family, or with the children or adolescents individually. The young person may be helped by talking through his experiences and traumas. Severely neglected and abused children can be difficult to look after, which means services are needed to support their carers. Parents may need to access help for their own issues with relationships or treatment for their own mental health problems.

Tips for families, teachers and friends

- If you are concerned about the immediate safety of a child, do not hesitate to call the police.
- If you suspect abuse or domestic violence is occurring in families and impacting on children you know, it is always a good first step to share your concerns with other people and colleagues. It is equally important to enquire about injuries on a child, to be sensitive to a child opening up and disclosing abuse, and to believe what the child is telling you and not minimize or dismiss her accounts. Your local Social Care Department or Health Clinic can provide further advice on what to do next.

Dr Sue Storey

INFORMATION

SUPPORT ORGANIZATIONS

NSPCC: national 24-hour Child Protection Helpline: 0808 800 5000. *www.nspcc.org.uk*

ChildLine: Helpline: 0800 1111. *www.ChildLine.org.uk*

www.everychildmatters.gov.uk – information about child abuse.

National Domestic Violence Helpline: freephone number available 24 hours a day: 0844 8044 999 or 08009 702 070. *www.ncdv.org.uk*. Run in partnership with Women's Aid and Refuge: 0808 2000 247; *www.womensaid.org.uk*

WEBSITES OUTSIDE THE UK

Australia

Child abuse: *www.childwise.net*

Lots of links for abuse and domestic violence at the Australian Institute for Family Studies: *www.aifs.gov.au*

Canada

Centre for children and families in the justice system: *www.lfcc.on.ca/calinks.html*

New Zealand

Child abuse: *www.parentline.org.nz*

New Zealand Ministry of Health – Domestic violence: *www.moh.nz*

FURTHER READING

Gerhardt, Sue, *Why Love Matters: How Affection Shapes a Baby's Brain*, Brunner–Routledge, 2004.

Glaser, Danya, 'Child Abuse and Neglect and the Brain – A Review', *Journal of Child Psychology and Psychiatry*, 41 (1), 2000; 97–116.

Roche, Peter, *Unloved: the True Story of a Stolen Childhood*, Penguin, 2007.

Yen Mah, Adeline, *Falling Leaves Return to Their Roots: the True Story of an Unwanted Chinese Daughter*, Penguin, 1997.

10 Worries and Anxieties

The Boy Who Wouldn't Play in the Park

Jack loved being outdoors, especially going to the playground at his local park. His mum took him all the time; he was a huge fan of the swings and the big slide.

One day, Jack was playing with his football on the grass just outside the playground. A man was walking his dog nearby and had let him off the lead. This dog was not terribly big, but neither was Jack at only six years old. The dog became very excited when he saw the ball being kicked about and started barking loudly as he ran towards Jack. Jack's mum saw this happen and was suddenly extremely fearful that her son would get hurt; she screamed and ran to him. Jack could see the dog barking and running towards him and his mum screaming and running towards him as well. Now he was really scared. His mum got to him just before the dog; she scooped him up in her arms as the dog reached her feet. The dog started playing with Jack's ball as his mother, still shaking, held Jack, who was now crying, and gave the dog's owner an earful about the animal not being on a lead.

After that, Jack became extremely frightened of dogs. He refused to go to the playground or to play outside except in his own back garden. He hated going out anywhere in case he saw a dog. He found it difficult to sleep at night, especially if he could hear dogs barking outside, and sometimes needed to sleep with his parents. He even became frightened of his picture books with dogs in, refusing to have them in his bedroom. One day, when he walked past a dog on the pavement, he became so scared that he let go of his mum's hand in order to run away and nearly ran into the road.

This was the point at which Jack's mum decided to get some help for him. The GP listened carefully to the story and referred Jack to a psychologist, who met with them a few times to understand what the difficulties were. She then treated Jack for what she called a 'dog phobia' by using a form of talking therapy called CBT (see p. 351), especially adapted for children of his age.

At the same time, Jack's mum came to understand how her own fear of dogs may have rubbed off on Jack. The whole family became involved in helping Jack with his CBT 'homework', which challenged his dog phobia in practical ways. Over several weeks, seeing the psychologist every week or so, Jack won the 'battle' with his phobia and made it back to the playground.

What is anxiety?

All children, like adults, get frightened from time to time. Fear, one of our most basic feelings, is provoked when we are in situations that we find threatening or dangerous. Fear can be helpful, as it tends to keep us out of harm's way. However, a small group of children and young people have extreme fear or anxieties that cause a lot of distress and can have a large impact on their everyday lives.

Types of anxiety

To help us think about how best to help, we tend to group anxieties based on what the fear or worry is about.

Simple phobias. Most young children go through phases of being scared of something, like animals, monsters or the dark. They tend to grow out of this sort of fear, or at least it becomes less intense with time. A phobia is different. It is an extreme fear which causes a lot of distress and affects the child's life significantly. For example, Jack's fear of dogs was called a phobia as it meant he wouldn't play outside, had trouble sleeping and was frightened of his story books. Phobias don't tend to go away on their own and most children need some help to learn to cope with them.

Separation anxiety. Worry about not being with their regular caregivers is a common experience for virtually all children. It normally develops at six months and is around to varying degrees during the preschool years, usually getting worse before it gets better. It can make going to sleep, parents leaving for work, or settling at nursery or school especially difficult. Help should be sought if it continues into later childhood or adolescence, or if it affects the child's development, education or family life.

General anxiety. Some children and young people feel anxious most of the time for no obvious reason. It may be a part of their temperament, or it may be something that is shared with other members of the family. If the anxiety becomes very severe, the child may worry so much that she

is not able to pay attention in class or socialize properly with friends. This sort of anxiety is more common in adolescence and can occur along with depression (see Chapter 17). It is also known to affect young people who may also have had a phobia or separation anxiety when they were younger.

Social anxiety. It may be helpful to think of this as an extreme, sometimes disabling, type of shyness. It means that although children are often fine in the company of familiar people and family, they find it extremely worrying to be in other social situations which, as a result, they usually avoid. This can have a major effect on their ability to make friends or manage in school. Adolescents with social anxiety often describe fear of humiliation, embarrassment or judgement by others, leading to their avoidance of social situations.

Panic disorder. A panic attack is an extreme episode of anxiety. The child will have all the physical symptoms of anxiety (see below) and will commonly also have frightening thoughts, such as thinking they are going to die, or 'go mad'. It is rare for children to suffer panic attacks without an obvious trigger, which is the hallmark of panic disorder, but this becomes more common in late adolescence and young adulthood.

How will I know my child is anxious?

This depends on how old your child is. Feeling frightened is only part of the picture. Anxiety is accompanied by lots of physical symptoms, caused by the chemicals released by the brain and body to prepare for the threatening or dangerous situation the young person thinks she is in. These symptoms include feeling breathless, having a racing heart, increased need to go to the toilet, stomach ache or 'butterflies', and headache. Children may also get irritable, restless and fidgety.

An older child or adolescent will be more able to tell you if they feel anxious or worried, and may even know what is worrying them; a younger child may not. Instead, they may cry, have tantrums, become clingy and have trouble sleeping.

What causes these worries and anxieties?

Temperament. Some children (and adults), by their very nature, tend to worry more than others.

Family history. Anxiety problems tend to run in families, so if parents or relatives are known to worry a lot, the children may be likely to do so too. Some of this will be in the genes, but children may also 'learn' anxious behaviour from watching their anxious relatives. They may continue to worry if their parents or care-givers do not have the ability to soothe them effectively.

Upsetting life events. Children who have to cope with stressful situations, such as bereavement, parental illness, divorce or bullying, often become anxious and insecure. They may be able to manage one event, but may struggle to cope if several difficult things happen together, such as parental divorce, moving home and changing school.

Parenting difficulties. If parents use harsh, inconsistent or over-protective methods of childcare, the children in turn may feel unsupported, confused and insecure. These patterns of parenting can be linked with separation anxiety in children. Young children can also feel worried and anxious if they hear or see their parents arguing or fighting.

Traumatic experiences. Children who have experienced a frightening or traumatic event, such as a road traffic accident, a household fire or an assault, may suffer from anxiety afterwards. They may also go on to develop post-traumatic stress disorder (see Chapter 24).

What can be done to help?

Self-help

A lot can be done to help children who are anxious without their having to see specialists. In the main, what you do will depend on what you think has triggered the anxiety in your child and on what sort of anxiety she has. For example, you may be able to identify a particular stressful recent event in your child's life. Knowing the cause of the problem will help you know where to begin trying to help. You could ask yourself if your child is picking up on your own anxieties and fears in certain situations. If you know she has a tendency to worry about things, you can help by giving her lots of gentle warning and encouragement when her usual home or school routines change. This should lessen any upsetting effects of the change when it occurs. Similarly, regular routines around bedtime and getting ready for school can help very young children with separation anxiety. Use star charts to reward your child for behaviour you wish to continue, such as sleeping in her own bed rather than yours. Above all, take the time to show your child that you are interested in her and her difficulties, and that you care.

Talking treatments

If your child is still distressed by anxiety despite trying these general tips, it may be helpful to seek some external help and support. Some children benefit from talking through their difficulties with an adult outside the immediate family, such as a family friend, teacher or grandparent.

It may also be helpful to seek the advice of your family doctor, who could refer your child to your local Child and Adolescent Mental Health Services (CAMHS). The type of specialist help offered will depend on what is causing the anxiety. The most common talking treatment offered for anxiety problems is cognitive behavioural therapy (CBT), but other talking treatments may be as effective, depending on the particular problem. In CBT, the child or young person will be helped to identify patterns between what she thinks, feels and does in situations which she links with being anxious. Help from her therapist and family will enable her to challenge her thinking processes and behaviour through practical 'experiments', often given as 'homework', which will, in turn, eventually decrease the intensity of the anxious feelings.

'Graded exposure' is a CBT technique used to treat anxiety problems. It involves the child or young person gradually overcoming the anxiety she feels in situations which become increasingly challenging as time goes on, until the ultimate fear-provoking situation is confronted and managed. For example, Jack may have started his dog-phobia treatment by being helped to manage the anxiety he felt when looking at a picture of a dog, then progressing to maybe seeing a dog in real life, followed by touching a dog and so on.

It can sometimes be more appropriate for the specialist to see the whole family to help a child or young person who has anxiety problems – especially if the anxiety was caused by an event that involved the whole family, like a divorce or illness, or is thought to stem from parenting difficulties. It is not uncommon for one person within a family, often a child, to 'carry' most of the distress caused by a problem or event that was experienced by everyone. Seeing the family together is really useful for unpicking those sorts of problems.

Medication

It would be uncommon for a child to be prescribed any medication for an anxiety problem, although there is some evidence that the antidepressants known as SSRIs (selective serotonin reuptake inhibitors) can help.

In adolescents and young adults, while talking therapy is always the first treatment option, medication may be added if the talking therapy alone is not enough. SSRI antidepressants may be used more widely for this age group, especially if the young person is also depressed.

Will my child always be anxious?

The good news is that most children do not carry on suffering from anxiety as adults. Many such problems get better with time and specialist help can be really effective, especially when sought reasonably quickly.

Dr Mona Freeman

INFORMATION

SUPPORT ORGANIZATIONS

Anxiety UK: promotes the relief and rehabilitation of persons suffering with anxiety disorders and advances public awareness of the causes and conditions of anxiety disorders and associated phobias. Helpline: 08444 775 774. *www.anxietyuk.org.uk*

Young Minds: national charity committed to improving the mental health and emotional well-being of all children and young people. Tel: 0808 802 5544 (parents' information service). *www.youngminds.org.uk*

Parentline Plus: national charity that works for, and with, parents. Helpline: 0808 800 2222. *www.parentlineplus.org.uk*

WEBSITES OUTSIDE THE UK

Australia
www.anxietyaustralia.com.au

Canada
www.anxietycanada.ca

New Zealand
www.phobic.org.nz

FURTHER READING

The Anxious Child, The Mental Health Foundation, 1997. Available free to download from *www.mentalhealth.org.uk*

11 ADHD and Autistic Spectrum Disorders

CHILDREN WHO HAVE PROBLEMS in their development, such as attention deficit hyperactivity disorder (ADHD) and autism-related disorders or learning disabilities, often have behaviour problems. In fact the problem behaviour may be the first or most noticeable feature. This group of problems is often referred to as neurodevelopmental disorders.

ADHD and hyperkinetic disorder

Lee is eight and his mother says that he is very creative, outgoing and friendly, but has always been 'a live wire'. Lee tended, however, to be quite reckless and accident-prone. When he was younger, he would wander off and get lost if not watched closely. When over-excited, he would get very silly and, despite his enthusiasm, rarely stuck to anything before moving on; he got bored very quickly. 'I don't understand it. When Lee makes a mistake he is always sorry, but he doesn't seem to learn, and he is always getting into trouble,' his mother would complain.

At school, Lee appeared younger than his classmates and

found it very difficult to settle in class. His teachers would complain that his behaviour was disruptive, and his work messy and careless, and would always say that he should try harder and could do much better.

Lee was rarely invited to parties because of his behaviour, and his parents started to wonder whether there was something wrong.

Eventually Lee was diagnosed and treated for ADHD. He has progressed at school and socially, and is now indistinguishable from his friends – apart from his great enthusiasm and charisma, which make him the life and soul of the party.

What is ADHD?

ADHD is a medical condition that is increasingly being recognized in the UK as a cause of severe behavioural problems. There is an increased risk of school failure and criminality if it is left untreated. Until recently, it has been under-diagnosed in the UK compared to the USA (where it is perhaps over-diagnosed). It is important to recognize the condition, as children with it can be incorrectly labelled as naughty, feeding into the vicious circle of blame described in Chapter 7. With the right treatment, most children with ADHD can lead a normal life.

ADHD, like most disorders, varies in the severity of its symptoms. The following terms are used to describe the three main degrees:

- Hyperkinetic disorder is the most severe form of ADHD, with severe symptoms in all three domains described below.
- ADD (attention deficit disorder) is a milder form, with inattention, poor concentration and impulsivity, but not over-activity.

- DAMP (disorder of attention, motor coordination and perception) is a name for ADD with dyspraxia (poor movement and co-ordination – see p. 146).

How can I tell if my child has ADHD?

To make the diagnosis, significant symptoms from each category described below have to be present in the child from a young age and must cause real and significant problems affecting the quality of the child's life. They include:

Hyperactivity/over-activity. A hyperactive child cannot sit still for any length of time. If sitting, he will constantly fiddle, fidget or make noise. This will be particularly noticeable at mealtimes or in school, where other children of a similar age are able to sit quietly and eat or work. Computers and videos are more likely to hold his attention. Even when playing, the child is constantly on the go, rushing, noisy, never completing tasks.

Hyperactive children can be accident-prone, as they are more likely to be climbing, running or jumping without 'looking before they leap'. In girls, it can manifest as over-talkativeness without other signs of over-activity.

Hyperactivity must always be assessed relative to a child's age and development. Most two-year-olds are very active compared to older children. By young adulthood, many may grow out of the hyperactivity while still having significant other symptoms that may need treatment.

Poor concentration/distractibility. Children with ADHD have a short attention span and may not be able to stick to any task for more than a few minutes at a time, though this may improve with age. They tend to underachieve, despite often being very bright. Their work tends to be careless or unfinished. The slightest distraction interrupts their concentration. They often forget what they were doing, so may appear to wander aimlessly, being led from one distraction to another and often inadvertently into trouble. Similarly, they lose things easily.

Impulsivity. Hyperactive children seem to rush headlong into things without thinking, which can sometimes involve risk and danger. This can include talking to strangers (despite knowing it's not allowed), blurting out answers out of turn in class, being unable to queue, running heedlessly across a road or climbing obstacles.

How is ADHD diagnosed?

If the above symptoms fit with those of the child, a careful history taken from a number of sources including parents, school, previous assessments and school reports, may help with the diagnosis. Screening checklists and specialist psychological tests may also help. The final diagnosis should always be made by an experienced specialist in collaboration with family and school.

There is no clear test for ADHD. It takes an expert in child development, psychological and medical problems to make the diagnosis. A family doctor should be able to refer the child to paediatricians or Child and Adolescent Mental Health Services (CAMHS) specialists who have the expertise to treat the disorder.

What causes ADHD?

The condition is due to a problem in the brain's regulation of attention, concentration and activity levels. Its exact nature is unknown, though the part of the brain affected seems to be the frontal lobes, involving a brain chemical called dopamine. The condition tends to run in families.

Brain trauma may be another cause, either following a difficult labour and birth or through direct trauma to the brain tissue – for example following a head injury or exposure to alcohol as a foetus.

Extreme deprivation or abuse in infants may also lead to irreversible developmental changes that do not respond to being well cared for in later life.

Some foods, such as those containing preservatives and additives, can make ADHD worse or can cause similar symptoms in some children, and eliminating these may be helpful. However, there is no evidence that these are the actual cause of ADHD.

How serious is ADHD?

ADHD can have a devastating effect on a child's life if it is not diagnosed and treated. The child is often in trouble and has difficulties at school, at home and with friendships. This all undermines his self-esteem and motivation to succeed in life, and sometimes it can lead to school failure, delinquency and criminality (see Chapter 19).

The effects of the condition at different ages are outlined in the table below. Resilience factors (see p. 158), such as intelligence, family support, hobbies and talents, can reduce the risk of these complications. Some people manage to live productive lives without treatment.

Treatment is usually very effective, especially if the family has other resilience factors, such as support and understanding from those around them. The outcome is, of course, worse the longer it is untreated and the more the child has been labelled as 'trouble' and 'bad'.

Common problems of ADHD at different ages

Infant				
Academic	**Decision-making**	**Risk issues**	**Relationships**	**Mood**
• Overactive. • Can't sit still. • Hard to control outside or to keep on task – e.g. listening to a story or watching TV.	• Can't wait – wants things now.	• Constantly on the go. • Wanders off. • Accident-prone. • Needs constant adult supervision.	• Responds well to close supervision, firm and consistent handling and immediate rewards, but can be exhausting for parents.	• Not a major issue, but some can be very temperamental and prone to severe tantrums.

Young child				
Academic	**Decision-making**	**Risk issues**	**Relationships**	**Mood**
• Can't sit still in class. • Disruptive.	• Poor judgement.	• Accident-prone – e.g. runs into road to get ball.	• Gets over-excited and over-intrusive in groups.	• Very changeable and reactive to situations. • Easily upset, excited or distracted.
Older child				
Academic	**Decision-making**	**Risk issues**	**Relationships**	**Mood**
• Motivated and enthusiastic, but underachieves, with careless mistakes and/or unfinished messy work. • Disruptive in class – can become class clown to get attention.	• Easily distracted and gravitates to excitement and trouble.	• Accidents.	• Starts to be aware of being told off a lot. • Becoming oppositional. • Family relations can be strained. • Can be left out of invitations to parties.	• Beginnings of lower self-esteem.
Early adolescent				
Academic	**Decision-making**	**Risk issues**	**Relationships**	**Mood**
• As above but worse. • Becoming aware of falling behind and gives up more easily.	• Trouble continues despite explanations, discussions and remorse. • Can't seem to learn from experience.	• Easily led by delinquent peers to minor misdemeanours, but first to be caught. • Given cautions.	• Oppositionality can worsen – answers back to peers and adults without thinking. • Told off more. • Arguments, hostility and aggression can escalate. • Relationships deteriorate.	• Low self-esteem. • Increasingly frustrated and aware of repeated failings.
Older adolescent				
Academic	**Decision-making**	**Risk issues**	**Relationships**	**Mood**
• Poor concentration becomes more of an issue with regard to coping with work and exams – high risk of educational failure.	• As above, but becoming more of an issue compared to peers, who seem to be maturing and to have better judgement.	• Higher risk of delinquency, conduct disorder, smoking and substance misuse, teenage pregnancy, fights and trouble with the law.	• Can be extrovert and friendly, but has trouble maintaining relationships, often saying thoughtless or destructive things without thinking.	• Higher risk of anxiety, depression and social isolation.

Older adolescent (continued)				
Academic	**Decision-making**	**Risk issues**	**Relationships**	**Mood**
• Forgetful, disorganized, loses things, scatty and chaotic. • Poor time management.	• Irresponsible behaviour continues. • Can't plan ahead and foresee consequences.	• Trouble managing money – likely to squander it without thinking and regret it later.	• Continuing criticism from adults as fails to become reliable and responsible compared to peers.	• Can't become self-reliant and increasingly frustrated at inability to manage simple daily activities (e.g. constantly late).
Young adults				
Academic	**Decision-making**	**Risk issues**	**Relationships**	**Mood**
• Can't stick to any training or job – higher unemployment levels.	• Impulsive, reckless behaviour. • Can become self-destructive. • Higher risk of impulsive self-harm.	• More driving accidents and fights (especially under influence of alcohol) and increased risk of criminality.	• Relationship failures. • Poor family relationships.	• As above. • Higher risk of psychiatric problems.

What can be done to help?

Most children respond at least partially to a combination of treatments. To begin with, it is important that an accurate diagnosis is made and that the school, relatives and others should be informed that the child is not just 'bad', but in need of help for this condition. This can reduce the criticism and blame that parents often suffer. It can also restore co-operation and improve motivation to work collaboratively to manage the problem.

Provision of support for the child, family and teacher is vital. This can be gained through contact with ADHD support agencies, the school (educational psychologists and advice with Special Educational Needs support), health services and possibly social services (for family support, financial advice or childcare support, if relevant).

Psychological approaches

- Parenting groups are very helpful in providing support between parents in a similar situation; in educating parents about the condition and how to manage it; and in giving those who do not have consistent parenting skills the necessary techniques to make this possible.
- Children may benefit from help in focusing their attention, managing their anger and frustration, building their self-esteem and coming to terms with their diagnosis and its implications, as well as coping with schoolwork. Parents and teachers can support them in all this, with extra help from specialist clinics.

Tips for parents and teachers

Self Speak. Ask the child to try 'self speak' to help keep focused. Get the child to ask questions and provide the answers to help keep himself on task: 'Where am I? Where am I supposed to be? I'm in the TV room and am supposed to be in the kitchen. OK, I'm now in the kitchen. What am I supposed to do next? Oh yes, fetch the milk from the fridge. OK, I have the milk. What am I supposed to do with it?', and so on.

Communication. Make sure the child is fully attentive to what you are asking. Position yourself so that you are face to face, so he isn't distracted by anything else, and establish eye contact. You may need to hold his head or shoulders gently to achieve this. Don't call out instructions if the child is not in the room, as you'll probably be wasting your time – he won't register. He may benefit from sitting near the front in class, as long as this can be done without embarrassing him.

Keep rules clear and simple. Communicate simply and briefly, in soundbites:

'Get the milk from the kitchen, please,' will be more effective than

'James, stop fiddling with the spoons. Get the milk and set the table. Come on, get on with it, we're late for school. Hurry up. Don't forget you have PE today and your shorts are on the landing. You'll need those.' With this latter approach, the child is likely to have forgotten what to do next after all these instructions! Give reminders calmly. Check that the child understands what to do by asking him to repeat what you asked of him before you let him go.

Follow up and praise him immediately before asking him to do the next task:

'Well done. Now, please pour some milk out in these cups. Great! Now . . .' If time is short, you can make it fun by trying to do it in a set time as a game.

Structure, 'scaffolding'. A child with ADHD will respond well to structure, routine, consistency, close monitoring and support. For example, help him to break tasks down into smaller steps with frequent praise and encouragement. This will keep him motivated and help him finish what he starts. You can help prevent loss, lateness and frustration by using checklists, diaries and alarms set as reminders (such as on a mobile phone). Help organize his belongings and keep them in place. Close supervision is necessary to prevent risks, redirecting him to safer options if he drifts towards trouble.

Keeping busy. Children with ADHD have loads of energy, so it helps to keep them occupied with a busy schedule to prevent them drifting towards boredom and trouble. Sometimes giving them things to fiddle with can help concentration and stop them having to get up and move around – doodling, a squeezy ball, playdough, origami, etc., can all be useful.

Be realistic. Allow for breaks when planning work times. In the heat of the moment, don't try to argue or reason, but allow time out for both of you to cool off and regain control. And try not to shout, nag, criticize, blame or give in 'for the sake of peace' – or give up! If possible, try not to react to bad behaviour, and ignore minor irritations. Follow through any pre-agreed consequences for problem behaviours. Save your undivided attention for the good behaviour, which is much harder to remember to do.

Medication

Although by itself it is unlikely to be a solution to all the problems, stimulant medication like methylphenidate (Ritalin) can dramatically improve the symptoms of ADHD in some children. It is helpful in most children if the diagnosis is correct, even if complicated by other conditions. It allows a child to stop and think before acting, to settle down and to live a more normal life. Although it can have side-effects, these are usually minimal, and the medication can always be stopped if it proves unsuitable. Ritalin is a classified substance as it is amphetamine-based. However, if used as prescribed, it actually reduces the likelihood of substance misuse, which is a common complication of untreated ADHD. For those who cannot tolerate stimulant medication, atomoxetine is a new class of drug that can also help.

In those with oppositional behaviours (where children have disruptive and oppositional behaviour that is usually directed towards authority figures, such as parents or teachers), medication will not prevent delinquency and further behavioural problems unless it is used in conjunction with behavioural and psychological approaches.

Complementary therapies and diet

The only complementary treatment for which there is some evidence of success is the use of omega-3 oil. Evidence suggests that it can have a modest effect when given consistently over a period of time at a high enough dose, although many people find that omega-3 does not replace the need for medication as well. It can be bought without prescription and is safe for use in young children, whereas it may be best to defer trying stimulants until five or six years old.

Diet. There is no evidence that a change of diet can cure ADHD, but it does help for some children to avoid foods that are known to make ADHD worse. These include caffeinated and fizzy drinks, E-numbers, artificial colours and preservatives such as tartrazine, excessive sweets, chocolate and sugary foods.

Extra help in school. Although most children with ADHD manage in mainstream education, often with careful behaviour management, some require extra help and very occasionally special schooling. See p. 130 for advice on what to do if this is the case.

What is the long-term outcome?

Although ADHD may never entirely go away, the underlying symptoms do improve with age. Adults with ADHD may have difficulties in concentrating or sitting still without fiddling, but often they do not need to continue taking Ritalin beyond their late teens. Currently a third of sufferers seem to outgrow the need for medication, a third don't and a third are somewhere in between – using lower doses, for example, or taking it only for particular situations such as exams.

The secondary complications of ADHD, such as delinquency, criminality, school failure, low self-esteem and associated mood problems, as well as poor peer relationships, are the aspects of the condition that are most likely to determine a child's future. If these are prevented early on with active treatment, the outcome can be very good.

Autistic spectrum disorders (ASD): autism and Asperger's syndrome

Callum is now fifteen but has always been different from his friends, brothers and sisters. He was late in starting to talk, but once he started he seemed very intelligent and quick to develop his language skills. He had extreme temper tantrums, couldn't cope with change and didn't really get on with friends at school, preferring his own company.

From an early age, Callum rarely smiled and he disliked cuddles and touching, except on his own terms. He had odd habits, such as smelling objects and rubbing his face on them, and looking at lights and mirrors close up. He liked watching things spin and was fascinated by planes. He also used to flap his hands when he got very excited. At nursery, he never joined in games, preferring to sit in his favourite corner in the playground lining up his cars.

When he started school, Callum was very advanced at spelling and was well ahead with his times tables. The teachers thought he was extremely bright and would, they hoped, 'grow out of his odd behaviours'. However, tests with speech and language therapists showed that he took language literally and had a very poor understanding of social situations. The educational psychologist found that his learning was patchy, being very poor in some subjects but above average in others.

Callum's parents were very relieved to find out that he had autism – knowing what the problem was helped them to understand and relate to him better. Both his parents and his teachers had far more realistic expectations for him and were able to plan for his longer-term educational needs.

What is autism?

Autism is a developmental brain disorder in which development deviates from normal. The spectrum is extremely wide. Some people may have very demanding behavioural difficulties and limited life opportunities. Others, at the opposite end of the spectrum, may have much milder problems and, with the right help and support, are able to lead relatively 'normal' lives.

Autistic spectrum disorders (ASD) are a form of pervasive developmental disorder. The term refers to a wide-reaching recognizable pattern of symptoms across a number of areas that makes the child markedly different from his peers (see the criteria on p. 197 and the table on p. 198).

The spectrum refers to the range of severity, from mild to severe, with varying levels of mental handicap and difficulty with speech. At the severe end, the child may have extreme learning difficulties, no speech and no social interaction. At the higher-functioning end, the child can be of normal or superior intelligence (some university professors can be classed at this end). In high-functioning autism, there is usually a history of speech delay, whereas in Asperger's (or Kanner's) syndrome there is no speech delay. However, by adulthood, it is usually not possible to distinguish between the two.

Even at this milder end, children may experience difficulties with day-to-day life. They may have to cope in a mainstream school with no extra support and, because they are bright and more is expected of them, they may be aware of just how different they are from their peers. This can be very upsetting.

ASDs are lifelong conditions for which there is no cure. The child's prospects relate mainly to his IQ, language ability and co-morbidities (associated problems). In one study at a clinic for ASD, 75 per cent of children also had a diagnosis of ADHD. Autism can be further complicated by epilepsy. Psychiatric disorders are common, especially anxiety, depression, obsessional symptoms and behavioural difficulties (temper and possibly aggression). ASD can also be complicated by tics (see Chapter 16) and other developmental delays.

People with ASD are socially vulnerable and may need lifelong support to prevent mental health and behavioural complications. Those at the high-functioning end can live successful independent lives, even if they remain 'different' or eccentric.

Early identification and intervention with the right support for the child and family can greatly improve a child's future.

How can I tell if my child has autism?

Unfortunately there is no diagnostic blood or laboratory test to tell if a child has ASD. Diagnosis depends on a careful history from a range of experts. There are, however, four main criteria:

Early lack of responsiveness. In children under the age of three, parents often notice very early on that the child seems different, less sociable or less interested in people, and may be less responsive than other children of the same age.

Social communication difficulties. These are sometimes severe. Children are often socially odd and aloof. They live in a world of their own and do not develop the 'to and fro' social conversations most people do. They often have abnormal eye contact, don't understand non-verbal gestures, and often can't work out what other people are thinking and feeling. For this reason they often lack empathy and may, for instance, respond inappropriately to someone getting hurt. They often do not become attached to their parents as normal children usually do, so can be very unresponsive. They may also (but not always) struggle with imaginative play. Mildly affected people can grow into 'eccentric professors', whereas the most severely affected individuals can end up sitting, rocking and spinning plates all day, with no other interests.

Language problems. At the severe end of the spectrum, the child may have no speech. At the milder end speech may be odd or stilted, with unusual words included; or the child may copy or repeat words (echolalia). When speech is present, the child tends to take language literally, and to use it literally too. Parents can ask, 'Go and get the milk', but if they fail to add 'and bring it to me' they could wait for ever as the child doesn't know to bring it back.

Insistence on routines and rituals. This manifests itself as having to do things a certain way all the time. Deviation from the routine can lead to huge upsets and tantrums. Even moving the furniture slightly can be very upsetting and traumatic. Rituals and mannerisms may arise, like spinning plates, flicking book pages over and over again, or hand-flapping when excited. These habits may develop into interests in things like train timetables, car models, lists and numbers.

Asperger's syndrome: common problems and solutions

ASD features	Problems	Solutions
• Speech delay in autism with expressive and/or receptive problems.	• Poor understanding. • Difficulty expressing self.	• Facilitate communication with pictures, cards, practice – e.g. visual timetables, communication systems like TEACH, PECS (see p. 203)
• Asperger's – subtle language problems – e.g. odd, over-formal or fussy, stilted.	• Takes language literally, answers back, misunderstands humour, sarcasm, bluffing.	• Use simple language and rules. • Avoid metaphors, similes, idioms, joking, sarcasm, etc.

ASD features	Problems	Solutions
• Social communication problems – e.g. avoids eye contact.	• Unable to manage 'to and fro' conversation or give and take – e.g. doesn't know how to have social conversation.	• Don't assume being rude. • Give a structured supported task with clear rules – teach him to ask about a subject he is interested in, e.g. pets.
• Doesn't know unwritten social rules of acceptable behaviour.	• Appears aloof or awkward.	• Don't insist on eye contact – e.g. can teach him to look at forehead to avoid appearing rude.
• Poor understanding of others' facial expressions or gestures.	• Misunderstandings.	• Teach how to behave in specific situations using social stories or role play.
• Difficulty expressing feelings and difficulty with 'to and fro' conversations.	• Trouble interacting, especially in new situations – e.g. asking for help. • Stilted conversations. • Anxiety.	• Check understanding, explain and help him express himself – e.g. with drawing/scales/pictures. • Use cue or time-out cards and offer help regularly. • Keep structure, routine and visual timetable. • Be supportive, flexible, clear, calm and consistent.
• Reduced imaginative play – lines toys up, spins them, sniffs or touches them rather than playing 'make believe'.	• Less interest in traditional toys. • Unusual attachment to objects or part-objects – e.g. wheels on toy car. • Less creative (don't pressurize over this).	• Work with strengths: prefers copying/repetitive play, collecting, lining up; often good at copying/drawing/models; good rote memory re facts. • Define rules very clearly.

ASD features	Problems	Solutions
• Rigidity – can't cope with change.	• Trouble coping with new people, places, situations, unexpected change, especially in unstructured social situations like lunchbreak at school.	• Warn, encourage and prepare for change, use visits, photos of new sites or people before new event. • Provide structure and support at key times, e.g. lunchbreak. • Use timers to warn about change.
• Hypersensitivity – to sound, touch, taste, smell.	• Upset by unexpected noises – e.g. thunder, fireworks, etc. • Faddy eater. • Faddy over clothes. • Extreme emotions.	• Multi-sensory stimulation can be used to calm, soothe and reward – e.g. fascination with lights, textures, spinning (wheels, fans, toys), collecting objects (has obsessional interests).

How common is ASD?

It used to be thought that ASD was very rare. However, we are now aware of the wider range of ASDs and the condition is much more frequently diagnosed. Recent studies suggest that approximately 1 child in every 1,000 shows severe autism and 6 in every 1,000 have ASD within the wider spectrum. ASD is more common in boys, with at least four boys to every girl affected.

What causes ASD?

Autism has a biological basis and is not due to bad parenting. It is a biological brain disorder which is often poorly understood but can be inherited genetically. Relatives may have very mild or similar traits.

Autism is related to a chromosomal disorder (abnormal genes like Fragile X, for example). Other factors may include viral infections in the womb, drug use in pregnancy and/or childbirth, birth injury, and measles and other infections such as meningitis. Research continues into its cause, but it is important that parents do not blame themselves and worry about everything that they may have done.

What should I do if I suspect ASD?

Children with ASD usually need a team of specialists to provide a full and detailed assessment as soon as possible in order to identify the right support early on. Quite often the school will identify the problem. But if they do not and you have concerns, it is important that you share these with the school or nursery as soon as possible and ask them to look into them. You can request assessment towards a Statement of Special Educational Needs (SEN) if you think your child has special needs. The school or nursery can then ask an educational psychologist to check for ASD. For a pre-school infant, your health visitor can advise at an early stage. At any age, ask your GP to refer your child to a paediatrician if you suspect this condition.

Assessment of ASD will involve some or all of the following professionals:

- Paediatrician – for medical diagnosis and associated conditions.
- Speech and language therapist – for language and social communication problems.
- Occupational therapist – for coordination problems, and assessing and advising about sensory hypersensitivities.
- Clinical and/or educational psychologist – to assess learning and behavioural problems and advise about behavioural management, recommend support needed at home/in school.
- Paediatric neurologist – for children with associated

neurological problems like epilepsy or unusual syndromes.

- Child psychiatrist – for very complex needs with associated conditions such as ADHD, Tourette's or depression (see Chapters 16 and 17), where there are extreme behaviours, or for high-functioning autism where the diagnosis is unclear.
- Social workers – may also be needed to help assess family/carer needs, including the needs of siblings, who may be entitled to support as young carers.

Possible early signs

Although autism can be reliably diagnosed in toddlers by about thirty months, Asperger's syndrome is not usually suspected until the child goes to school.

You must refer the child to the nurse, health visitor or GP if any of these arise:

- no babble or gesture by one year old
- no single words by one and a half years old
- no spontaneous two words (not copied) by two years old
- loss of language or skills at any age

Consider referral as above if by two or three years old you are aware of:

- communication problems:
  verbal: language delayed or odd (e.g. echolalia, repeating words)
  non-verbal: little or no smiling or social response
- poor social skills: e.g. little or no sharing of enjoyment, difficult relationship with other children and sometimes with adults
- poor imaginative play; rigid or obsessive play
- aloof, 'in a world of his own', lacking interest in others
- poor eye contact

- Difficulty coping with change, leading to:
  - extreme emotional reactions (especially if for no apparent reason)
  - hypersensitivities: to touch, taste, smell, light, food (faddy eater)
  - odd behaviours: self-injury, head-banging, hand-flapping, odd movements

What can be done to help?

Although there is no specific treatment or cure for ASD, research shows that early identification and giving the right help can make a big difference. So it is important to refer to a specialist as soon as the problem is suspected and not just 'wait and see'. There are now more assessments available to detect the condition at an earlier stage than previously, so getting to a specialist who knows about autism can make all the difference.

Targeted ASD support

It is vital that all concerned have a detailed understanding of the child's strengths and weaknesses so that they can work out how best to support him. A child with ASD needs structure, routine, warning and preparation for change in a calm setting, with communication strategies which can include:

Picture Exchange Communication System (PECS). PECS is helpful for children who are non-verbal or have severe language and communication problems. It teaches the child to exchange a picture of a desired item with a teacher, who rewards him with this item. The key is that the child learns to initiate requests, and is not dependent on being prompted. Children are also taught to comment and answer direct questions.

Teaching and Education of Autistic Children and Handicapped Children (TEACH). TEACH provides a systematic approach to learning and structure for the individual and is used with both children and adults. It is about adapting the setting of the child at home and school so that the environment is more autism-friendly, more structured and less overstimulating. Special and mainstream schools often use similar strategies.

Social stories. These are simple stories created to describe a new social scenario, teaching the child what to expect and how to respond in order to help him prepare and know what to do. The table on p. 198 outlines some of the strategies that can be helpful in dealing with various problem areas. But each child will respond differently, so a key issue is maintaining consistent care with individualized approaches.

Who should change, the child or the environment?

This is an important issue. Some children have families and schools adapting to their every need, which keeps them content and easy to manage. The risk of this is that they will never cope in a mainstream environment.

Other schools and families won't accept that an autistic child should be treated any differently and this can lead to friction and upset. A careful judgement must be made about teaching the child to learn to manage change at his own pace, so that he has a better chance of coping with the 'real world' and accepting discipline, rules and sanctions without tantrums.

School

Children with ASD often require additional help in school and many, depending upon their ability level, will require special schooling, either in a special unit or a special school. (See p. 127 on extra help in school and special schools.) All assessments should be sent to the educational psychologists, who will be able to recommend an individualized package of support and learning. This may include speech and language input at school (possibly with access to social skills training), and use of communication systems (as above) so that the child can access the curriculum. The right placement and provision can make all the difference.

Home

Parents in the UK can currently attend a 'HELP' course about ASD for parents of newly diagnosed children. This is invaluable in understanding more about the condition and what to do. There are specialist courses on parenting, parent support groups, advice available about how to help the family cope, where to get help and benefits if needed, and specialist schools in your area if relevant. The National Autistic Society will know about the local services in your area and advise where to get the best help.

Specialist (CAMHS) interventions

- Individual and parenting treatments.
- Specialist parenting and behavioural advice can be tailored to a child with complex needs. Cognitive behavioural therapy (CBT) may help for anxiety and phobias (see Chapter 10), but young children often cannot cope with play therapy or 1:1 work, in which case work is done via parents and school.
- For children with associated emotional and behavioural problems, treatments are available as described for the other conditions in this book, but tailored to a child with ASD.
- Family work or therapy may be helpful if the family as a whole is struggling to cope, and relatives want to work together to improve their situation.

Medication

Risperidone is a major tranquillizer, usually used in psychosis. Recently it has been shown to be extremely helpful for treating high levels of agitation, upset and aggression in children with ASD – if taken in very low doses. It is not a substitute for good environmental and behavioural support, but can be very helpful, especially in the short term when all else fails. There are major side-effects, however – including weight gain and associated complications (such as raised blood pressure or the development of diabetes) – that need to be discussed carefully in weighing up the risks and benefits.

Antidepressants can be effective in children with ADHD and ASD and sometimes can improve sociability. Medications can be helpful when the child is unable to access individual support because of communication problems or high levels of upset. A child psychiatrist will be able to advise more about this.

Medication can also be used for associated conditions, such as ADHD, depression or anxiety, when relevant (see p. 193).

There is sometimes a tendency to add too many medications. This can make things worse and children with ASD can be sensitive to side-effects. Sometimes the most helpful intervention is reducing medication, so this must always be used with caution as part of a wider care plan and must be closely monitored.

Complementary therapies and diet

There is no evidence that complementary therapies are helpful, although the advice given for ADHD regarding omega-3 oils and diet (see p. 193) may also be useful in ASD.

Because of their hypersensitivities, however, therapies or activities based on smell (aromatherapy), relaxation (hydrotherapy or gentle massage, or cranial osteopathy) may be relaxing and improve the quality of life for children with autism. They also often respond well to multi-sensory environments (access to sand, water, scented gardens, spinning toys, coloured lights, music, lava lamps, bubble baths, etc.). It is best to experiment with these to see what works.

Remember that a bottle of bubble bath can be much cheaper and more effective than a specialist unproven therapy. Parents are often vulnerable to exploitation and need to be aware of the lack of evidence base before parting with large sums of money for unproven treatments.

Tips for parents

Although not always the case, parenting an autistic child can be extremely exhausting and demanding. Parents can get demoralized and depressed, which in itself can prevent the development of the usual attachments with the child. Because the child does not show the attachment behaviour expected for his age, it can be very frustrating for parents. Also, at times the parent may be 'unavailable' to the child emotionally because of exhaustion and burn-out.

Having an accurate diagnosis together with the right support, however, can make a huge difference. Once you are emotionally available, even if your child is less responsive than others, it is still possible to achieve much mutual pleasure. There is a capacity for a rewarding bond to develop between you as you get to know, understand and accept your child. Autistic children do develop attachments.

Other points to consider:

- Is the assessment complete? Has anything been missed (e.g. specific learning difficulty in a bright child with ASD)? Remember that ASD is associated with a lot of other conditions, many of which are treatable.
- Does the child have the right support in school? Do his helpers have experience or training in ASD and, if not, could they access this? Remember to be consistent and to keep close communication between home and school.

- Do you have the right help? Do you have enough help? Think through the problem list in the table above and consider some of the solutions. Have all angles been covered? If not, get the right help and advice to do so. Don't be embarrassed to ask for help and support – you are likely to need it and are entitled to it, but may not get it if you do not ask.
- Keep an active regular routine, including in the holidays, and use a visual timetable to plan together. Consider activities for young people with special needs, especially in school holidays. Check what is available in your area through your local disability networks.
- Remember to plan carefully for any changes. Change is usually the main problem for making things worse and can usually be managed better with more planning.
- Deal with one problem at a time, and take time out for yourself.

Dr Dinah Jayson

INFORMATION

SUPPORT ORGANIZATIONS

Attention Deficit Hyperactivity Disorder (ADHD): LADDER (National Learning and Attention Deficit Disorders Association), PO Box 700, Wolverhampton WV3 7YY.

ADD/ADHD Family Support Group: Helpline: 01454 772262. *http://beehive.thisisbristol.com*

Hyperactive Children's Support Group: *www.hacsg.org.uk*

National Autistic Society: *www.nas.org.uk*

Afasic – unlocking speech and language: *www.afasic.org.uk*

I-CAN: supports the development of speech, language and communication skills in all children, with a special focus on those who find this hard. *www.ican.org.uk*

Asperger's syndrome: OASIS (Online Asperger Syndrome Information and Support). *www.udel.edu/bkirby/asperger*

Kids (Good) Behaviour: *www.kidsbehaviour.co.uk*

FURTHER READING

Attwood, Tony, *Asperger's Syndrome: a Guide for Parents and Professionals*, Jessica Kingsley, 1998.

Taylor, Eric, *The Hyperactive Child: A Parent's Guide* (2nd edn), Vermilion Press, 1995.

WEBSITES OUTSIDE THE UK

Australia and New Zealand
www.anzhealthpolicy.com

Canada
www.phac-aspc.gc.ca
www.ldac-taac.ca
www.chaddcanada.org

12 Culture and Society

Nancy is a fourteen-year-old girl who came to the UK two years ago from Zimbabwe, where she had been living with her grandmother on the outskirts of Harare and attending a private girls' school. She had lived with her grandmother since the age of five, when her parents had to leave the country for political reasons. Her parents decided two years ago that it was time for their family to be reunited as they had settled well in the UK and secured their right to stay.

Nancy also seemed to settle in well and made an excellent start at the local school. However, after about a year her parents took her to the GP saying she had headaches, stomach pain and tiredness. Despite lots of tests by the paediatric service, no physical cause was found, so Nancy was referred to the local Child and Adolescent Mental Health Services (CAMHS) as everyone was at a loss to explain her symptoms.

When Nancy was assessed, they found no evidence of a mental health disorder. She was given an opportunity to talk alone with the psychiatrist and confided that she missed Zimbabwe, her grandmother and the private school, which was very different from the local comprehensive she now attended. She felt that admitting this to her parents might make them angry or think she did not want to live with them.

The psychiatrist was able to work with her parents to help them understand that adjusting to life in the UK had been more difficult for their daughter than they had realized. This enabled Nancy and her parents to talk about her early childhood and the move. Openness in the family meant that she no longer had to hide her sadness at having left Zimbabwe. Her parents were also able to talk to her about what she missed.

Over the next few weeks, Nancy's physical symptoms got better. Her parents said that she had now started joining in more things at school and was feeling happier and more settled.

What is culture?

Although there are clear definitions of 'culture' in the dictionary, in practice it often means very different things to different people. How often have you heard the statement that Britain is now a multicultural society and that that is a good thing? Do you find yourself agreeing or disagreeing?

Quite often we think that culture is the same as ethnicity. But it isn't. Culture depends on many different factors, including ethnicity. Culture may be better explained as the group or groups with which a person identifies. Your cultural identity may be based on heritage (such as race, ethnicity, language, country of origin) as well as on your circumstances (age, gender, sexual orientation, social class, physical ability) and on your personal choice (religious/spiritual beliefs). All these factors may affect such things as communication style, diet preferences, health beliefs, family roles, lifestyle, rituals and decision-making processes. Culture, while not always linked to race or ethnicity, does affect how we interpret and interact with others.

It is important that each of us is allowed to define ourselves rather than be defined by others. We all develop our unique sense of identity and culture as we grow into adulthood. We already know that people's cultural backgrounds can affect:

- the way they think about mental health and mental health problems
- the way they make sense of certain symptoms and behaviours
- the services they find helpful
- the treatment and management strategies they find useful
- the way in which those who have mental health problems are perceived

Culturally appropriate care is the care that is right for any particular person at that particular point in time, taking into account their perspectives. It is also care that the person understands and is comfortable with. In the case of children, while the parents' views and agreement are important, so too is the child's.

Any good healthcare professional should be able to discuss what will help and answer any questions you may have. Providing help that fits with culture is not just about good communication and choice. To offer culturally appropriate care, the professional needs to be constantly aware of what life is like for the young person and her family, and how this may be affecting her in asking for, or getting, help. Other factors may be important, such as different expectations of what boys and girls should, or can, do, and at what ages.

Cultural expectations

Gareth is sixteen years old and from a traditional English background. He was seen in A&E after taking an overdose of paracetamol. He told the psychiatrist who assessed him after the overdose that he was gay and wanted to die because someone at school had found out about it. This person was threatening to tell Gareth's father, the local vicar. Gareth was aware that his father has views that homosexuality goes against what God wants.

Gareth was referred to the local CAMHS, where he saw a community psychiatric nurse for some counselling. Over the next few weeks, he realized that he had to be honest with his parents. To his surprise he found that, while his father struggled with Gareth being gay, he loved his son and wanted to support him. The family was put in touch with a local support service to help them talk about things. In this case, different attitudes towards homosexuality caused problems for the young person.

There are very few culturally specific problems – that is, problems that occur only within specific cultures. In other chapters, you will read about some disorders that are more likely in some contexts than others – for instance, the eating disorder anorexia nervosa is more common in 'Western' contexts than in others.

Younger children will often accept what their families tell them and so have the same views as their parents. As they move into adolescence, cultural expectations may influence their developing sense of identity.

They may question the values that their parents hold. There is often an assumption that differences between parents and young people are more likely in ethnic-minority families. The explanation given is that the parents may hold views consistent with their ethnic origin, whereas adolescents face the task of integrating the wider culture in which they have grown up with their family's culture. For example, some may believe that 'Eastern cultures' have a more collective sense of identity and 'Western cultures' are more focused on the individual. However, these are stereotypes and sometimes individuals are assumed to be like that stereotype. In fact, families usually have a unique culture of their own. As we have already seen, this sense of culture can mean different things to different people, so it would be wrong to assume that everyone in a family will have the same views.

Cultural practices often vary between the private (usually the home) and public (school or work). At home families may speak the language of the culture of origin and raise their children in particular ways, but in more public contexts may speak English and conform to the 'majority' norms. Different families and young people manage in different ways. Some may take on the culture of origin and the culture of the new country; others may switch between these cultures depending on the context. Others may blend both cultures to produce a unique culture of their own. It is a mistake to think that young people (and their families) are exposed to only two cultures. Most young people are exposed to a range of cultures and often 'pick and mix' different components. Music is a good example. Both bhangra and hip hop could be said to be specific to certain cultures; however, lots of young people (and adults!) from many cultures listen to this type of music.

Children who have grown up without their parents may begin to ask questions about their backgrounds in early adolescence to help them make sense of who they are. Mixed-race children may be curious about their cultural background, especially the one they are not predominantly brought up in.

Issues that may give rise to problems are:

- pressures to practise their family's religion or other things that young people may not want to do
- pressures to fit with gender roles expected by their family's culture (such as boys wanting to enter careers generally thought to be for women, such as nursing and childcare, and vice versa)
- pressures to conform to social norms – e.g. an expectation to go on to further education despite this not being what they want
- pressures to conform to family expectations that differ from what the young person wants (for example, an expectation that the young person works in the family business)
- sexual orientation
- impending forced marriage
- difficulty in reconciling the culture at home with that at school/work

Young people may try to cope with these pressures by:

- being argumentative and challenging every aspect of their parents' authority
- doing things they know will upset their parents – e.g. not doing their homework if the parents value education; not observing religious rituals
- harming themselves
- becoming moody
- taking substances to cope with the pressures
- becoming depressed, especially if they feel there is no possibility of things getting better

What can be done to help?

If there is a specific mental health problem, this will need to be discussed within the family and managed in an appropriate way – see the relevant chapters of this book. It may be that some approaches need more discussion and negotiation because of cultural differences. Parents may be surprised when clinical staff want to involve the young person in decisions about himself. Work with the young person or the family will usually be needed to bring out and help issues related to culture. The young person may be helped to think about his views and identity. Working with the family may be needed to resolve conflict. Things will get better if everyone is able to compromise and be flexible.

Tips for families

It is really important to remember that young people are developing and part of that process is questioning what their parents and elders take for granted. This does not mean that they are being disrespectful, but that they are thinking of what their values are. The more strongly they are discouraged from doing this, the more likely they are to rebel. This strategy can often be self-destructive, but the young person may feel he has no other option.

✔ **DO**

- keep open all communication and talk a lot together
- listen to young people with sincerity
- be consistent and clear about your expectations
- try to have another adult with whom the young person can talk things through (such as an aunt or uncle), as their relationship with the child may not be as intense as that between parent and child

✖ **DON'T**

- assume the young person is going to share all your values

- assume that just because they don't share all your values they don't value any of them
- write off the young person just because they have made some mistakes

Dr Nisha Dogra

SUPPORT ORGANIZATIONS

There is remarkably little in terms of broad support available about the above issues, although it is an area that is being increasingly researched. General mental health websites should give some attention to cultural issues.

Mind: mental health charity in England and Wales. Helpline: 0845 766 0163. *www.mind.org.uk*

Mental Health Foundation: charity that provides information, carries out research, campaigns and works to improve services for anyone affected by mental health problems. *www.mentalhealth.org.uk*

WEBSITES OUTSIDE THE UK

Australia
Centre for multicultural youth issues: *www.cmyi.net.au*

Canada
Canadian International Development Agency: *www.acdi-cida.gc.ca*

13 Dealing with Loss

Gemma was fifteen years old and an only child. She had taken very little notice when her mum first told her she was ill. She was busy getting on with her own life as a teenager and not particularly interested. Then her mother went into hospital, leaving Gemma without any transport to places she wanted to go. Mum had always done so much for her, supporting her in whatever she wanted to do. Gemma was angry with her mum for letting her down and for not being there when she needed her. She thought her mum was being 'hard work' and was irritated when she complained of being tired. When her mum died, Gemma felt guilty about her feelings.

Her dad now had to work very long hours away from home in order to pay the bills and Gemma was at home alone most nights. Even when her dad was there, things were no better as he always seemed tired and bad tempered. She now had to do the housework, cooking and shopping, and they were very short of money. She was becoming isolated from her friends, who seemed to be having 'normal' lives. She felt different from them. She had her GCSEs coming up but was finding it difficult to concentrate on schoolwork.

Gemma had not spoken to anybody about how she felt – it didn't feel as if there was anybody there. She did want to talk to somebody, but didn't know where to turn for help. A schoolfriend who was worried about her suggested she drop in to see the school nurse one lunchtime, so Gemma did. She was a bit nervous at first, but the nurse was so kind and helpful that Gemma found it a great relief to be able to talk about her situation. The nurse put Gemma in touch with a Connexions adviser, Young Carers and the school counsellor.

Illness and death are part of our human condition. They create stress for a child and a family, but this stress does not often lead to lasting mental health problems. Indeed, over time, most children, teenagers and their families come to terms with these difficulties and go on to lead happy and fulfilled lives. In the long run, people can even develop strengths through adversity. There will be times when the support of family and friends is needed and occasions when the help of support organizations, clergy, school nurses, school counsellors, health visitors, GPs and specialist services may be helpful.

Children and young people are constantly subjected to loss and change, because they are developing – physically, emotionally, socially, spiritually – in their thinking and in their experience of the world. At every stage of development they lose some of the advantages of an earlier stage, while gaining new and different ones.

In a study of schoolchildren in the UK, 92 per cent of eleven- to sixteen-year-olds had experience of bereavement when pets were included, and 66 per cent of them had lost at least one grandparent. Five per cent had lost a brother or sister through death, 4 per cent a parent, 11 per cent a close friend and 23 per cent an aunt or uncle. This means that children frequently have to deal with death within the family and sometimes among their close friends.

Some children and young people find it helpful to talk about their loss, but others don't. There is no 'right way' for children to deal with loss and grief. Each child needs to do so in his own way, and if he does want to talk to someone he should be able to choose when that happens and whom he would like to see. There are organizations and services to support this.

If death is sudden, violent or by suicide, this makes it more difficult for children to come to terms with, and is more likely to lead to health problems. Children might also struggle if they had relationship problems with the person who has died.

Children often go through other types of loss. For example, the rates of divorce in Western countries are very high; parents, teenagers and children experience illnesses or accidents which may cause a disability; and families often move house.

Whose loss is it?

Sometimes a change is seen as a gain to some members of the family but a loss to others. So, although the same event may occur in several people's lives, the experience of it may be very different for each of them. For example, a house move into a more well-off area may be positive for the parents; to their children, however, it may mean loss of friends, loss of familiar surroundings and routines, and loss of cherished aspects of the former school and home.

After divorce a parent may feel relief, whereas the children may have very different feelings which are difficult for the parent to appreciate.

Shared loss may be easier in some ways, but more difficult in others. For example, a child who has lost a brother or sister may not want to speak to her parents about how she feels for fear of causing further distress or worry.

Death in the family

When someone the child knows or cares about dies, it is important to consider the following.

✔ **DO**

- ❖ remember to notify your children's school about what has happened before your children return following the death
- ❖ provide information to your children at a level appropriate to their ages and ability – what has happened, why it happened, what will happen next
- ❖ be honest – even if they do not like what you say, it is better for them to know rather than to worry or guess
- ❖ listen to what they have to say and support them
- ❖ encourage and support them to be involved if they want – e.g. by attending the funeral
- ❖ take them to visit the place where the funeral will be held if they want, in order to explain what they will hear and see
- ❖ explain that the person who has died can no longer feel hot, cold or sad and that they can't feel pain
- ❖ use books to help with this if it is too difficult for you
- ❖ let them find and use their own sources of support
- ❖ seek help if you are concerned that your child might be becoming depressed, too clingy or withdrawn
- ❖ look after yourself – you need time, space and support
- ❖ use the help that is around you

✖ **DON'T**

- ❖ be surprised if each child reacts differently
- ❖ be shocked if your children appear flippant about the loss – that is a normal reaction for a child when the feelings are too strong

- ❖ be afraid to cry in front of them – it is OK for them to know you are upset

Children's grief at various developmental stages

Age	Concept of Death	Grief reaction
0–2	• No concept of death, separation or despair.	• At 4–7 months protests at separation. • May cry with strangers. • May regress. • May have feeding difficulty. • May have disturbed sleep.
2–5	• Magical thinking: may see death as reversible; may feel they have caused it.	• May show anger at changes in routine. • May show regressive behaviour. • May have disrupted sleep. • May show fear of abandonment and separation. • May show signs of despair and protest loudly.
5–11	• More understanding of the permanence of death.	• May express a variety of emotions – anger, fear, sadness. • May show regressive behaviour. • May try to be brave or try to be the 'perfect child'.
11+	• Understanding that death is permanent. • Disbelief that it has happened.	• May withdraw. • May express stages of grief – denial, anger, sadness, acceptance. • May show regressive behaviour. • May act inappropriately.

Divorce and separation

When talking to a child about divorce or separation, please:

✔ **DO**

- ❖ tell your children about your decision to live apart as soon as you are certain of your plans (tell them together, if possible)

- ❖ tailor the talk to your children, bearing in mind their age and maturity
- ❖ reassure them that they are not to blame
- ❖ give them information to prepare them for the changes in their lives
- ❖ answer their questions honestly and reassure them about how life will change and what will stay the same
- ❖ keep it simple
- ❖ acknowledge that their feelings are understandable and OK
- ❖ be patient and understanding if children take time to come to terms with the changes or even appear indifferent

✖ **DON'T**

- ❖ discuss feelings of guilt, anger or blame
- ❖ blame the children or get angry with them
- ❖ deceive them in an effort to protect them
- ❖ give them more details than they need

It is important to help children cope with a divorce or separation by doing the following:

✔ **DO**

- ❖ encourage honesty
- ❖ help them put their feelings into words – sometimes children and teenagers struggle to find the words and you can help them with this
- ❖ acknowledge and accept their feelings
- ❖ offer support
- ❖ keep yourself healthy, physically and emotionally
- ❖ keep details to a minimum
- ❖ get help for yourself through this difficult time – look for support groups, friendships and counselling

- expect resistance and difficulties if the children have to adjust to your new partner or your new partner's children (you may need to ask for additional support at this point)
- try to avoid financial hardship for the children
- try to provide consistency in family structure and routine
- try to maintain good-quality planned contact with the non-resident parent (except where protection from abuse or violence is needed, in which case you will need to seek professional help)
- look out for warning signs of divorce-related depression or anxiety in your children and get help if they are there

✖ **DON'T**

- criticize your ex-partner in front of the children, even if you are still angry or feuding
- fight in front of the children
- use the children as messengers or go-betweens, especially when you are feuding

Chronic illness in a child or young person

George was fourteen and had lived with kidney failure since he was seven. He had been on a very strict diet for years and had to take lots of medicines, including some that tasted foul. He was sick of it. He had to go for dialysis at the hospital three times a week, each session lasting for several hours. He had missed so much school that he didn't feel part of it. He preferred people at school to think he was playing truant rather than that he was ill. He felt people treated you differently if they knew you were ill, and they often thought they might catch something. A boy he used to talk to at the hospital died a few months ago and the same could happen to him.

George didn't go out much because lots of activities enjoyed by his schoolfriends involved food that he wasn't allowed to eat. He would have quite liked a girlfriend, but didn't know if anyone would fancy him. At home he felt like a burden to the family. His mum had been depressed and he felt guilty because he knew she worried about him a lot. There was a great deal of work involved in taking him to and from appointments and he didn't always stick to his diet or take his tablets, which led to arguments.

George's mum and dad couldn't relax when it came to their son. He wanted a bit more independence, but his parents were scared to let him do things. He wanted them to talk to him more about things that were not to do with his illness.

George was now in Year 10 and planning his work experience in a shop, but it would be difficult to arrange – what should he tell them? It felt as though everything was more difficult for him. People had no idea.

Then he heard that there was a teenagers' group running at the hospital where he would be able to meet with other young people in a similar situation to his own, so he went along. It was good to talk with them – they understood what it was like and it was interesting to hear about their difficulties and how they managed, especially the older ones.

Dealing with chronic illness can be very challenging. Families are subjected to many pressures, such as juggling hospital appointments, school runs, work, shopping and housekeeping. These all take their toll, so it is not surprising that mental health problems are more common in families of chronically ill children.

When families have the added burden of illness, they lose autonomy and privacy. They often need outside help, which can sometimes feel like interference, and they become subject to the deficiencies of the professional systems with which they have to interact.

When parents have a child with a disability or a child different from the one they had expected, this can be experienced as a loss. Parents can undergo a process of grieving and, until they have worked through this, they can struggle to accept the child they have in front of them.

It is also possible that the needs of brothers and sisters of a chronically ill child can be overlooked by families and professionals alike. Sometimes the illness of the child manifests in such a way that the siblings are repeatedly and seriously challenged physically, psychologically or socially.

While illnesses can cause children and young people stress, they can also lead to short-term benefits for the child, such as reduced expectations, fewer challenges, compassionate responses, increased attention and the prevention of changes or other losses. However, it is important to help the young person to keep in mind their long-term best interests, and to listen to them carefully about how they feel.

Some children and young people suffer from severe and chronic pain. As many as 15 per cent of children suffer from headaches and abdominal and musculoskeletal pain, but 2 per cent have pain symptoms that can be severe enough to interrupt sleep, limit physical activity and prevent them from attending school. The practical pressures on the family as a result of their child being at home full time, in hospital or needing transport to medical appointments, coupled with their helplessness in the face of their child's distress and feelings of vulnerability, can all have a major impact on the family. Parents report high levels of anxiety, marital problems and financial difficulty. Some are unable to work because of the demands involved in looking after the child.

However, research from the Pain Management Unit in Bath has shown that, even for children and adolescents with the most severe pain and disability, it may be possible to reduce the impact of the pain on their lives and the lives of their families through psychological treatments. Such treatments may include cognitive behaviour therapy (CBT; see p. 351), family therapy (see p. 355), or help for a struggling or depressed parent.

Practical support for the family on a day-to-day basis is important and can make a difference. This support can be provided by family, friends, social care, tailored education where appropriate, voluntary agencies and health services. Services that are consistent, flexible and child- and family-centred can help the child and family to cope with the challenges.

Psychosomatic problems

It is not possible to separate body and mind, as they work together and affect each other. 'Psychosomatic' is a term we use when physical symptoms are made worse by worry or anxiety. For example, some days a child might feel able to go to school despite a bad cold, but on a day when they have a test the combination of the cold and the test might feel like too much. If they are worried about the test they might notice the physical symptoms more, or even get extra symptoms caused by the anxiety. This is a normal reaction that probably happens to everyone at some point. But if the pattern becomes frequent a vicious circle is set up, where the child might fall behind, lose confidence, worry more and as a result feel less well physically.

Where you suspect psychosomatic problems in your child:

✔ **DO**

- take her to the doctor to see if anxiety is making her worse
- be consistent in talking about the problem
- talk to your child about her feelings

- be sympathetic and reassuring but firm
- help the child to use simple relaxation exercises and distraction techniques
- tell her that you understand that she feels unwell, but don't make a big deal out of it
- explain to the child that stress can make physical symptoms worse and will make the symptoms go on longer, even when the physical cause has gone away
- encourage activities and behaviour that are not illness-related. Going to school will help to distract them from the symptoms, and the teachers can ring you if their symptoms get worse or can arrange for them to see a school nurse
- make sure that the child does not miss school, with the help and support of school staff if necessary

✖ **DON'T**

- question the child's truthfulness – she does feel the pain
- be shy of asking for professional help if things aren't getting better

Parents as patients

In 2007 a research project collected the views of children and young people when their parents were in hospital with mental health problems. Children and young people reported feeling worried for themselves and for their parents – confused, isolated, afraid, abandoned and frightened that their parents would not return home. Those questioned stressed the importance of maintaining regular high-quality contact with their parents, but they struggled with the practicalities – getting lifts to and from hospital, for example. They also had problems with the stigma of having parents in hospital as a result of mental illness, and they disliked and feared the hospitals and the other patients.

The young people reported that it helped them to feel less anxious if they could telephone any time and if the ward staff were welcoming, helpful and caring. It helped if they had a private and comfortable space where they could spend time with their parents, and if there was a room with toys and activities this made them feel that the hospital welcomed children and families.

When a parent is ill mentally or physically, children may become angry about the parent's physical or emotional unavailability. This in turn can lead to feelings of guilt. Alternatively, the children might worry about the parent and try to care for him or her. They might try to look after the parent and expect more from themselves than they can possibly do. When a parent seeks professional help in such circumstances, this can lift a great burden from their children. There is an organization called Young Carers which supports children and young people who find themselves caring for a family member (see Support Organizations, p. 231).

When parents are ill, they may be less able to fulfil their responsibilities and children may even suffer neglect. Mothers with postnatal depression may, through no fault of their own, be less able to stimulate their babies than usual (see p. 77). Asking for help as soon as you become aware that something is wrong is best for you and best for your child.

Dr Lucy Harrison

Bereavement and loss

SUPPORT ORGANIZATIONS

The Child Bereavement Trust (CBT): national charity that helps bereaved families when a baby or child has died, or when children are bereaved of someone important in their lives. It trains and supports those who come into contact with child bereavement in the course of their work within healthcare, education, social care, the emergency services and the voluntary sector. It also offers a confidential information and support service for professionals and families, providing a listening ear and, if appropriate, signposting to further local and national sources of support specific to the particular situation. Information and support helpline: 01494 446648. *www.childbereavement.org.uk*

CRUSE Bereavement Care: promotes the well-being of bereaved people and aims to enable anyone bereaved by death to understand their grief and cope with their loss. Helpline: 0844 477 9400. Young person's freephone helpline: 0808 808 1677. *www.crusebereavementcare.org.uk*

Winston's Wish: charity supporting bereaved children and families. Helpline: 08452 03 04 05. *www.winstonswish.org.uk*

Divorce

Divorce Aid: run by an independent group of professionals, it provides advice, support and information on all aspects of divorce. *www.divorceaid.co.uk*

The Children's Society: produces a series of leaflets for children and parents. See *Focus on Families – Divorce and Its Effects on Children*, The Children's Society, 1988. Tel: 0845 300 1128. *www.childrenssociety.org.uk*

Citizens Advice Bureaux: your local branch is listed in the telephone directory. *www.nacab.org.uk*

National Family Mediation: organization specifically to help families who are separating. It has a useful booklist, which includes books for children of different ages. Tel: 01392 271610. *www.nfm.u-net.com*

Parents as Patients

Young Carers: YCNet: *www.youngcarers.net*. If you have a question about something you have read on the site, please email: *youngcarers@carers.org*

Royal College of Psychiatrists, *When a parent has a mental illness.* Young carers talk about their lives caring for a parent with mental illness; narrated by a young carer herself. *www.rcpsych.ac.uk*

Emotional Support for Young Carers: A report prepared for the Royal College of Psychiatrists by The Children's Society Young Carers Initiative and The Princess Royal Trust for Carers (2007) *www.rcpsych.ac.uk*

FURTHER READING

Heegard, Marge, *When Someone Very Special Dies – Children Can Learn to Cope with Grief*, Woodland Press, Minneapolis, 1991.

WEBSITES OUTSIDE THE UK

Bereavement and loss

Australia
The Australian Child and Adolescent Trauma, Loss and Grief Network: *www.earlytraumagrief.anu.edu.au*

Canada
The Compassionate Friends of Canada: *www.tcfcanada.net*

New Zealand
www.skylight.org.nz

Divorce

Australia
Relationships Australia: *www.relationships.com.au*

Canada
Canadian Children's Right Council: *www.canadiancrc.com*

New Zealand
Family and community services: *www.familyservices.govt.nz*

14 Drugs and Drink

Youth is a time of increasing experimentation and independence. The use of drugs and alcohol by young people is common, and some people would even say it is a normal part of growing up. However, drugs and alcohol affect those who use them, altering their state of mind and leaving them vulnerable while intoxicated. They can also have severe and long-lasting effects on physical and mental health, and can lead to many problems, including dependency. These factors lead to continuous debate on the legal status of drugs and the availability of both drugs and alcohol to young people.

Some young people use substances to escape from difficult feelings, such as anxiety, depression or anger. Sometimes identifying and treating the underlying causes results in significant improvements in the substance-misuse problem. In other situations substance misuse requires a different approach.

Alcohol, cigarettes and 'softer' drugs, such as cannabis, are seen by some as 'gateway' substances into a world of 'harder' drugs, such as heroin and crack cocaine. But for most people, their substance use will progress no further. A lot of research has been aimed at working out who will go on to develop a substance-misuse problem (commonly referred to as an addiction or dependence) and who won't.

Research shows that by the age of sixteen up to half of young people have tried an illegal drug. The number of young people who have tried any drug increases with age, and the average age of first use is falling.

There is some evidence that current rates of drug use are static or even falling after increasing during the late 1980s and 1990s. The most commonly used illegal drug is cannabis.

However, the number of young people entering into programmes for the treatment of dependent drug use is increasing, and the ages of these young people are falling.

Worryingly, rates of alcohol use are rising, both for regular small amounts and for binge-drinking.

Thomas is a fifteen-year-old who started smoking cannabis when he was ten. He lives in an area where cannabis use is common and drugs are easily available. He smoked cannabis with his mates whenever anyone had any money. By the time he was twelve he was smoking daily and was starting to steal to buy drugs. He began to lose interest in school and stopped attending. His family life was chaotic. His relationship with his mother deteriorated and she appeared to give up on him, feeling that she had no control over him. His drug use continued and he started using other drugs, including cocaine, amphetamines, ecstasy and other pills.

Thomas's drug use eventually came to light when he was arrested for various offences that he had committed to fund his increasingly expensive drug habit. He was referred to the drug treatment service for young people and started to work on controlling his drug use. This involved looking at managing his emotions without turning to drugs and working on his relationship with his mother. He eventually returned to education and started college. With the increased structure to his day and with the support he received, his drug use decreased and his relationship with his mother improved.

Shannon is a seventeen-year-old girl who came to adolescent mental health services when she started getting increasingly paranoid. She had been smoking cannabis for the past two years but had not used any other drugs. She drank a lot of alcohol at weekends when she was out with her mates. She was going to school and had been managing her A-level coursework with no difficulty. Then her parents noticed she had begun to miss school and become withdrawn. They also noticed a change in her level of self-care. Before she came to the service she had refused to eat for a few days, saying she thought someone might have poisoned her food.

Shannon was assessed by staff and found to have some symptoms of a psychotic illness. She was hearing voices and had various paranoid beliefs. She was advised to stop smoking cannabis and started on some antipsychotic medication. The symptoms got better with treatment. It was thought that Shannon's symptoms were due to her cannabis use and she was diagnosed as having a drug-induced psychotic episode.

Kieran started smoking cannabis with his older brother when he was ten years old. Most people he knew smoked cannabis and he described it as 'normal' behaviour. His mother had depression, which had started when she was in a relationship with Kieran's father, who was physically and emotionally abusive. Kieran and his siblings witnessed this abuse and were also victims of emotional abuse from their father. His parents' relationship had broken down when Kieran was seven years old. Since then, his mother had had other abusive relationships, which had resulted in Kieran and his siblings spending periods of time in the care of the local authority.

At the age of twelve Kieran started trying other drugs. He tried heroin for the first time when he was fourteen while he was running away from care and mixing with older people. By the age of fifteen he was physically dependent on heroin and was also using crack cocaine. It took several prison sentences over a two-year period before he recognized he had a problem and accepted help from specialist services.

What do drugs do?

Different drugs produce different effects. There are the effects of intoxication, of withdrawing or 'coming down', and other effects that occur once dependence on substances develops. Most substances can be categorized into one of three groups: uppers, downers and hallucinogenic.

Downers include alcohol, benzodiazepines (including diazepam (valium), temazepam, lorazepam) and heroin. These drugs are likely to make you feel more relaxed and contented, but are addictive if taken regularly.

Uppers include stimulants such as amphetamine, cocaine and crack cocaine. They generally make you feel livelier and energetic, but can also make you feel anxious and scared.

Hallucinogenics include cannabis (in high concentrations), ecstasy and LSD. Ecstasy also has some stimulant properties. Hallucinogenic drugs can cause you to see strange things or alter your perception of colours and shapes. Users can have bad experiences (known as trips) and they can go on to have flashbacks where they re-experience these feelings. Flashbacks can recur for a long time after the drug was taken. Withdrawal effects are variable, but generally are the opposite to the effects of intoxication.

What can be done to help?

If you are concerned about a young person's drug or alcohol use, the first step is to try to find out as much as you can about the substances you think he may be using. Try to talk to him about your concerns in an open and non-confrontational way, and offer help and support rather than getting angry. It is important to encourage the young person to talk to you about what may be happening in his life and to try to understand. This may increase his confidence in you. Have the contact details for organizations that may help (see Support Organizations and websites, p. 240). Keep an open mind. Remember that this may not be the beginning of an addiction but just adolescent experimentation. If this is the case, then it's important that the young person understands the risks of taking drugs or of drinking, and how he can keep himself safe.

If your child is involved with problematic drug or alcohol use, he may need professional help. Accessing help relies on the person recognizing that he needs help – it is difficult to force someone to get help if he does not believe it is necessary. Agencies that deal with young people with substance-misuse problems can help them recognize that they have a problem and that they need help. These organizations use techniques such as motivational interviewing to increase motivation to help address the underlying difficulties. However, sometimes young people are just not ready to accept that they may have a problem.

Treatment can have different aims. Staying off drugs or alcohol is not the goal for all young people and sometimes a 'harm reduction' approach may be more appropriate. This can help engage a young person in a treatment programme through which he may move on to consider abstinence as an achievable goal. The approach will therefore be influenced by the young person's goal.

Talking treatments

Psychological interventions are useful in addressing substance-misuse problems. These work best when they are tailored to the person's needs and when they think about all aspects of his life, including family, school and the wider environment. This is because substance misuse in young people usually develops as a result of complex difficulties across all areas rather than any one cause.

Useful treatments include:

- Providing information about substances and the potential pitfalls of using them.
- Brief interventions with a harm-reduction approach, such as informing people of safer levels of drinking and offering advice on how to keep safe when using alcohol and drugs.
- Family therapy and individual approaches using a cognitive behavioural model (CBT; see p. 351). Multi-systemic therapy – an approach involving relevant therapies, professionals and families – has been identified as a useful intervention for substance-misuse problems. This uses an intensive package of interventions with children and their families, and is more comprehensive than just family or individual therapy.

Medication

Medication can be used to treat underlying difficulties, such as low mood or anxiety. It can also be used to treat symptoms that occur as a result of substance use. Medication should not be used alone, but rather as part of a package of care which would be likely to include other interventions such as talking therapies and educational approaches.

In situations where a young person is assessed to be dependent on drugs and detoxification is required, substitution medication can be prescribed, such as methadone or buprenorphine for heroin dependence. Sometimes treatment for the withdrawal symptoms is all that is required. For some drugs, however, there is no medication to treat the dependence and the only treatments available are psychological ones, such as individual interventions and family work. This can include identifying the triggers to the substance misuse, and developing strategies to avoid them. Family work is often useful in identifying the difficulties which contribute to the continuing substance misuse, and it strengthens the support for the young person.

Tips for families and teachers

With any young person growing up, it is important to be observant of behaviour, to notice any changes or behaviour that is out of character. This could be a loss of interest in activities that he used to enjoy, or changes in mood. It is difficult to detect the effects of occasional drug and alcohol use, but where there is regular or frequent use there is likely to be a noticeable change in behaviour patterns. There is no definite indication that a young person is using drugs, but some of the following things may increase your suspicions. (**REMEMBER**: it does not necessarily mean that he is using drugs – he may just be stressed or have other problems.)

Physical signs:

- changes in eating and/or sleep pattern
- he may smell of a substance
- his eyes may become red and watery; pupils may be larger or smaller than usual
- he may feel sick or be sick or sweat a lot
- he may be shaky

Changes in behaviour:

- his general attitude may change and he may become less interested in the family
- he may stop doing things he used to enjoy and drop old friends
- schoolwork may become a problem
- he may become moody, silly or paranoid
- he may start stealing, or selling his things

Notice who your child is friends with. Take an interest in what he is doing and where he is going. Learn about the effects of drugs and alcohol, and talk to him about these effects – both good and bad. Encourage him to be responsible about drugs and alcohol and to feel that he can talk to you about any worries or concerns he has.

INFORMATION

If you are concerned and the young person will not agree to talk to a professional, you can still contact support organizations yourself. They may be able to help you to understand the problem and advise you on what to do.

Dr Ruth Marshall

SUPPORT ORGANIZATIONS

Talk to Frank: free, confidential drugs information and advice for young people and parents. Helpline: 0800 776600. *www.talktofrank.com*

NHS Direct: provides help and advice on any aspect of drug and alcohol use. Tel: 0845 4647. *www.nhsdirect.nhs.uk*

Addaction: offers help, information and advice on drug or alcohol problems. *www.addaction.org.uk*

Alcohol Concern: works to reduce the incidence and costs of alcohol-related harm, and to increase the range and quality of services available to people with alcohol-related problems. *www.alcoholconcern.org.uk*

Alcoholics Anonymous: National Helpline: 0845 769 7555. *www.alcoholics-anonymous.org.uk*

Al-Anon: provides understanding, strength and hope to anyone whose life is, or has been, affected by someone else's drinking. *www.al-anonuk.org.uk*

WEBSITES OUTSIDE THE UK

Australia
Government of Western Australia Drug and Alcohol Office: *www.dao.health.wa.gov.au*

Canada
Health Canada: *www.hc-sc.gc.ca/hl-vs/alc/index-eng.php*

New Zealand
Alcohol Drug Association New Zealand: *www.adanz.org.nz/ADANZ/Home*

FURTHER READING

Crome, Ilana, Ghodse, Hamid, Gilvarry, Eilish, and McArdle, Paul, *Young People and Substance Misuse*, Gaskell, 2004.

15 Eating Problems, Weight Problems and Eating Disorders

Three-year-old Joe had feeding difficulties. His mother was concerned about his faddiness and unwillingness to try new foods. She discussed this with the health visitor, who thought that Joe's problems stemmed from an anxious temperament and his mother's worries in dealing with her first child. Parents often have concerns about eating at all ages and they sometimes inadvertently reinforce a child's difficulties.

David was an overweight ten-year-old. He dealt with the sadness of his parents' separation by comfort eating, turning to junk food as a way of managing his emotional difficulties. This was compounded by the family's existing poor diet and inactive lifestyle.

Emma was a fifteen-year-old with anorexia nervosa. Her primary concern was a fear of fatness. Her underlying difficulties included poor self-esteem, lack of self-worth and insecurity about her inability to cope with the physical and social demands of adolescence.

Chloe, a nineteen-year-old university student, coped with the pressures of moving away from home, dealing with adult responsibilities and breaking up with her boyfriend by binge-eating. She then became very conscious that she was putting on weight. Because she was unable to restrict her eating, she attempted to control her weight by making herself vomit.

What are eating problems and disorders?

'Eating problems' is a general term for difficulties with food and weight, whether or not a psychological disturbance is involved. Eating problems include a range of difficulties, from feeding disorders in infancy to more serious and life-threatening conditions like anorexia nervosa and bulimia, which most commonly occur in adolescence and young adulthood.

Feeding difficulties are quite common in infancy in both boys and girls. These can take the form of refusing food, failure to gain weight or difficulties in weaning. They may occur with behavioural disturbances, such as crying or tantrums, and parents often feel they are involved in a battle of wills with the child.

Young children with weight loss, failure to gain weight or excess weight, may cause concern. As steady growth is normal throughout childhood, weight loss should always be taken seriously. While weight loss or excess weight gain may be an indicator of an eating difficulty, the overall mental and physical health of a child is a better measure of well-being.

Over-eating, lack of exercise and subsequent obesity are increasing problems in children and adolescents. It is estimated that 8.5 per cent of six-year-olds and 15 per cent of fifteen-year-olds in England are obese. Psychological issues may play a part in over-eating, particularly when children eat in response to difficult emotions, often referred to as 'comfort eating'. Obese children often suffer low self-esteem and bullying.

Eating disorders are relatively rare. Most people will have heard of anorexia nervosa and bulimia nervosa. There are a few atypical eating disorders which share similarities but do not qualify for these diagnoses; however, they still cause difficulties.

Anorexia nervosa and bulimia

Anorexia and bulimia predominantly occur in females and the most common feature is a fear of 'fatness' with a distorted view of the importance of weight or shape.

In anorexia nervosa, young people usually weigh less than 85 per cent of their ideal body weight. This extreme weight loss has usually delayed the completion of puberty or stopped the young woman menstruating.

In bulimia, there are attempts at weight control, based on a similar preoccupation with body weight, but the person loses control of her food intake through binge-eating, and subsequently vomits or purges as a way of regaining control over weight.

What does it feel like?

In infants and young children, feeding problems can manifest as a battle of wills. The child may find that this is a way of securing their parents' attention, but often feels overwhelmed by the power she wields. Parents can often feel frustrated at being unable to get a toddler to try new foods, or else offer too many choices and feel disempowered.

In middle childhood, a sedentary lifestyle and the consumption of high-calorie foods contribute to obesity. Young children who have an unhealthy lifestyle to begin with often exaggerate these habits as a way of coping. For instance, the ten-year-old who experiences bullying might find it 'safer' to fill time with eating than to dwell on her relationship difficulties.

Other children might restrict eating as a way of ensuring that parents and other people notice their sadness or unhappiness. Drastic changes in eating, either under-eating or over-eating, can be a way of communicating distress.

In early adolescence, changes in body shape associated with puberty can make young people feel as if they have no control over what is happening to them. Perfectionist young people with poor self-esteem can feel they are failing in everything unless they have 'control' over their eating and attain unreachable targets. Although restricting dietary intake is a coping strategy, those with anorexia are generally unhappy, fearing the potential loss of control if they stop restricting food. For those with bulimia, regular loss of control is a frightening reality.

What can be done to help?

Eating and weight patterns tend to be quite entrenched. Thus any help needs to address long-term lifestyle changes.

Preventing eating or weight problems requires family, school, health service and social agencies' commitment to promoting healthy-eating practices and a healthy lifestyle.

Education and advice are helpful in the initial stages of simpler problems. For example, most feeding disorders of infancy sort themselves out in time. You can ask your health visitor for advice on staying in control and not feeling stressed, or you can ask to be put in touch with other mothers who have experienced similar difficulties. Mother and toddler support groups can be a good means of helping you. Reassurance and simple suggestions can ease your worries.

For children who are not yet at school, simple guidance on behavioural strategies can be helpful. Advice on establishing a routine for mealtimes, offering healthy snacks and not using food as a threat or a bribe can work with many difficulties.

In young children who resort to eating as a way of dealing with their emotions, it is important to address the cause of the emotional difficulty. It is also essential to teach children other coping strategies, as there is a risk of using over-eating or control over food as a way of dealing with stress. It is important to find other ways to boost the child's self-esteem and confidence and to give her better ways of coping with life's challenges. Talking to her in a supportive way can help deal with her anxieties and worries. Nutritional advice and guidance on healthy living can promote well-being.

Eating disorders are more complex and will require more specialist help. Anorexia nervosa in younger adolescents requires family-based work; this helps parents to feel more in control in managing their child's eating.

Individual therapy that tackles the young person's underlying beliefs about weight, shape and control is also helpful. Weight gain is essential to improve physical health, which will allow the young person's brain to be well enough nourished to engage in therapeutic work.

In older adolescents and young adults with anorexia or bulimia nervosa, individual therapeutic work is the mainstay of treatment. In addition to addressing beliefs about the importance of weight and shape, it often focuses on mood and interpersonal relationships, as well as ensuring physical recovery.

Treatments and therapies

If these feeding disorders do not improve through the simple measures mentioned above, the child will be referred to paediatric services to rule out any physical cause that could be contributing to the problem.

Obesity requires a change in eating and activity. Sensible dieting and appropriate exercise are the cornerstone of managing the condition. This can be provided at home or in school after any indicated physical investigation. Drugs like sibutramine and orlistat have been effective in producing weight loss in adults. Gastric banding and other surgical procedures are used as last-resort measures for extreme obesity with acute medical risks.

Eating disorders are treated by family and individual work in primary care services, in child and family services, or in more serious cases at specialist Eating Disorder Services. Management is usually on an outpatient basis, with in-patient treatment reserved for severe or resistant anorexia nervosa.

Outpatient management involves individual psychological therapies, exploring factors that led to the development of the condition and those that maintain it. Therapies aim to improve self-esteem and to address fears of growing up and the responsibilities associated with it. They teach the young person coping strategies and help her develop confidence in being able to deal with changes in her body, her life and her future.

In-patient management can be required when there are severe physical problems, or if intensive psychological therapy is needed. An in-patient admission can address physical concerns and may offer restoration of weight and help in reducing risk. However, mere restoration of weight is not the 'cure' for anorexia nervosa and it is essential to address the beliefs that maintain this illness.

Intensive day programmes offer an alternative to in-patient management. Group work and creative therapies often feature in such programmes, and communicating with others with similar illnesses can make the young person feel supported and understood.

Family work is generally available, sometimes delivered as multi-family therapy with a number of families seen at the same time. This approach addresses how family members support each other and make behavioural changes, particularly around meal preparation.

There is a limited role for medication in the treatment of anorexia. However, there is research evidence to show that antidepressants like fluoxetine are effective in reducing binge-eating and are sometimes useful adjuncts to psychological therapies.

Self-help, whether guided by a therapist or in which the participant works through exercises from a book or DVD, is a growing field. There are now a number of internet sites offering resources and discussion forums.

Tips for families, friends and teachers

Children with eating problems rarely approach services themselves, so families, friends and teachers are important in identifying a difficulty and then encouraging the young person to seek help.

Parents can play a preventative role by advocating healthy eating habits, making more healthy foods available and emphasizing good mealtime behaviour. Parents play a vital role in supporting the child or young person, encouraging her to tackle her difficulties and having expectations of behavioural change.

Friends can be supportive during mealtimes. Having a friend around who understands can be crucial for a young person who feels socially isolated as a result of either being obese or having an eating disorder.

Teachers can provide links with health services, can monitor and encourage healthy and appropriate eating during lunchtimes, and can encourage social integration. Schools are becoming increasingly aware of the importance of promoting self-confidence, self-esteem and emotional literacy (see Chapter 8) for the physical and emotional well-being of children.

Professor Simon G. Gowers and Dr Anandhi Inbasagaran

SUPPORT ORGANIZATIONS

Voluntary organizations can be a valuable source of help. They offer information on self-help networks, online support, social-networking forums, and information on local services.

beat: UK National Eating Disorders charity providing information and help for those with eating disorders and their carers. *www.b-eat.co.uk*

Kooth.com: website aimed at young people and offering online support. *www.kooth.com*

HandsonScotland: online resource for anybody working with children and young people. *www.handsonscotland.co.uk*

WEBSITES OUTSIDE THE UK

Australia
www.thebutterflyfoundation.org.au

Canada
www.nedic.ca

New Zealand
www.eatingdisorders.org.au

FURTHER READING

Fairburn, Christopher, *Overcoming Binge Eating*, Guilford Press, 1995.

Lock, James, and Le Grange, Daniel, *Help Your Teenager Beat an Eating Disorder*, Guilford, 2005.

Schmidt, Ulrike, and Treasure, Janet, *Getting Better Bit(e) by Bit(e): A Survival Kit for Sufferers of Bulimia Nervosa and Binge Eating Disorders*, Psychology Press, 1993.

Treasure, Janet, Smith, Gráinne, and Crane, Anna, *Skill-based Learning in Caring for a Loved One with an Eating Disorder*, Routledge, 2007.

16 Tics and Obsessions

TICS, TOURETTE'S SYNDROME and obsessions may sound rather strange to people who don't know what they are. But anyone who has suffered from them will know how distressing they can be for young people and their families. In the past there has been a tendency not to talk about them, but in recent years they have been more openly discussed and several celebrities from the worlds of TV, film and sport have described having them, what it feels like to have them and how they deal with them.

Tics and Tourette's syndrome

Adam was a ten-year-old boy who was referred to his local Child and Adolescent Mental Health Service (CAMHS) by his GP. Both his parents and his teachers at school had noticed that he regularly blinked and made facial grimaces, often smacking his lips many times a minute, to the extent that it had resulted in his being teased by other children at school. He also sometimes made a noise to clear his throat, even when there was nothing there to clear; this too happened every few minutes.

Adam's parents had noticed that he had a tendency to eye-blink from the age of five, but the grimacing, lip-smacking and throat-clearing had all come to their attention in the few months preceding the referral. Adam had an uncle on his father's side who had also had tics as a child, but these had settled as he grew up. Adam's father could remember his brother being told off at school for making 'faces' and being teased about his eyes blinking all the time.

Adam had noticed that when he was worried his movements became worse, and they were also worse if someone drew attention to them. He did not notice them at all when he was playing football and the throat-clearing didn't happen then either.

He had some blood tests and a brain scan that showed no problems. A child psychiatrist explained what the tics were and that they would settle as he got older, just as his uncle's had. The child psychiatrist and the psychologist helped him think of how to deal with them at school and what to say to his friends and teachers about them; they also talked to Adam's family about helping him manage these tics. He was given a tablet, called clonidine, that also reduced his tics. He came back regularly to the clinic to say how he was getting on and to discuss any problems, as well as to see the doctor to check that his tablets were working well.

Things are now much better for Adam – his tics have reduced and he doesn't worry so much about them any more. He also isn't teased at school now and is feeling much happier.

What are tics?

Tics are purposeless repetitive movements that are not under your control. They can involve the face, neck, arms and other parts of the upper body, such as eye-blinking, facial-grimacing, mouth-opening or neck-jerking. They are defined by doctors as either 'simple' or 'complex' tics according to how much of the face or body is involved. Complex tics can involve touching or jumping.

Tics can change from day to day or week to week in type, strength and frequency and usually come and go.

How common are tics?

Tics are common in children and up to about 20 per cent of children may have a simple tic at any time. In about 1 in 100 children these tics may be more long-lasting. Tics are more common in boys than girls. They usually begin around five years old and are at their worst around the ages of ten or eleven, disappearing in as many as half of young people by the time they reach eighteen.

What is Tourette's syndrome?

Tourette's syndrome is a neurological condition in which the young person has vocal and multiple motor tics that last for longer than a year. It is less common than simple tics – fewer than 1 per cent of children have Tourette's syndrome. Motor tics are as described above. Vocal tics can include making repeated sounds, for example making a specific noise or clearing the throat repeatedly. Coprolalia (saying rude words) is the most well-known symptom of Tourette's syndrome, but it occurs in only a small number of children with the condition.

The syndrome is named after a nineteenth-century French neurologist, Georges Gilles de la Tourette, who first described the illness in nine of his patients. Since then it has been described all over the world and it affects all races and ethnic groups equally.

What causes tics and Tourette's syndrome?

The causes of both tics and Tourette's syndrome are not fully understood. Researchers have suggested that they could be caused by a genetic factor, by difficulties around birth and even by infections.

What other conditions occur with tics and Tourette's syndrome?

Several other conditions may occur with tics and Tourette's syndrome, including obsessive compulsive disorder (OCD; see p. 258), ADHD (see Chapter 11), depression, anxiety, learning difficulties and difficulties at school.

How are tics and Tourette's syndrome diagnosed?

Although your GP can diagnose these conditions, he is likely to refer a child for an assessment at the local CAMHS. An assessment usually means a meeting with a child psychiatrist, child psychologist or other child mental health professional. They will talk to your child and the family about the problem, about the symptoms and about your child's early development and your family history. They will also ask about other aspects of the child's life, for example school, and how the tics interfere with this. They may refer your child for a scan or to have some blood tests.

What can be done to help?

Many simple tics do not require any treatment at all. The child and family will be given detailed information on how to deal with the symptoms. Behavioural therapies may also help a young person to manage his tics. Most people find that stress and anxiety make tics worse, and so relaxation and anxiety-management techniques can make a difference. If the problem is accompanied by OCD or depression, behaviour therapies and CBT (see p. 351) can also help with these.

Family therapy can help family members understand the condition better and show them how to cope and give support.

Medication

Severe tics and Tourette's syndrome may be reduced with the help of medicines such as clonidine or risperidone. But they will not stop the problem completely and should be used in addition to psychological and/or behavioural treatments.

The other conditions that sometimes occur with tics and Tourette's syndrome can also be helped by treatment: see Chapters 11 and 17, and p. 258.

How to manage tics and Tourette's syndrome

If a young person has tics or Tourette's syndrome, it is important to advise him to try not to worry about the tics, and not to stop doing the things other young people do.

Lots of people won't understand tics, so helping them to learn what they are is important. It may be useful for a child or young person to have a simple explanation ready to give others – for instance explaining that he can't control the tics and that they come and go in different situations.

Many people find that when they are anxious their tics get worse, but when they are concentrating on something they disappear altogether. Some young people find that playing music or fiddling with a rubber band on their wrist helps reduce the tics. It is important to try out what works well for each individual; they may then be able to plan for their tics – for example, sucking a sweet or having a drink if it is a throat-clearing tic.

Being able to relax often also helps tics go away and a young person can try anything that helps him to relax. Exercise – such as football or swimming – can reduce tics. Find out if any of these things is effective for the young person and then advise him to keep practising what works.

How to manage at school

School can be the most difficult place to manage tics, and many young people worry about being teased or bullied. Telling friends and teachers about tics is a good place to start if the child feels able to do this. Practising what they are going to say about tics helps many young people to worry less when other people ask them about their tics, as they have an answer ready.

If young people with tics or Tourette's have special learning needs, help is available through the school – see Chapter 7.

Do tics and Tourette's go away?

Most of the symptoms of tics and Tourette's syndrome disappear before or around the age of eighteen in as many as half of young people. In most, the symptoms reach their peak at the ages of ten or eleven, then slowly improve. However, they may recur in later life at times of stress and anxiety.

Obsessions and compulsions

Ahmed was a nine-year-old boy who began to have recurrent fears that objects around him were dirty and covered in germs. Whenever he touched something, such as a door handle or a telephone receiver, he felt that his hands were unclean and infected. He could feel clean again if only he washed his hands thoroughly five times before drying them. If he was interrupted while washing his hands, he would have to start the whole routine from the beginning again. As a result, Ahmed was often late for school in the morning and was finding it difficult to take part in his usual day-to-day activities. Deep down he knew that there was no logic to his thoughts, but he just could not stop worrying about them.

His mother took him to meet a psychologist who asked them both about Ahmed's difficulties, as well as more general questions. The psychologist explained that Ahmed was not going mad, but that he did have an illness called obsessive compulsive disorder (OCD). The psychologist offered to help and they agreed that they would work together to help Ahmed feel less anxious about touching things. This work included talking about the things he feared and practising dealing with the feelings that these caused. After a few weeks, his difficulties gradually disappeared and he learned how to keep himself well if ever the thoughts should return again.

What are obsessions?

Obsessions are repeated ideas, images or thoughts that keep coming into your mind again and again, no matter how much you try to stop this happening.

These thoughts are usually distressing and often seem ridiculous. For example, a person may have the thought that his hands are dirty even immediately after washing them. He may keep thinking that he has left the door unlocked after leaving the house, no matter how often he returns to check on it.

Other examples of obsessions include fears of hurting other people, sexual thoughts, or the idea that everything should be lined up or placed in some kind of order.

What are compulsions?

Compulsions are repeated behaviours that you feel you must carry out again and again. These behaviours are not enjoyable and often seem pointless, but you think that this is the only way to stop obsessive thoughts from coming true. For example, a person may feel that his hands will never be clean until he has washed them thoroughly five times, or he may have to carry out a set of actions in a particular order. Other examples of compulsions include checking things repeatedly, counting or tapping.

What is OCD?

Children and young people of different ages will often seem to develop rituals or apparent obsessions. Small toddlers will often insist on a fixed routine being followed at bedtime ('Mummy, say goodnight to Teddy before you tuck me up'). Primary-school children may be fixated on the rules of a game ('I'm not playing because he's cheating!'). Teenagers may develop a fascination with a certain celebrity or pop group ('I love David Beckham'). However, these common behaviours do not cause the child or young person any significant harm, and can often help the development of social relationships and future independence.

Someone is considered to have OCD if he suffers from either obsessional thoughts or compulsive behaviours, or both, on a regular daily basis. These symptoms will take up a lot of time each day and may interfere with school, family or other social relationships.

The symptoms of OCD often change over time, and their course and severity can also vary from person to person. OCD can often occur in a person with another condition such as ADHD, Tourette's syndrome or depression. At other times, rituals or repetitive behaviours are seen in conditions such as autism or schizophrenia, and can seem like OCD.

How common is OCD?

It is common to have an occasional obsessive thought ('Did I turn the tap off?') or compulsive act ('If I don't step on the cracks in the pavement until the end of the street, I'll pass my maths test'). However, about 1 person in 100 is affected by OCD. Their symptoms are more serious and often cause them unhappiness or become quite disabling. These problems are equally common in boys and girls.

What causes OCD?

OCD often seems to run in families, so it may be that a tendency to OCD is inherited from our parents. Very rarely, OCD can suddenly develop after a very sore throat.

How is OCD diagnosed?

Although OCD can be diagnosed by your GP, it is more usual for a child to be referred for an assessment to the local CAMHS. The assessment will usually be carried out by a child and adolescent psychiatrist or psychologist, although sometimes another child mental health professional may be involved.

An assessment involves an interview with the child and his family and will include questions about the symptoms described, as well as other important information such as the child's early history and the family history.

Sometimes questionnaires are used as part of the assessment, and occasionally a more in-depth assessment of the child's learning abilities can be helpful.

What can be done to help?

When a child is diagnosed with OCD, the psychiatrist or psychologist usually spends some time with the child and family explaining the condition and its treatment; this is sometimes called 'psychoeducation'.

Unless the condition is very severe, the treatment used for OCD usually involves the talking therapy cognitive behavioural therapy (CBT; see p. 351). CBT involves discussing the obsessions and compulsions with a psychiatrist or psychologist, and considering ways to challenge them. This can often involve the child experiencing the feared thought and then using a technique to stop him avoiding the thought until such time as his distress has diminished.

For instance, if a young man has repeated thoughts that his hands are dirty even after washing them, a plan may be made not to allow him to wash them again for a certain time. At first he is likely to become quite anxious about this, but after a while this anxiety lessens. With practice, he will become less concerned and have fewer such thoughts.

Medication

Some young people with more severe OCD will be prescribed medication for their symptoms. Typical medications used include fluvoxamine, sertraline and clomipramine. If a child does require medication, the doctor will discuss the effects and possible side-effects of these drugs with both the child and his family.

Will OCD go away?

Although rituals can be very common during childhood, recurrent obsessions or compulsions in the form of OCD can be very distressing and disabling to children and their families. However, these symptoms can often be helped with treatment. Treatment helps the child to learn strategies to control the OCD rather than it controlling them, the skills to manage obsessional thoughts and urges to complete rituals, as well as distraction techniques to manage the anxiety.

Dr Helen Bruce and Dr Graeme Lamb

SUPPORT ORGANIZATIONS

Tourette's Syndrome (UK) Association: produces a range of leaflets and runs a helpline. Tel: 0845 458 1252. *www.tsa.org.uk*

Oaasis: a resource for parents and professionals.
Helpline: 0800 197 3907
www.oaasis.co.uk

OCD UK: national charity working with and for people with obsessive compulsive disorder (OCD). *www.ocduk.org*

OCD Action: Support and information: 0845 390 6232
www.ocdaction.org.uk

WEBSITES OUTSIDE THE UK

Australia
Tourette's Syndrome Association for Australia:
www.tourette.org.au
www.anxietyaustralia.com.au

Canada
Tourette's Syndrome Foundation for Canada: *www.tourette.ca*
www.anxietycanada.ca

New Zealand
Tourette's Syndrome New Zealand: *www.tourettesnz.com*
www.mentalheath.org.nz

FURTHER READING

Veale, David, and Willson, Rob, *Overcoming Obsessive Compulsive Disorder: Self-help Guide using Cognitive-Behavioral Techniques*, Constable & Robinson, 2005.

17 Mood and Behaviour: Psychosis, Schizophrenia, Bipolar Disorder and Depression

MOOD IS AFFECTED BY MANY different things. Most people are aware of how their mood changes in an ordinary way in response to happy or sad events, exciting news or disappointments, and also to internal factors such as hormonal changes or physical illness. Behaviour is closely linked to mood and is often the outside indicator of how we are feeling. We have different expectations of behaviour for children and teenagers at different ages and different stages of their development.

Children, and especially adolescents, experience changes in their mood and behaviour as they develop in an ordinary way. It can be a challenge to separate these changes from the symptoms of mental illness. Families, teachers, friends and others who work with children and young people all have an important role to play in the recognition of problems and in accessing appropriate help.

Most young people experience mood swings and feel fed up, anxious or frightened at times. We can all think we are misunderstood by family and friends and believe nothing is going right – these sorts of experiences are part of everyday life. However, for some young people things can get so bad that they feel out of control and unable to cope or get on with their lives. Some reach a point where they cannot concentrate on anything and become withdrawn, isolated and unable to attend school or college. Some have feelings of wanting to be dead.

Others may show very difficult behaviour and become restless, irritable, argumentative or even violent.

For these young people life is extremely difficult – they are unhappy and do not feel well. They are experiencing severe mental health problems. This could be due to a relatively mild illness that will get better quickly, or to a more severe mental illness resulting in the young person feeling confused, out of touch with reality and unable to cope. In cases like this specialist help is required to enable the child or young person to recover and get on with her life.

This chapter is about the mental illnesses psychosis, schizophrenia, bipolar disorder and depression, all of which significantly affect mood and behaviour. Each disorder is described separately to aid understanding. However, it should be noted that, especially with children and young people, the diagnostic categories are not always clear. Often a young person's mental health problem can change from one type to another over time. Mental health professionals may try to avoid 'pigeonholing' children and young people into the categories described below, preferring to keep an open mind and assess regularly, managing symptoms as they arise.

Psychosis

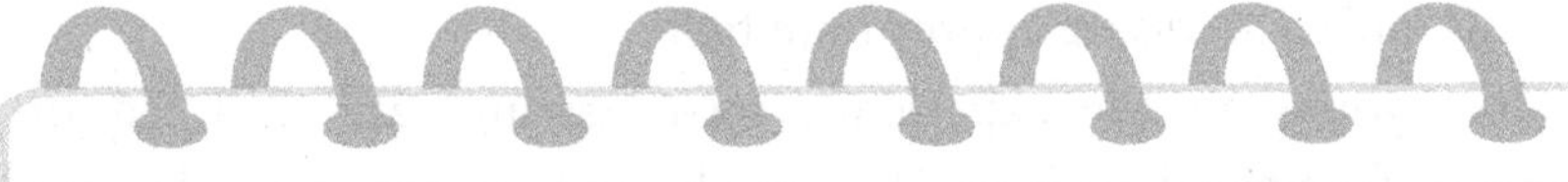

Helen is a sixteen-year-old girl who, over the last eight months, has not seemed herself to family and friends. She has been talking increasingly about her suspicions that something strange is going on and recently told her schoolteacher that someone is controlling her thoughts with a 'special' mobile phone. The teacher was concerned, as Helen has also been very distracted in lessons. Helen's teacher discussed her concerns with the school nurse, who referred Helen to the specialist Child and Adolescent Mental Health Services (CAMHS). Following assessment, she was diagnosed with psychosis. She was treated with a combination of psychological treatments and medication and has since been doing much better. She has been able to complete her GCSEs and is no longer troubled by her experiences.

What is psychosis?

Psychosis can occur in many mental disorders and illnesses. It is one of the most serious conditions that can affect a young person and around 1 in 200 suffers with it. It usually first occurs when people are young – 80 per cent of first episodes of psychosis occur between the ages of sixteen and thirty, and 5 per cent in children aged fifteen years and under. It is a mental illness in which the person loses touch with reality and cannot tell the difference between what is real and unreal, which leads to strange thinking, strange feelings and unusual behaviour. The most common causes of a psychotic illness are bipolar disorder and schizophrenia (see pp. 271 and 267). It can also occur by itself as a one-off episode. Episodes of psychosis can be precipitated by illicit drug use and in rare cases are due to a physical illness such as epilepsy, certain diseases of the immune system or even a tumour.

What does psychosis feel like?

The symptoms of psychosis are often described as either positive or negative. Positive symptoms are unusual experiences such as hallucinations and delusions.

Hallucinations cause a person to see, hear or taste things that are not really there. Hearing voices is one of the most common types: 'I can hear people talking about me even though I can't see anyone around.' To the sufferer, a hallucination appears to be totally real.

Delusions make a person believe something that is not true. The sufferer might believe she is famous or has special powers, or that people are talking about her or trying to harm her: 'I can control the weather'; 'My stomach has melted away'; 'My mother is trying to poison me'. There are other types of delusions in which a person believes her body, thoughts or feelings are being controlled by an outside force: 'Ideas are being transmitted into my mind by the FBI', or that reference is being made to her by ordinary day-to-day things: 'The man on the TV was trying to tell me something. When he touched his desk it meant that I should go to London.'

A negative symptom occurs when something that should be there is missing, such as the loss of ability to think clearly or the loss of motivation to do things.

Confused thoughts. People with psychosis often find it hard to think. Sometimes thoughts can feel speeded up or slowed down. Some young people experience the inability to think at all – thoughts simply disappear from their minds. Sometimes thoughts do not join up in the normal way, making it difficult to follow someone's train of thought when they speak. When this absence of thought-stream becomes severe, the person can say what appears to be a series of random words. This is the loss of the ability to 'think straight'.

Lack of motivation or drive. Parents, family, teachers and friends may notice that a young person is becoming increasingly withdrawn and losing interest in her usual activities: 'She wasn't down or depressed – it just felt like she'd lost her zing, as if her personality wasn't getting through any more.' A young person may feel as if she has lost her emotions and find it hard to react, or in some cases even to get out of bed.

What can be done to help?

If psychosis is present, it is very important that the young person and her family access specialist help. A young person with psychosis may be very frightened and confused and may have suicidal ideas or plans. If you notice that a young person is worrying about things more than usual; losing interest in things she usually enjoys; becoming preoccupied with unusual ideas or hearing voices; having difficulty relating to peers or keeping friends; having problems with sleeping, eating and looking after herself; or feels there's no hope for the future, then it is important to seek help.

There are many effective treatments for psychosis which are usually available through specialist mental health teams to which a GP can refer a sufferer. A specialist will give the young person and her family time to think and talk about worries and problems, and will offer advice on what will help. Getting help early gives the best chance of getting better faster. If caught very early, it is sometimes possible to delay or even prevent the onset of psychosis.

Schizophrenia

What is schizophrenia?

Schizophrenia is a serious mental illness characterized by psychosis. It affects around 1 person in 100. The age of onset is usually between fifteen and thirty-five; it is rare for a pre-adolescent child to develop schizophrenia. It may be hard to recognize in its early phases and diagnosis in children and adolescents should be made by someone with specialist experience in child and adolescent mental health. The cause of schizophrenia is not known, but current research suggests that brain changes, biochemical, genetic and environmental factors may be involved. Prolonged cannabis use increases the risk of developing schizophrenia. Early diagnosis and treatment are very important. Schizophrenia involves episodes of psychosis that tend to recur throughout a person's life and may need ongoing treatment.

There is a common misconception that schizophrenia means 'split-personality': this is not correct. People suffering from schizophrenia are not generally dangerous. In fact, someone with schizophrenia is more likely to be a victim of crime than a perpetrator.

Who gets schizophrenia?

Schizophrenia and similar illnesses tend to run in families. Some street drugs, especially cannabis, can cause schizophrenia in people who are vulnerable to the illness. People from all races and cultures can suffer from this condition.

What does schizophrenia feel like?

Suffering from schizophrenia can be an extremely frightening and lonely experience. Everyone is different, but generally it affects family, social and academic life. The symptoms of psychosis have been described above. Young people suffering from schizophrenia might have a mixture of 'positive' and 'negative' psychotic symptoms and might be totally preoccupied by their experiences. Suspicion and paranoia may interfere with a young person's ability to ask for help from those whom he would usually trust. Suicidal ideas and plans are common.

What can be done to help?

Children and adolescents with schizophrenia must have a thorough evaluation by a specialist mental health team. Getting help as early as possible improves the long-term outcome. A GP can make a referral to a specialist, who will be able to discuss the treatment options with the young person and her family. Sometimes hospital admission to a child and adolescent in-patient unit is a useful way to undertake a thorough assessment and get a head start with treatment.

There are a number of recommended treatments for schizophrenia. A combination of medication, individual and family therapy, and social interventions (support with finances, education or training) is often needed.

Medication

There are many different types of antipsychotic medication, which work slightly differently and have different side-effects. Treatment with antipsychotic medication will usually be for a year, or longer if needed. If episodes of psychosis recur, lifelong treatment may be required. Medication has a role to play in the treatment of the symptoms of schizophrenia, and also in protecting against further episodes of the illness. Whatever the medication and the time-scale of the treatment, it will need to be carefully and regularly monitored by a psychiatrist.

Psychological and social interventions

There are a number of psychological and social approaches that may help. The most popular psychological treatment is cognitive behavioural therapy (CBT; see p. 351). CBT can help the sufferer monitor and change his thoughts, feelings and behaviours. Some psychological work might be suggested for his family; improvement in his social environment can help a great deal in the treatment of schizophrenia. The child and adolescent mental-health team will be able to discuss the kinds of social adjustments and psychological interventions that may be helpful.

Complementary therapies and diet

Some people believe that omega-3 fish oils and other food supplements can help, though there is no strong evidence one way or the other. Food supplements should not replace the medication, psychological and social interventions that have been proven to help, but may be complementary to them.

Tips for families, teachers, friends and others

Schizophrenia can be very gradual in its onset, sometimes making it difficult to spot. 'Negative' symptoms can be particularly tricky to recognize. Ordinary changes in adolescence can confuse the picture and mask the onset of the illness. Changes in personality, lack of motivation, withdrawal and odd behaviour may be signs that something is wrong. However, it is important to get help as soon as possible, which may mean seeing a GP even if the young person does not want to attend.

A young person with schizophrenia may have strange beliefs and behaviours that are symptoms of psychosis. It is not generally helpful to comment on or argue about them. Arguments, criticism and emotion or outbursts are known to make episodes of schizophrenia worse, so it's important to try to maintain a calm atmosphere at home. Seek help from your GP or other trusted professional if you are finding it hard to cope.

Bipolar Disorder

Rachel is a fifteen-year-old girl who has suffered episodes of depression in the past. Two months ago she started to talk very quickly and seemed to have lots of energy. She was excited about everything and was making all her friends laugh a lot. Over a three-day period Rachel barely slept or ate and started to say things that did not really make sense; for example, she told her friends that she was a princess in Taiwan. She also started swearing and became extremely flirtatious, which was out of character. She is quoted as saying, 'I've never felt so great – I'm flying. I'm eleven on a scale of one to ten.'

Rachel's parents were very worried and on the fourth night of her not sleeping, they took her to the local A & E department, where she was seen by a psychiatrist who arranged for her to stay in hospital. A diagnosis of bipolar disorder was confirmed and treatment was given to bring Rachel's mood back to normal. She now has treatment to help prevent episodes of both depressed and abnormally high mood in the future. She has also been working with a community psychiatric nurse to improve her ability to recognize her own mood state and take measures to protect herself from further episodes.

What is bipolar disorder?

Bipolar disorder is the modern name for 'manic depression'. Ordinary reactions to life's ups and downs will be familiar to most of us. However, young people who suffer from bipolar disorder experience episodes of extreme happiness (elation) and/or sadness (depression) which are outside the normal range of emotion and not necessarily related to events going on in their lives. There is a difference between the episodes of illness in bipolar disorder and having strong emotional reactions in general.

Who gets bipolar disorder?

People from all backgrounds and cultures can develop bipolar disorder. Many people develop the condition in their late teens or early twenties. It can occur in children who have not yet reached puberty, but it is rare in this age group and more difficult to diagnose. Diagnosis of bipolar disorder in children and adolescents should be made by someone with specialist experience in child and adolescent mental health. It affects between 1 and 4 people in a 100 and tends to run in families, so it is probably linked to our genes. Triggers for illness episodes can be any event that is stressful to the mind or body. For example, sad events like the death of a friend or exam stress could trigger an episode. Strangely, happy events too can trigger episodes of either depression or elation. Strain on the body can also trigger an episode – for example, physical illness, eating irregularly or losing sleep.

What does bipolar disorder feel like?

Young people with bipolar disorder have episodes of 'mania' and episodes of 'depression'. The disorder may begin with an episode of either depression or mania. Most people show depressive symptoms first, but in order to diagnose bipolar disorder in young people, mania must be present.

Symptoms of depression

A depressive episode usually builds up slowly over a few weeks or months. A number of changes in the young person's thoughts, feelings, behaviour and physical well-being are likely to become noticeable. These are described in the section on depression in this chapter – see p. 276.

Symptoms of mania

During a manic episode a young person will have feelings of extreme happiness (elation) or feeling high. She may also feel very irritable. Young people often say they feel 'buzzy' or 'giddy'. They may become suddenly very active and rearrange their bedrooms for hours, or feel the urge to start a number of creative projects all at the same time. Boundless energy, fast thoughts and speech, excitability, poor judgement, increased sex drive and an apparent lack of the need for food or sleep are all features. When a manic episode becomes more severe, a young person may feel invincible, engage in dangerous or promiscuous behaviour and not want to hear anyone's advice. People in a manic phase can take big risks that are often completely out of character.

If the illness advances without being picked up, mania may develop into symptoms of psychosis. Hallucinations and delusions (see p. 266) can build in intensity until the young person is strongly convinced, for example, that she has wonderful powers and abilities or that she has special relationships with famous people: 'Don't try to tell me what to do – I know Wikipedia off by heart. I am the boss of the internet.' During both depressive and manic phases it is common for young people to experience strong suicidal ideas.

Sometimes episodes can include a mixture of depressive and manic symptoms – these are called 'mixed affective states/episodes'. Between episodes the person tends to be well and is usually able to function normally.

What can be done to help?

Early detection of bipolar disorder is very important. If a young person is diagnosed and receives effective treatment early on, she is likely to have a good outcome. It gives the young person and her family a chance to find out about the illness and ways to manage it and prevent relapse. Admission to a specialist hospital for children or young people is sometimes necessary for detailed assessment and safe management.

Talking therapies

There are very effective treatments for young people with bipolar disorder. These usually include educating the sufferer and her family about the illness, medication and psychotherapy, as well as individual counselling/talking therapy (CBT) and family meetings.

Medication

Different medications are used for different phases of the illness. If the young person has mania she may initially be treated with a medicine called an antipsychotic. If this is not effective then a mood-stabilizing medicine, such as lithium carbonate or sodium valproate, will be offered. During a depressive episode treatment may involve specific talking treatment and medication. This will usually be a mood stabilizer, as above, but in some cases an antidepressant medicine may be offered. Any medication given in bipolar disorder must be supervised by a specialist team.

Complementary therapies

Complementary therapies may be of help and some people believe that omega-3 fish oils are particularly useful. However, the herbal remedy St John's Wort, often used to relieve the symptoms of depression, may trigger a manic phase and cause other side-effects, and is best avoided in children or young people with bipolar disorder.

Tips for families, teachers, friends and others

Symptoms of a manic phase might easily be confused with normal changes in adolescent behaviour. The person may have previously been depressed, so the difference between her former depression and current elation and energy might at first seem a positive thing. Specialist assessment is very important, but a young person with bipolar disorder might need a lot of encouragement to get help because she may not believe that there is anything wrong with her in the first place.

If you are worried about a member of your family or someone you know, your GP is the first point of call. He can provide you with information, support and advice, and can make a referral to a specialist multidisciplinary mental health team.

Preventing relapse

The prevention of relapse into either phase of illness is important. There are lots of things that young people can do to protect themselves against episodes once bipolar disorder has been diagnosed. The lengths of time for which someone is well can be lengthened by self-help – for example, looking after physical health, regular sleep and eating patterns, the avoidance of unduly stressful situations, and the avoidance of mood-altering substances like alcohol or drugs. Cognitive behavioural techniques can also help prevent recurrence of depressive episodes. In addition to talking therapies, medication usually has an important role to play in keeping someone well between episodes, as well as treating the depressed and manic episodes themselves.

Depression

Jamie was seven years old when his father died. Over the subsequent twelve months he was understandably upset. Following the anniversary of his father's death, Jamie started to refuse to attend school. When he was forced to go, he tended to get into trouble for misbehaving. He ignored teachers in class and when he was told off he cried or sometimes shouted, and on one occasion he locked himself in the toilet. Jamie told his mum that he wanted to die and join his dad in heaven. He also cried a lot at home, lost his appetite and didn't seem interested in anything any more.

Jamie's GP asked for help from the Child and Adolescent Mental Health Team, and a community psychiatric nurse met up with Jamie on a regular basis. He was able to make use of a talking treatment for depression and slowly got back to his normal self. He was always sad about his father's death, but was able to get on with other things and enjoy his life again.

What is depression?

Most people, children as well as adults, feel low or 'blue' occasionally. Feeling sad is a normal reaction to experiences that are stressful or upsetting. However, when these feelings go on and on, or dominate and interfere with your whole life, it can become an illness.

Depression is defined as an illness when the feelings of sadness and hopelessness persist and interfere with a child or adolescent's ability to function. All children feel sad or needy sometimes and many adolescents experience times of brooding and melancholy. However, there are some children and young people who experience disturbing and distressing periods of low mood that are beyond the normal range of sadness. Depression is very common – around 1–2 per cent of children and 4–5 per cent of adolescents are suffering from it at any given point in time. The behaviour of depressed children and adolescents may differ from the behaviour of depressed adults. It is a treatable illness and early diagnosis and treatment are very important.

Who gets depression?

Anyone can suffer from depression, but some people are more prone to it than others. It is not a sign of a weak character. Many high-achieving and determined people have suffered with the illness. Depression is more likely to occur in poor and socially deprived families, but can happen to someone from any background or culture. Although not entirely hereditary, it can run in families. Stressful events, especially those that are ongoing or involve loss, increase the risk – for example, bereavement, parental divorce, bullying, abuse, friendship difficulties and other adverse social events. Having other problems, such as anxiety disorders, physical illness, disability or learning difficulties, can also increase a child's risk of getting depressed.

What does depression feel like?

Depression causes a number of changes in thoughts, feelings and behaviour. Features of depression in children and young people include low mood, sadness that will not go away, irritability, persistent boredom, tearfulness, problems with decreased or increased sleep, loss of appetite and eating too little, or eating too much, loss of motivation and loss of interest in activities, even those that are normally enjoyed, such as sport, music, talking to friends or watching TV. Depressed children may start to complain of aches and pains, find it hard to concentrate or to manage schoolwork, refuse to go to school, have outbursts of emotion or anger and threaten to run away. Other symptoms include feeling hopeless, worthless or guilty, being very sensitive to rejection or failure, and being self-critical. Children have different ways of expressing sadness or distress. Some might start misbehaving, others may stop wanting to go out of the home. Others may start lying for no obvious reason. Depression is often accompanied by anxiety, which can be overwhelming and distressing (see Chapter 10).

Adolescents and even young children with depression may think that life is not worth living and experience suicidal thoughts or thoughts about death. Depressed children and adolescents are at increased risk of self-harm and attempted suicide (see Chapter 18).

What about psychotic symptoms in depression?

When depression gets very severe it can cause symptoms of psychosis, which are described earlier in this chapter (see p. 265). In depression, a person might start to believe that she has done something terrible when she has not, or she might think that her body is not working properly any more, or that she is in terrible debt. Psychotic symptoms in depression tend to be related to low mood – that is, they are negative, depressive and often hostile and critical.

What can be done to help?

Early diagnosis and treatment are essential for depressed children and adolescents.

Talking treatments

When depression is mild it will often go away by itself. However, if it lasts longer than four weeks help should be sought. There are many different types of help for depression. Most involve talking to someone who will listen, understand the problem and have some practical suggestions about what to do next. With a little guidance, many young people and children can be supported to help themselves.

It may be useful to undertake activities that help to describe feelings – for example, writing a poem or song or keeping a diary. Some young people find it helpful to draw or paint. Eating a healthy diet, sticking to regular mealtimes and getting regular exercise are also beneficial.

When depression is moderate or severe or lasts a long time, other treatment is needed. Talking-based treatments work for most people. There are many types of talking treatments (see Chapter 25), some of which involve one-to-one sessions with a mental health worker. Problem-solving therapy, interpersonal therapy and cognitive behavioural therapy (CBT) are all examples. Sometimes CBT can be undertaken in a group setting. Family therapy can also be useful in the treatment of depression (see p. 355).

Depressed adolescents may use alcohol or other drugs as a way of trying to feel better. It is important that they avoid this, as it can make depression worse.

Medication

When talking therapies are not enough, or if the depression is severe, medication can be helpful. Antidepressants are usually only prescribed for older children and adolescents following an assessment by a specialist in child and adolescent mental health and are used alongside talking therapies.

Complementary therapies

St John's Wort is a complementary (herbal) treatment for depression. It should be given to children only under specialist supervision and not as an alternative to talking therapies. The dosage for children is not necessarily the same as it would be for adults and it can cause side-effects. It is thought to work in a similar way to antidepressant medications.

Tips for families, teachers, friends and others

Listen to the child or young person, give her time and space to say how she feels. Try to be sympathetic and don't expect too much. Avoid telling her to 'pull herself together' or 'snap out of it'. Try not to criticize her: it is easy to take criticism to heart when you are depressed, so avoid any kind of teasing or bullying. If you know of specific problems, where possible try to help solve them. Finally, unless the depression goes away by itself within a few weeks, encourage the young person or family to get help.

Dr Clare Lamb and Dr Habib Behi

SUPPORT ORGANIZATIONS

Young Minds: national charity committed to improving the mental health and emotional well-being of all children and young people. Tel: 0808 802 5544 (parents' information service) or 0207 336 8445 (general). *www.youngminds.org.uk*

Rethink: works to help everyone affected by severe mental illness recover a better quality of life. National Advice Service: 0845 456 0455. *www.rethink.org*

The Bipolar Association: works to enable people affected by bipolar disorder to take control of their lives. *www.mdf.org.uk*

WEBSITES OUTSIDE THE UK

Australia
www.beyondblue.org.au

Canada
Children's mental health Ontario: *www.kidsmentalhealth.ca*

New Zealand
www.ranzcp.org

FURTHER READING

Graham, Philip, and Hughes, Carol, *So Young, So Sad, So Listen*. Gaskell, 2005.

18 Self-harm and Attempted Suicide

Jake had had enough

Dear Mum,
By the time you read this I'll be somewhere else and all my problems will be over. I can't take the arguing and fighting any more. I wish you and Dad hadn't split up and I'm pissed off being the one you're angry with all the time. I'm sorry Mum but I can't take any more. Now I'm gone, you can get on with your life. I hope things work out for you. If you see Dad tell him I love him and miss him and maybe I will see him again, who knows? Tell Mandy I love her and she can have or sell my things. Have a good life Mum.
Love, Jake

Jake is fourteen and attending secondary school. He was diagnosed with attention defecit hyperactivity disorder (ADHD) (see Chapter 11) when he was eight and takes medication for this. He also has some learning difficulties. He lives at home with his mum, Eileen, and his younger sister, Mandy, who is ten.

Jake's dad, Paul, left home eighteen months ago when Eileen discovered he was having an affair with a colleague at work.

Paul and Eileen hadn't been getting on well for quite a while, but had stayed together 'for the sake of the children'. For the last few years, Paul had started drinking very heavily as well.

Eileen had found it very hard to cope with his affair and his drinking and often criticized him in front of Jake. Jake sometimes thought Eileen took all her anger out on him because he looked like his dad. Jake fantasized about running away to stay with his dad, but Paul's new girlfriend actively discouraged him from seeing his children. Paul had hardly seen Jake in the last eighteen months and had stopped phoning.

Another problem for the family was that Paul had not contributed any maintenance to Eileen, who was increasingly short of money. Last week, Jake asked to borrow £20 so that he could go out to the cinema with his friends, but Eileen said she couldn't afford it and told Jake to ring his dad. Jake then stole the money from his mother's purse and went out anyway. Eileen reported this to the police and Jake was cautioned as a result. Jake was so angry with Eileen that he told his best friend he was 'going to teach her'.

One morning, Jake pretended to go off to school as usual, but doubled back and let himself into the house, unbeknown to his mum who had gone out. He then wrote the suicide note, found his mum's medicines and took a variety of them, including ten paracetamol.

Fortunately, Eileen was taking her car to the garage that morning and had forgotten her car service book. She came home and discovered Jake half asleep on her bed, soon after he had taken the last of the tablets.

He was treated in hospital for paracetamol poisoning. Luckily, his liver had not been damaged. The consultant told Eileen they had got Jake 'just in time'. He was referred to the on-call self-harm nurse of the local Child and Adolescent Mental Health Service (CAMHS), who came to see him on the ward the day after his admission to hospital.

On the day of this assessment, Jake was interviewed alone and also in the presence of his mother. The nurse was also able to talk to Paul, who came to see Jake separately. The nurse found evidence that Jake was upset and confused about his self-harm but that, if he could believe things could get better, he wouldn't want to die.

His parents agreed to attend the CAMHS outpatient department with Jake in the weeks following his discharge from the paediatric ward. At these meetings, Jake was assessed for evidence of a psychiatric disorder by a child and adolescent psychiatrist but, apart from the need to get his ADHD under control, no evidence was found for a new disorder that could be causing or be adding to his unhappiness. The possibility that Jake's ADHD medication was causing increased thoughts of self-harm (which both Paul and Eileen had been worried about) was also carefully ruled out. Instead, the diagnosis was that Jake was experiencing a normal reaction of stress to a situation over which he felt he had no control (his parents' poor relationship). The psychiatrist explained to the parents that they had to re-establish a proper parenting role with Jake and try to resolve their differences in a more civilized manner. Jake would then feel more in control of his life.

Over the next few weeks, Jake became a happier child and was able to rebuild a warmer, more mutually respectful relationship with both his parents. He was offered regular CAMHS follow-up for his ADHD, which included monitoring his mood and possible mood-related side-effects of his medication.

Deliberate self-harm (DSH)

Mental health practitioners use the term DSH for people who deliberately harm or injure themselves. It is about 100 times more common than completed suicide in childhood or adolescence and often does not come to professional attention.

There are several kinds of DSH, including:

- self-poisoning (overdosing) with medications
- cutting, hitting or burning yourself
- picking your skin or hair
- trying to strangle yourself

DSH can also include drinking excess alcohol or taking illegal drugs. Before the age of twelve, it is commoner among boys than girls. But this pattern is dramatically reversed in adolescence, when about five times more girls than boys try to harm themselves. The commonest method of DSH is self-poisoning, especially in girls.

Suicide and attempted suicide

Completed suicide before the age of twelve is very rare. In the UK, there are about five suicides per million in the ten to fourteen age group, with this rate increasing to thirty suicides per million in the fifteen to nineteen age range. Adult rates, particularly in the elderly, are much higher. Completed suicide is always more likely in males than females, whatever the age. Teenage suicide rates in Europe and the USA have increased since the 1950s, with some evidence of a flattening out of this trend since the 1980s.

What causes DSH in young people?

First and foremost, everyone is an individual and all people (including children) are complex. This means they sometimes think and behave in ways that may seem irrational or mysterious, even to experienced parents, carers or clinicians.

Research has shown that there are various factors associated with DSH. The more severe or complex these factors, the higher the risk that they will prompt a more severe form of DSH, and so attempted self-harm will become attempted suicide. Factors leading to self-harm may include the following:

- The child does not experience a supportive relationship with a caring adult. DSH is often associated with 'broken homes' and family relationships that have broken down, possibly after years of disharmony. Boys whose fathers have left home often report conflict with their mothers.
- Children who harm themselves have often been living with family members who have a psychiatric disorder, commonly fathers with serious alcohol problems. There may also be a history of DSH in the family.
- Some children who self-harm have a psychiatric disorder, particularly dependence on substances such as alcohol or drugs, but also other conditions such as ADHD or depression (see Chapters 11 and 17). However, most are not depressed. Instead they are unhappy and feel trapped by a cycle of negative feelings about their problems, which they can't sort out. DSH is often then seen as a way of regaining control or relieving tension.
- Some children have a history of abuse (emotional, physical or sexual; see Chapter 9). This can cause feelings of guilt or shame that become unbearable. These children develop an urge to punish themselves and constantly think about self-harming. Alternatively, some young people develop feelings of detachment, and discover that self-injury helps them re-connect with themselves or their environment and even makes them feel more alive.

- It is common to find a history of academic problems, and older adolescents who self-harm are often unemployed.

About 20 per cent of children and young people who self-harm have tried it before. Most DSH is impulsive: half of the young people affected have only thought about harming themselves less than 15 minutes before acting on these thoughts. The impulse is usually triggered by an argument with a family member or friend. Thoughts of self-harm are more likely to be acted out if the child or adolescent has access to prescription or 'over-the-counter' medication. Paracetamol is a particular risk, due to widespread ignorance about its potential to cause permanent liver damage, or even death, at relatively low doses.

What signs can predict serious suicidal intent?

Evidence suggests that children or young people who really want to die:

- have been thinking about killing themselves for a long time
- tell people what they are planning to do (e.g. with apparent 'off-the-cuff' remarks that people later realize were meant seriously)
- make preparations before their death (e.g. arranging who will get the things that are precious to them)
- take steps to avoid being found and then harm themselves in a place and/or at a time they think they won't be discovered
- do not tell anyone about the fact that they have self-harmed (e.g. they might take an overdose, but try to carry on as normal until they become unconscious)
- leave a suicide note

Are there patterns at different ages?

It is hard to generalize about anyone's state of mind, whatever their age. However, evidence suggests that most children do not fully develop an adult concept of death until they are about seven or eight years old; this can probably be explained by how the brain develops. Because of this, children younger than eight may not fully understand that death is permanent. For this reason, different behaviours in younger children – such as running away – may be the equivalent of attempts at self-harm by older children.

What can be done to help?

Any kind of DSH by a child or young person, no matter how insignificant it may seem, should always be taken seriously. Someone, preferably a responsible adult, needs to give the child a clear message that they are available to help, understand what he has been feeling, and are willing to help, at the child's own pace. The adult needs to be able to stay calm, to control their own feelings and separate them from those of the child. Mental health professionals often call this important process 'containment'. It is similar to what any good-enough parent does instinctively with their child, every day of the week.

The adult also needs to give the message that practical solutions to the child's difficulties will be attempted. But it is unhelpful (although entirely understandable) to offer solutions that cannot be guaranteed. Many of these children have repeatedly experienced being let down by adults (for example, children who have been abused) and if they are to change the pattern of their self-harming behaviour they need to build at least one meaningful, trusting relationship with someone to whom they can turn in a crisis.

If it is possible to guarantee that such a person will be available for the child in future, then it is important for them to tell the child that if he ever feels like harming himself again, he should tell this person about how he is feeling. This guarantee and offer will then, it is hoped, make sense to the child (particularly one who is unsure whom he can trust) and be more likely to be acted upon in future.

Specialist help

Even if the child or young person appears well after a self-harm attempt, all patients who have self-harmed deliberately require an urgent assessment by a doctor. For example, in overdoses of paracetamol, complications of toxicity can take days to develop and even minor overdoses can cause serious illness or death.

If the young person has been admitted to hospital, he should have a specialist mental health assessment before being discharged. This is usually carried out by a clinician from the local CAMHS, who may be either a specialist nurse or a doctor. An assessment is a bit like detective work and is designed to find out why the young person has acted in this way. It is important that parents and carers take part and the clinician will nearly always request this. At the end of this assessment, the CAMHS clinician will decide on the next steps. Often it will involve a plan for more in-depth assessment in a CAMHS outpatient department, because clinicians know that if a young person who has self-harmed does not get the help he needs, it is very likely that he will make another (perhaps more dangerous) attempt.

CAMHS assessment includes individual and sometimes family work over several meetings. This should enable any psychiatric disorder to be recognized. Sometimes treatment will involve psychological therapies (individual and/or family work) and sometimes it involves a trial of medication (while monitoring the benefits of any effect against evidence of side-effects). These interventions may require CAMHS specialist input over a sustained period of time (several months, even years). A small number of children and young people may require admission into an age-appropriate day service or psychiatric in-patient unit.

Finally, it is essential for parents, carers and clinicians to be aware of the constant possibility that the child or young person, for whatever reason, does not trust the adults responsible for his safety, or does not want to tell anyone what he is planning to do. Therefore, if you have any reason to suspect that the child for whom you are responsible is at risk of self-harm, you should always consult his GP for advice. In this important area of child and adolescent psychiatry, it is always better to be safe than sorry.

Dr Iain McClure

INFORMATION

SUPPORT ORGANIZATIONS

National Self-Harm Network: *www.nshn.co.uk*

Self-harm: recovery, advice and support. *www.selfharm.org.uk*

The Samaritans: 24-hour service offering confidential emotional support to anyone who is in crisis. Helpline: 08457 909090 (UK); 1850 609090 (ROI). E-mail: *jo@samaritans.org* *www.samaritans.org*

A CD-ROM designed for 13–17-year-olds on mental health which looks at depression and self-harm: *Changing Minds: a Multimedia CD-ROM about Mental Health*. Further details from the Royal College of Psychiatrists, tel: 020 7235 2351, ext. 146; *www.rcpsych.ac.uk/publications/books/rcpp/1901242927.aspx*

WEBSITES OUTSIDE THE UK

Australia
Sane Australia: *www.sane.org*

Canada
Canadian Mental Health Association: *www.cmha.ca*

New Zealand
Mental Health Foundation New Zealand: *www.mentalhealth.org.nz*

19 Antisocial Behaviour: Conduct Disorder and Delinquency

EVERYONE CHANGES THROUGHOUT LIFE, whether for the better or for the worse. People can be affected by adversity, but they can also be affected by the positive influences in their lives.

What we fear as parents

It is natural for parents and grandparents to want their children to be safe, whether as infants or as teenagers. No parent or grandparent wants to face the fact that their child has ended up in the criminal justice system, having harmed another human being, and is destined for a juvenile prison.

Juvenile crime and delinquency are significant social and public health concerns. Many children and adults are increasingly fearful of the rise of random violence and the potential for serious harm.

What is delinquency?

Delinquency, conduct problems and aggression are all 'antisocial behaviours'. They represent a failure of the individual to respect the rights of other people and to conform to society's expectations of him.

Antisocial behaviours can range from mild conflicts with authority figures (such as the police), to major violations of societal norms (such as mugging), to serious violations of the rights of others (such as rape).

The term 'delinquency' implies that the acts could result in the person being convicted, although this sometimes doesn't happen.

What is conduct disorder?

Antisocial behaviours are the commonest causes for referral of young people to Child and Adolescent Mental Health Services (CAMHS). Where the child shows persistent disruptive, deceptive and aggressive behaviours over time, and especially when these are of a marked degree, the child may be assessed as having conduct disorder. Younger children, where the disruptive, deceptive and aggressive behaviours are confined to the home, may be diagnosed as having oppositional defiant disorder (ODD).

We know that conduct disorders cause children, families, schools and, at times, their local community distress. For the young person it can lead to social and educational impairment. If they are not helped early there can be negative outcomes for the young person in adolescence, with the onset of criminal behaviours and, in adulthood, development of antisocial personality disorder.

No single risk factor is either necessary or sufficient on its own to lead to the development of conduct disorder, but we are beginning to learn that where several risk factors come together, conduct disorder can be the result. In Child and Adolescent Mental Health Services (CAMHS) it is very common to find that a child has more than one disorder (co-morbidity; see p. 35). In no other mental health issue is this truer than in conduct disorder. The majority of adolescents with a diagnosis of conduct disorder have another diagnosis, most frequently ADHD, depressive disorder and substance misuse.

Research tells us that there are at least two developmental patterns for conduct disorder. There is early onset, associated with ADHD, overall lower intelligence and being male, and adolescent onset, which is related more to the influence of peers and substance misuse.

Does this matter? The answer is yes, because early onset conduct disorder is more linked with violence and delinquency in adolescence and offending in adulthood. Early diagnosis of the conduct disorder and other difficulties is very important so that early support and treatment can be given to the child within the contexts of his home, school and the community.

Although all individuals differ, we know that engaging with families early, working in partnerships which utilize their strengths and treating all of the child's disorders, including help for learning difficulties, will have the best chance of a successful outcome.

For conduct disorder, treatments can include many of those described later in this chapter and in Chapter 20, as well as those listed below:

In 3–12-year-olds:

- Parent management training
- Child therapies, especially cognitive behavioural and social skills therapy
- Intervention in school, focusing on positive behaviour, group interventions and behavioural management
- Promotion of academic engagement and learning

In the teenage years:

- Family-based intervention, such as functional family therapy and multisystemic therapy

Use of medication

Medication should, except in exceptional circumstances, only be used to treat co-morbid conditions, such as ADHD.

More treatment programmes are becoming available to support families and the child who has conduct disorder. The key to effective treatment is to try and change the environment around the young person, to enable her to increase pro-social behaviours and control her impulsiveness. Often the main task is to enable her to stop and reflect about how to respond safely when she perceives a world around her that is hostile and unforgiving.

What are the facts?

Overall the crime rate has not increased in recent years, although more girls are being convicted of offences than before. There has been a rise in violent crime since 1991. The number of juveniles cautioned or convicted for violence, drug offences and robbery has also risen, and the proportion of young people receiving custodial sentences has increased.

Much media publicity has recently been given to the rise in 'gang culture' in the UK and the increase in violent crime involving young people, both as victims and perpetrators, linked to the possession of guns and knives. Despite the fact that England and Wales now imprison more young people than any other European country, two thirds of young offenders who have been imprisoned re-offend within twelve months of their release.

In 2006–2007 in England and Wales, 295,860 criminal offences were committed by young people. The most common offences recorded were theft and handling (19.2 per cent), violence against the person (19.1 per cent), criminal damage (13.9 per cent) and motoring offences (12.4 per cent). Nearly half of these offences (48.6 per cent) were committed by sixteen- and seventeen-year-olds. The majority of offences (79.9 per cent) were committed by young men.

Who is at risk?

Poor mental health and substance misuse are important risk factors. These can increase once the young person enters the Youth Justice

System. However, we also know that in some neighbourhoods it is far more difficult to keep children out of the way of older antisocial peers. It is a sad truth that fewer than 1 in 10 families in any community accounts for more than half of that community's criminal offences. Some families have inbuilt difficulties and pressing social problems. We also know that poverty is not good for mental health or antisocial behaviour. Where there is little adult supervision of children, harsh discipline and poor bonding between a parent and child (see Chapter 4), antisocial behaviour is more likely to follow.

We know a great deal about the negative effects of maltreatment on children and its link with antisocial behaviour. The negative impact of marital conflict and domestic violence is also well documented (see Chapter 9).

Outlined below are some of the factors that increase the risks of children and young people offending and coming into contact with the criminal justice system. Also highlighted is the proportion of young people who have mental health problems and learning difficulties which make them particularly vulnerable to involvement in crime. Based on recent research, there is a brief overview of some of the interventions that different agencies can provide which may help reduce the risks of offending, both in the short and the longer term.

- Most adolescents commit some delinquent act, but usually this will be some minor infraction.
- The majority of children in prison have a background of social exclusion (homelessness, been in public care, low income, poor housing, poor schooling/exclusion); a significant proportion have been subject to violence at home and 1 in 3 females and 1 in 20 males report a history of sexual abuse.
- 70,000 school-age offenders enter the criminal justice system in England and Wales every year, according to Prison Reform Trust reports.

- Young offenders under twenty years old account for more than half the violent crimes in the country.
- Half of the group of young people who commit serious and violent offences are 'active' in crime by the age of twelve or thirteen.
- Robbery is the commonest reason for children to be given a custodial sentence.
- The age at which most violent crime is committed is seventeen.
- Only a small proportion (around 6 per cent) of adolescent offenders are the persistent offenders who account for the majority of violent acts within this group.
- Perpetrators aged between ten and twenty account for 20 per cent of convictions for all sexual offences in the UK.

What increases the risks of young people getting into trouble?

- A history of family disruption, poor parenting and parental conflict (a minority of young offenders live with both parents).
- Higher than average rates of loss, bereavement, abuse and violence experienced within a family setting (see Chapters 9 and 13).
- Relatives with a history of offending, or absence of positive role models in the family.
- Low educational attachment, attendance and attainment.
- Higher levels of young people who have been in institutional care than in the general population.
- Peer-group pressure.
- Higher than average levels of drug and alcohol use (not necessarily related to offending behaviour; see Chapter 14).
- Higher than average mental health needs, estimated at around 30 per cent, including depression, self-harming behaviour,

post-traumatic stress disorder, anxiety disorders, ADHD, conduct disorder, emerging personality disorder, substance misuse and learning difficulties (figures from the Youth Justice Board).

What do we know about gangs?

There has been a significant increase in the number of gangs in larger cities in the UK during this decade. In south London alone, there has been a sixfold increase since 2000. Membership can include children as young as five years old, ranging up to early–mid-twenties. Gangs are frequently linked to specific housing estates and fighting often occurs between rival gangs. In some cities they have been modelled on 'American-style' gangs, such as those in cities like Los Angeles. These gangs often have access to and are willing to use weapons with little or no apparent motive to do so.

The BBC reported that 25 per cent of gun crimes committed in 2007 were committed by under-eighteens. More than half of killings today appear to be gang-related.

The impact of gangs, not only on young people and their families but on the community as a whole, can be very significant. Police forces and other agencies, including the voluntary sector, have developed multi-agency gang strategies to actively reduce gang membership and prevent gun crime in the areas worst affected.

A recent survey by the children's charity NCH (now known as Action for Children) identified that many young people did not think they were safe in their communities, feeling demonized by adults and dismayed by the gun and knife crime. They wanted to be involved in helping tackle the problems in their communities. Many children believed drugs, self-protection, image, peer pressure and revenge were reasons for their peers becoming involved in gun and knife crime. They considered that music and violent computer games could also have some influence. They highlighted a need for more community-based activities.

What can be done to help?

The principal aim of any Youth Justice System is to prevent offending by children and young people under eighteen years of age. For example, there are 157 Youth Offending Teams in England and Wales. These are multi-agency teams (Health, Justice, Education and Social Care).

There are around 3,000 custodial places for young people under the age of eighteen in prison service young offenders' institutions, local authority secure children's homes and private-sector secure training centres.

Sometimes we need to focus on things within the young person himself, looking at what is happening at home or in the community in which he lives. Treatment is tailored to the individual and his family. Many young offenders are not engaged in mainstream education and health services, and it is critical that they are helped to access the mainstream and specialist services they need.

Many different treatments have been used to reduce offending, such as cognitive behavioural therapy, or medication if a young person has a particular condition such as ADHD or psychosis (see Chapter 25).

As a society, we can do much to prevent young people becoming antisocial – for instance 'Communities that Care' schemes, in which the community targets five main behaviours that are damaging the lives of adolescents and the communities where they live.

As a young person travels further down the road of crime, the interventions needed become more intensive. For those at risk of custody, therapies have been combined to help the individual and his family bring about positive change. For example, multisystemic therapy (MST) is about directing the intervention not just at the young person and his family, but also towards the social contexts in which the young person lives, so works with the family, school, peers and local community.

Often violent youngsters see the rest of the world as hostile and out to get them. Some of the following interventions help them cope:

- social skills training helps them to walk away from confrontation
- education and training can open up new opportunities on release from custody
- help with drug and alcohol problems
- working with the family to encourage positive behaviour

Recently multi-agency teams have been engaging with parents before their child reaches the courts. It is important that they are involved at an early stage.

Still a taboo?

There is still very little known or documented about children who are violent towards their parents. This is surprising given the level of concern about antisocial and violent behaviour committed by children in school or in the community.

As a parent, admitting that you fear your own child can bring about a sense of shame and failure. But help is available through professionals and self-help groups.

Once a young person has entered the criminal justice system, it is hard to change his behaviour. None the less, we now have good evidence that, with the right treatment programme, young people can come through as young adults who give back to the community and, more importantly, can themselves become good parents.

My professional life has involved me in working, together with an art therapist, with the few youngsters who have killed or raped. We are in for the long haul, and have seen how over the years young people can gain an understanding of the dreadful harm they have caused. We can work with the origins of this final act with care, time, attention and good aftercare, enabling them to return safely to society as adults.

Professor Sue Bailey

SUPPORT ORGANIZATIONS

The Youth Justice Board: oversees the Youth Justice System in England and Wales, working to prevent offending and re-offending by children and young people under the age of eighteen, and to ensure that custody for them is safe and secure, and addresses the causes of their offending behaviour. The website describes the different parts of the Youth Justice System and how it works.
www.yjb.gov.uk/en-gb

WEBSITES OUTSIDE THE UK

Australia
www.aic.gov.au

Canada
www.library.ualberta.ca/subject/law/youngoffenders/index.cfm

New Zealand
www.justice.govt.nz/youth-justice/youth-strategy.html

20 The Mental Health of Young Offenders

Stephen was seventeen when he was first referred with depression to the Mental Health In-Reach team in the young offenders unit where he had been sent on remand for a serious assault. He had very poor recollection of the incident, as he had been drinking heavily at the time. He had one previous conviction for fighting and had spent two months in prison at the age of sixteen.

He was brought up in the north-west of England and had an older brother and a younger sister. He couldn't recall having any difficulties when he was small, although his parents fought often and sometimes he had witnessed his father physically assaulting his mother when he had been drinking. Stephen thought his problems started in primary school, where he was bullied and struggled with literacy. He still found reading very difficult, but loved sports and was good at drawing. His older brother used to protect him in school.

In secondary school, however, things became worse. His brother was moved to a different school, the bullying continued and Stephen didn't think his parents or teachers were able to stop it. He continued to struggle academically, was in bottom sets for all his subjects and could not recall receiving any extra help. When he was fourteen he was beaten up in the school toilets by a gang of youths. He fought back, believing he had to 'stand up for himself', and assaulted one particular lad. As a result of this he was excluded from school and never returned to formal education.

When Stephen was fifteen, his father died of complications from his alcoholism. Stephen was with him when he died and he still had flashbacks of his father when he was dying. He was close to his dad and found it very difficult to talk about the way he was feeling afterwards. He was twice sent for counselling but stopped going because it was too painful. Instead, he resorted to using alcohol regularly, drinking with a group of older boys who knew his brother. He said this 'numbed the way he was feeling'. His mother became depressed and he did not feel able to talk to her. He helped care for his younger sister. He also began to use crack cocaine at weekends, combined with alcohol, and was getting into lots of fights. He knew alcohol made him more aggressive. He described fluctuating low mood, irritability, feelings of hopelessness and thoughts of suicide, all of which were worse after cocaine and binge-drinking.

Stephen had briefly had help from an alcohol counsellor following his previous offence, but this had been withdrawn and he had resumed drinking heavily. He was depressed and had very low self-esteem. In addition to medication to treat his depression, he required counselling to help address his unresolved grief following his father's death and educational support to improve his literacy. After release from prison, he is likely to require ongoing support to help him abstain from alcohol and illicit drugs, and will possibly also benefit from the involvement of a local community mental health service.

Mental health problems in young offenders

We know that children with conduct disorder (see Chapter 19) and ADHD (see Chapter 11) are at much greater risk of committing delinquent acts in adolescence. Therefore, it is really important to treat conduct disorder and ADHD early.

A small number of young people with autistic spectrum disorders (see Chapter 11) may also fall into crime because their social naivety means they are easily led into criminal acts by others. Aggression can arise if their routines are disrupted. Antisocial behaviour may happen because of their lack of understanding of what is happening, or if they misread social cues. Very occasionally, crimes may reflect their particular obsession, especially if their obsession involves a fascination with violence or fire.

Unfortunately, children whose learning disability has not been recognized early in education can find themselves excluded from school and then they become very vulnerable to the negative influence of other peers. Children in the Youth Justice System have far higher than average levels of reading difficulties.

There is a slightly increased risk of violence if a young person develops psychosis (see Chapter 17) and has active symptoms, especially if he also misuses drugs or alcohol.

It is important to recognize that depression (see Chapter 17), anxiety (see Chapter 10) and post-traumatic stress disorder (see Chapter 24) are very common in young offenders. Feeling depressed affects self-esteem and can make us irritable, hostile and angry. We are more likely to lash out when we feel others are getting at us. People working with young offenders have to be constantly alert to the risks of deliberate self-harm and completed suicide (see Chapter 18), especially for young offenders in juvenile prisons.

- The most common mental health problems for young offenders are emotional disorders, conduct disorders and attentional disorders.

- Substance abuse, which can cause or exacerbate mental health problems, is also common. Studies vary in estimating that between one third and over a half of young people are affected by one or more of these problems.

- Young offenders have been widely documented as having high levels of need in a number of different areas, including mental health. In addition, about half have had problems with relationships (with family and peers), and a third have experienced significant problems with education or work.

- Formal studies have shown that about 25 per cent of young offenders have an IQ lower than 70 and a significant number have learning difficulties. Problems with communication and social difficulties are also common.

- A study for the Youth Justice Board showed that a third or more of young offenders have a mental health need. Almost 20 per cent are depressed, and 10 per cent reported a history of self-harm in the previous month, with a similar proportion suffering from anxiety and post-traumatic stress disorder (see Chapter 24). Hyperactivity was reported in 7 per cent and psychotic symptoms in 5 per cent.

- Although a much smaller group, female offenders have relatively higher mental health needs than males. Young offenders from ethnic minorities have also been described as having higher rates of post-traumatic stress.

What about girls?

Overall, levels of offending are far lower in girls, but in general they share the same risks for offending as boys. Girls can be aggressive in their own right and are more likely to choose a violent partner. If they become adolescent mothers, they may be less sensitive and responsive as parents.

What about drugs and alcohol?

We know drug and especially alcohol misuse are associated with offending because:

- Under the influence of drugs and alcohol young people, like adults, become more disinhibited.
- Once addicted to drugs and/or alcohol, some young people commit crimes to pay for their habits.
- A study revealed high rates (approximately 75 per cent) among young offenders of dependence on one or more drugs. Of these, 28 per cent were dependent on heroin and crack, and 94 per cent reported frequent use of cannabis, although only 10 per cent were dependent on it. Harmful levels of alcohol use also featured prominently among this group.
- Many had psychological and emotional problems which needed to be addressed in parallel with their drug and alcohol use.
- Research has suggested an education and harm-minimization approach in combating young males' substance-misuse problems, combined with an emphasis on thorough care while in prison and on release.
- Some police forces estimate that up to 70 per cent of all crime

is drug- or alcohol-related. Alcohol is thought to be a feature in 80 per cent of domestic violence and 40 per cent of child abuse cases.

What can be done to help?

In younger children:

- Early identification of and support for children and families with clear psychosocial risk factors. High-risk groups, such as young expectant mothers, may be targeted with help, especially if they've experienced harsh parenting themselves.
- Identification and treatment of children at an early stage with ADHD, oppositional defiant disorder and conduct disorder who are more at risk of developing seriously aggressive behaviour, offending as adolescents and adults, and also developing personality disorders when they are older.
- Engaging families with children who have conduct problems and delivering parent-training programmes (Webster Stratton or Positive Parenting Programme, for example).
- Interventions in schools to promote positive behaviour, identify children with learning difficulties, and implement strategies to promote academic engagement and learning.

In adolescents:

- Initially, a careful, structured assessment of risk and mental health needs is essential to plan for any interventions that may be necessary. This should be done by the local Youth Offending Team, who will involve the local Child and Adolescent Mental Health Services (CAMHS) team as required, or by a mental health worker who can liaise with the local CAMHS.

- Multi-systemic therapy (MST) is a multi-modal approach focusing on the individual, the family and the peer group (see Chapter 19).
- Recognition of depression (see Chapter 17), which can cause irritability, hostility and anger in teenagers, and of post-traumatic stress disorder, which combined with anxiety can increase the risks of developing antisocial personality disorder in adult life if untreated.
- Awareness of other developmental disorders, such as autistic spectrum disorders (see Chapter 11), sometimes in combination with learning difficulties, which are being increasingly recognized in populations of young and adult offenders.
- Identification of adolescents at risk of, or already having, problems with substance misuse and offering interventions to them, including for children as young as ten.
- Early referral for assessment and treatment of young people with sexually abusive behaviour.
- All interventions should be tailored using a cognitive behavioural and problem-solving skills training approach (see Chapter 25), based on an assessment of risk, needs and learning abilities.
- Those with moderate and severe mental health problems should be identified and referred to the appropriate agency.
- Anger management and social skills training in older adolescents.

Dr Theresa McArdle

SUPPORT ORGANIZATIONS

Addaction: provides help, information and advice on drug or alcohol problems. *www.addaction.org.uk*

National Association for Youth Justice: operates as a campaigning, training and membership organization with an over-arching philosophy and policy regarding the Youth Justice System. *http://nayj.org.uk*

Muslim Youth Helpline (MYH): provides faith- and culturally sensitive services to Muslim youth in the UK. Helpline: 0808 808 2008. *www.myh.org.uk*

PAPYRUS – Prevention of Youth Suicides: UK resources and support for those dealing with suicidal behaviour, depression or emotional distress. HOPELine UK – 0800 068 41 41. *www.papyrus-uk.org*

Depaul Trust: Depaul Prison Project offers advice, advocacy, immediate support and routes into the community for young people leaving prison, and preventive work to help stop young people ending up in prison and to reduce re-offending. *www.depaulnightstopuk.org*

Barnardos: runs almost 400 projects around the UK, whatever the issue – from drug misuse to disability, youth crime to mental health, sexual abuse to domestic violence, poverty to homelessness. *www.barnardos.org.uk*

WEBSITES OUTSIDE THE UK

Australia

www.aic.gov.au

Canada

www.library.ualberta.ca/subject/law/youngoffenders/index.cfm

New Zealand

www.justice.govt.nz/youth-justice/youth-strategy.html

21 Sexuality and Sexual Problems

NAVIGATING THE TURBULENT WATERS of identity, relationships and sexuality is crucial in adolescence. Young people often mature physically before they have the emotional awareness and life experiences needed to manage their sexuality well. This is a time that can be bewildering for young people as well as for their parents.

Some young people look to adults they trust for guidance, but most confide in friends. Magazines and television are full of messages about sex and relationships – not all of them helpful. This only serves to reinforce that parents do have a key role to play.

In this chapter we will focus on key issues affecting teenagers: relationships, sexual orientation, promiscuity, pressure and the role of alcohol and drugs in affecting choices, and on sex and young people with disabilities.

Relationships

First of all, what exactly is a relationship? Is it saying you are 'going out'? Do you actually need to spend time together in person to be in a relationship? Or can you be in a relationship with someone over the internet? How long do you have to have been 'going out' with someone for before it counts as a relationship? Are you only in a relationship if it's physical? And how physical do you have to be to say you're having a physical relationship? Would it mean you're having sex, and what exactly does that mean? Does the relationship have to be with only one person at a time?

Some cultures have clear, even strict, rules about relationships, but for many people in modern-day Britain there aren't universally agreed rules about relationships. Ideally, the young people involved will both decide if they are in a relationship and what the rules are for their relationship. Of course, it doesn't always work that way and one person may have very different ideas from the other about the 'relationship rules'.

The popular image of the teenage romance is that such relationships, even if they are intense, are fleeting. In terms of research, teenage relationships have not been looked at as much as issues around sex, so to an extent we tend to rely on collective wisdom and personal experience to guide our thinking about them.

Recent research from the USA found that as many as 80 per cent of teenagers have had some sort of romantic relationship by the time they are eighteen. Despite their temporary nature, these relationships are often intense. The researchers found that boys are more shy and awkward about communicating their feelings than girls, who tend to have better decision-making capabilities and are more prepared for emotional involvement. Girls are also more likely to talk to friends about their relationships, giving them a broader perspective. Overturning a common myth, they also found that boys feel things just as strongly as girls. A difficult but important life experience is learning to cope with these intense feelings for the first time. Adults can help by recognizing that the young person's feelings are genuine and taking them seriously, while trying to retain a degree of balance.

Working out one's views in terms of what we expect from others in relationships and what others can expect from us is important. Most teenagers have already had experience of this in family relationships and other friendships and, despite the odd hiccup, negotiate this quite successfully.

Occasionally parents may worry that their son or daughter is becoming over-committed, or that a relationship is becoming too important, causing them to neglect other friends or activities. Many parents worry that, despite their disapproval, any intervention may lead to a *Romeo and Juliet* situation, whereby the young people are pushed even closer together. It is important to try to work out whether the apparent neglect of other friendships or 'over-commitment', is caused by the relationship itself becoming too exclusive, or whether the relationship has become so important as a consequence of problems or insecurities in other relationships. Remind your son or daughter that they are important to you, giving them space to talk about any worries. Let them know that you are available if they need you. Whether you need to do any more than this depends upon the level of concern, but quite often these types of problems sort themselves out.

Parents may also worry that their son or daughter is being taken advantage of or treated badly. This may be more likely to happen if, for some reason, the young person is less secure. Although it is probably uncommon, teenage girls can sometimes be victims of violence from their boyfriends. Women's Aid has recently launched a campaign called Expect Respect to raise awareness of this issue. If parents suspect their daughter is experiencing violence, it is important to raise this with her, to let her know you are concerned and to make sure she is safe (see Support Organization at the end of the chapter).

Sexual orientation

It is usually during the teenage years that individuals begin to realize whether they are heterosexual, homosexual or bisexual as part of an understanding of their own identity. For homosexual and bisexual young people, their sexual maturation has an extra layer of complexity. They have to decide if, or when, to 'come out' and face the possibility of disappointment, rejection and hurtful comments from loved ones, peers and strangers alike. It is important to remember that teenagers 'try out' different roles until they find one that fits them and experimentation with sexual orientation can be part of this normal process. Despite this, it is important that parents let their children know that they accept their sexuality and make it clear that they will support them. Social attitudes towards sexuality have changed a great deal, but lesbian and gay people can still experience prejudice and rejection. Family support is essential in helping weather this storm.

Hearing that your child is gay or lesbian can come as a bit of a shock and parents may sometimes struggle to accept it. They may worry that their child will face a lifetime of prejudice, or they may feel a sense of loss or sadness or worry as their image of their child's future may suddenly have changed. Talking to other parents who have had similar experiences can be helpful. There are useful support groups, such as Families and Friends of Lesbians and Gays. If groups aren't your thing, there are also helpful internet sites, including the Channel 4 health site. The key is realizing that you will find a way through it, that being lesbian or gay is part of normal life and not an illness or some sort of psychological disturbance. As parents, you haven't made your child heterosexual or homosexual or bisexual. Whatever your child's sexuality, they still need you.

Pressure and promiscuity

Pressure to have sex younger, and with more people, is higher than it has ever been. With the UK having the highest teenage pregnancy rates in Western Europe and an increasing prevalence of sexually transmitted diseases such as chlamydia, gonorrhoea and HIV in young people, the consequences of promiscuity are serious. Two young people can feel more or less ready to have sex and this can cause one partner to feel under pressure. There can be pressure coming from peer groups as well. Young people need to get the message that there is no set 'right time' to start having sex – it's a personal choice.

The media's glamorization of promiscuity, sexual freedom and liberation, in addition to the advertising industry's active choice to target 'tweenies' (pre-teens) in marketing campaigns that utilize the notion of 'sexiness' in order to sell clothes, cosmetics and music, adds to the pressure young people feel to be sexy and sexually active. Young people are constantly bombarded with sexual images via TV, music videos, films, magazines and the ever-popular social networking sites in a way in which older generations were not.

There is evidence that talking to your children about sex and relationships is more likely to encourage them to delay having sex and to use contraception.

Sex and relationships education plays a vital role in informing young people about important topics such as contraception and how to protect themselves against sexually transmitted diseases. If done well, such education goes further than this. It explores issues of pressure, feelings, autonomy, self-respect and respect for others. Testament to this is the fact that in the Netherlands, where sex education is introduced comprehensively (with practical skills, such as how to put a condom on, included), the teenage pregnancy rate is the lowest in Western Europe. It follows that to be informed is to be empowered. So the next big question is, who should do the informing? Should it be parents, schools, the health service or another agency? The answer is, both schools and parents, and sometimes older siblings. It is beyond the scope of this chapter to go into detail about how to do it – most parents know their children and know best how to approach them. Of course, they may still be embarrassed and want advice from a sourse other than family or friends. Internet sites, such as Parentline, can provide useful tips.

Teens can also go to sexual health clinics or to their GP for confidential advice, sexual health checks, pregnancy testing and free condoms. Young people should also understand that both parties involved are responsible for contraception and protection. If they are not able to have these conversations to make a decision on what will work best for them, they should question whether they are ready to be having sex at all.

A tricky issue for parents can be the fact that young people under sixteen, if they are deemed to have sufficient understanding and it is thought to be in their best interests, can receive confidential contraceptive advice without their parents' knowledge.

Sex and drugs and alcohol

Britain's current problems of binge-drinking and a teen drug culture can fuel promiscuity and unsafe sex in young people. Intoxication with substances is well known to impair decision-making ability. It also increases impulsivity and this impacts upon the decision whether to have sex or not, with whom, where and whether to consider and use protection against sexually transmitted diseases and pregnancy. Young people who make important decisions such as these, under the influence of substances, run the risk of making themselves vulnerable and also of doing things they may live to regret both in the short and long term.

It is important to take binge-drinking and drugs seriously – but one of the most effective protections against them is for young people to have a sense of connection with their parents. Doing everyday things such as eating together and spending time with each other regularly helps families bond.

Sex and young people with disabilities

Talking to your child about sex if she has a disability may be difficult, partly because sex and disability are still something of a taboo subject. Contact-a-Family has a number of useful tips:

- Talk to your child about sex early so that problems are less likely to arise – certainly before puberty.

- Talk openly and casually, as this gives the message that it is not something secretive or to be afraid of.
- Take advantage of everyday cues – e.g. a television programme which might help trigger a conversation.
- When talking about sex, take into account your child's disability and be realistic – e.g. it might take longer; it might mean experimenting a little.
- Try to make sure that your child understands as much as possible about love and sex and the difference between wanting to touch and kiss someone and being made to do something that feels wrong or scary.

Your child may, because of her disability, have less privacy than other young people and may be more dependent upon you to help her go to the GP for contraception. She may also be less able to experiment without your knowing. This can be difficult for both of you. As with most things, talking to others can be helpful. Working out what are your own fears and emotions is important.

Sexuality is part of healthy adult relationships. To consider only the problems and potential pitfalls of sex would be an unbalanced view of the topic. Provided that there are no child protection concerns, that the young people involved are making informed choices with which they are happy (and healthy), and are respecting themselves and others, then this should be viewed as part of normal development and maturation.

Dr Margaret Murphy and Dr Taryn Tracey

SUPPORT ORGANIZATIONS

For parents

Family Planning Association: *www.fpa.org.uk*

NHS Choices: Talking with teens about sex.
www.nhs.uk/livewell/sexualhealth/pages/talktoyourteen.aspx

Parentline Plus: national charity working for, and with, parents. Helpline: 0808 800 2222. *www.parentlineplus.org.uk*

For young people

Brook: provides young people under the age of twenty-five with free and confidential sexual health advice. Helpline on 0808 802 1234. *www.brook.org.uk*

www.likeitis.org: click on to the country – likeitis gives young people access to information about all aspects of sex education and teenage life. Topics include: teenage pregnancy, help and advice, periods, lovebugs (sexually transmitted infections), sex, peer pressure, sexuality, contraception, emergency contraception and puberty.

Information and advice for young people on love, sex and relationships: *www.ruthinking.co.uk*

Site for teenagers, including the facility to email questions on medical/sexual issues *www.teenagehealthfreak.org*

Sexual health

Family Planning Association: *www.fpa.org.uk*

Young People's Sexual Health: *www.ypsh.net*

Orientation

Families and Friends of Lesbians and Gays: national organization. Helpline: 0845 652 0311. *www.fflag.org.uk*

London Lesbian and Gay Switchboard: information and support for any issue relating to lesbian, gay or bisexual life. Helpline: 020 7837 7324. *www.llgs.org.uk*

Other

Women's Aid: national charity working to end domestic violence against women and children. *www.womensaid.org.uk*

WEBSITES OUTSIDE THE UK

Australia
www.healthinsite.gov.au

Canada
www.sexualityandu.ca

New Zealand
www.everybody.co.nz

22 Atypical Gender Development in Children and Adolescents

George who wanted to be Georgina

George was a nine-year-old boy who said that he had wanted to be a girl since he was four years old. He enjoyed dressing up in his mother's and older sister's clothes and playing with dolls. He would often tell his family and friends that he was really a girl and would introduce himself as Georgina. At school he played with girls and avoided rougher games like football with other boys.

George's family were worried that, as he got older, he would be teased or bullied by other children at school, so they asked their GP for some advice. Their doctor felt that George and his family would benefit from some support and referred them to the Gender Identity Development Service for Children and Adolescents.

George and his family were seen and were able to talk openly about him wanting to be Georgina, and they were encouraged to talk about their feelings, worries and concerns. George had the opportunity to talk both on his own and with his family, and they felt very supported and listened to. George's school was also contacted in order to help them support George and ensure that he was not being teased or bullied. George was seen at the service until he was fifteen, by which point he no longer felt that he was or that he wanted to be a girl and felt instead that he was gay.

Lucy who wanted to be Max

Lucy was a sixteen-year-old girl who called herself Max and wanted to be referred to as 'he'. (Lucy will now be referred to as 'Max'.) Max hated his female body, especially after going through puberty. He dressed in a masculine way and would bind his breasts. He looked like a male, and said he had felt like a boy for as long as he could remember. Max was generally accepted by his peers, although he did get teased and was called names by some other teenagers at school. Max also felt very uncomfortable about going to the girls' changing rooms and toilets and would often avoid going to the toilet while at school. His family were worried about how unhappy he was feeling about his female body and asked their GP to refer him to a specialist service.

Max was very relieved when he and his family were offered an appointment. He asked to be called Max by the team and to be referred to as 'he'; having this request acknowledged made him feel that his distress had been understood. He said he wanted to have a sex-change operation as soon as possible as he was sure he was really a male.

It was explained to Max that he would need to continue to

be seen at the clinic regularly over a period of time, along with his family, so that they could all have a chance to think about and explore his feelings without rushing into any physical treatments. Initially he felt disappointed and frustrated by this, but he also realized that he needed to be certain about changing his body and to be sure that the features of his gender identity disorder had persisted over a period of time. Clinic staff also visited his school to discuss gender identity issues with his teachers, and the school made arrangements for Max to use separate changing rooms and toilets.

After six months of meetings at the Gender Identity Service, it was felt that the features of a gender identity disorder had persisted and Max was referred to a paediatric clinic where he had some physical investigations, and was also asked to think about whether he might want children in the future. It was important to make this decision before starting hormonal interventions.

The test results were all normal and, as Max decided he might want to have children in the future, his eggs were frozen.

Max was then prescribed 'hormone blockers', which is the first stage of the treatment. These stop female hormones being produced and are reversible – i.e. the effects do not last when the medication is stopped. Max had an injection every month and was very relieved that his periods had stopped.

It was explained to him that staff could not prescribe him male hormones and he could not have a sex-change operation until he was at least eighteen years old, at which point he would be referred to an adult Gender Identity Service.

What is gender identity?

The gender identity of a child is their perception of whether they are male or female. This may be reflected in their behaviour, play or statements about themselves, such as 'I am a girl' or 'I am a boy'.

The majority of young children and adolescents have a gender identity which matches the sex into which they were born (biological sex); most girls have a female gender identity and most boys a male gender identity. In a small number of children, however, the sex they were born does not match their perception of their gender. A child born as female may feel that she is really a boy and vice versa. The degree to which the child identifies as being the opposite sex varies, can often be part of normal child development and may be transient.

Patients often do not like the label 'gender identity disorder'. However, this diagnostic category has made it possible to develop further understanding and research in specialized services.

Gender identity disorder in children

Some children may have the features of what is called a gender identity disorder, and may identify very strongly as the opposite sex. They may make statements about feeling that they are of the opposite sex, dress up in clothes or play games usually associated with the opposite sex, and identify more with children of the opposite sex. For example, boys may prefer playing with dolls and girls a more rough-and-tumble type of play. They will often describe feeling distressed about their biological gender.

Gender identity disorder in adolescents

Adolescents with a gender identity disorder often feel very uncomfortable with their biological sex and strongly identify with the opposite sex.

The experience of going through puberty in particular is an extremely distressing period. Young women can become very upset with the onset of breast development and menstruation, and young men with growing taller, developing facial hair and with the more sexual changes associated with male development.

Adolescents will often dress 'in role' – that is, as the opposite sex – and also change their names to something they feel fits their identity more. This can sometimes lead to difficulties in being accepted by family or friends or in educational or social settings.

Associated difficulties

Children and adolescents with a gender identity disorder may have associated difficulties, including feelings of unhappiness, isolation and depression. Some may feel suicidal. They may feel others do not generally understand or accept them, and may be the victims of harassment and bullying at school or in other social areas.

Parents and siblings of these children may feel confused, unsure what to do or say, and may also feel very alone.

What can be done to help?

Self-help

Much can be done to help children and teenagers who have issues regarding their gender identity without needing to consult professionals. Young people may feel embarrassed about feeling different, and enabling them to talk about how they feel may help them feel less isolated and more understood. It is important to try to be non-judgemental and supportive. There are also self-help organizations that can offer advice and support, as well as the opportunity for young people and their families to meet others in a similar position to themselves. This form of help is complementary to the help offered by professionals.

Professional help

If your child appears distressed or troubled, and you feel you may need some professional help, your GP can advise you and offer support. If there are other concerns about the child's mental health, a doctor will also be able to refer you to a Child and Adolescent Mental Health Service (CAMHS), or to a Specialist Gender Identity Development Service.

Specialist services work with the whole family in exploring the gender identity of the young person. They take a staged approach, first involving psychological assessment over a period of time to ensure that the young person continues to feel the same way about his or her gender identity before any physical investigations or treatments are considered.

Talking treatments

A number of different talking treatments are available (see Chapter 25). These include the young person talking about their feelings and difficulties to a professional on their own in order to help them gain a clearer sense of their gender identity. Teenagers in particular may find the opportunity to talk in private very helpful. Verbal and non-verbal communication is used to explore factors that might have been involved in the development of the atypical gender identity. This might include attachment issues, particular experiences of loss in the family, etc.

The aim of therapeutic interventions is not to change the atypical gender identity in itself. However, it is possible that a person's understanding of the factors involved in gender identity may affect their future gender identity development.

Family meetings can be very helpful. They provide an opportunity for the entire family to talk about and explore their feelings about the gender identity disorder and to gain a better understanding of how it impacts on the family as a whole, as well as on the individual family members.

Group therapy is also available, and provides the opportunity for the young person or their parents to meet others in a similar position, and reassures them that they are not alone.

Support with education

Professionals are also able to provide advice and support to schools and colleges. This can often improve the young person's relationships with teachers and peers, as well as offering practical advice about issues such as the use of toilets and changing areas.

Some children and adolescents will be helped by talking treatments alone and may not need or want further help.

Medication

The introduction of drug treatments in adolescence should be done only after an individual has been psychologically assessed over a reasonable period of time (usually six months) and after a clear diagnosis of a persistent gender identity disorder is made by professionals.

In the UK, current protocol suggests the prescription of hormone blockers in young people take place near the end of pubertal development. These have the effect of producing a hormonally neutral state, and can alleviate the distress caused by puberty. In females they will stop menstruation and further breast development. In males they will stop further growth in height and body-hair growth and block sperm production.

Hormone blockers can only be prescribed by specialists following some investigations to ensure there are no other physical problems and also to measure bone density. Young people are also counselled about whether they may want to have children in the future, and will be offered the opportunity to have their sperm or eggs frozen before the start of hormonal interventions.

The effects of hormone blockers are reversible, so if they are discontinued there are no permanent changes. They are given by injection fortnightly or monthly. They should not be prescribed long term, as their use can be associated with risks such as a reduction in bone density.

At the age of eighteen, a referral can be made to adult services, where hormones can be prescribed and gender-reassignment surgery carried out, both of which are irreversible. These steps are undertaken only after further psychological assessment.

How common is it?

Gender identity disorders are relatively rare. As previously mentioned, it is important to have a non-judgemental approach to the child or young person, and to allow them to talk about their feelings openly. They can often feel unhappy or distressed and may feel very isolated.

The majority of children who have the features of a gender identity disorder in childhood do not go on to become transsexual adults. Most develop a homosexual orientation, while others may be bisexual or heterosexual.

Professionals can offer help and support, and it is important that the young person is assessed for a period of time before any physical treatment is offered.

Dr Victoria Holt

INFORMATION

SUPPORT ORGANIZATIONS

Tavistock Clinic Gender Identity Development Service: provides therapeutic support to children and adolescents (and their families) when the young person is unhappy with the gender they are born with. Support is also given to children of transsexuals. *www.tavi-port.org*

Mermaids: charity for gender-dysphoric children and adolescents and their families. *www.mermaids.com*

WEBSITES OUTSIDE THE UK

WPATH: The World Professional Association for Transgendered Health. *www.wpath.org*

23 Sleep, Fatigue and Chronic Fatigue Syndrome

FATIGUE IS COMMON: at any one time 1 teenager in 3 complains of it. Feeling tired is part of everyday experience, particularly after exercise or a sleepless night – and teenagers don't tend to get good nights' sleep. Their natural body clock keeps them up late, as does being up with friends, with schoolwork, or with worries. However, in about 0.05 per cent of young people, a debilitating and chronic fatigue can occur. This chapter looks at various aspects of sleep, fatigue and chronic fatigue syndrome.

Sleep problems and sleep hygiene

We do not know exactly what sleep is for. It might help with conserving energy, 'recharging the batteries', consolidating memories, resolving emotions, or promoting healthy nervous and immune systems. But we do know that the wake/sleep cycle in humans is controlled by a kind of 'master clock' in the brain: melatonin is a substance produced by the brain's pineal gland that reinforces sleepiness. During the day, light suppresses melatonin production and stops us from feeling sleepy. When we do sleep, there are several different stages of sleep, each with its own electrical brain-wave pattern.

A child's sleeping pattern changes as she gets older, reflecting her maturing brain. Sleep duration shortens, from 18 hours at birth to 12 hours at four years and 7 hours for a late-teen. In the years prior to adolescence, children are highly efficient sleepers and are alert during the day. However, in adolescence insomnia becomes more common. The amount of 'deepest' sleep increases, more sleep is required, and the onset of sleep tends to be delayed. In 'delayed sleep phase syndrome', the delay in getting to sleep may last for hours and lead to problems getting up in the morning, as well as daytime sleepiness and fatigue. This can be helped by chronotherapy, which brings the sleep phase into line by gradually advancing it, or delaying it, stepwise 'round the clock', depending on how delayed sleep onset is. However, this requires considerable motivation and an unequivocal wish by the young person to normalize the sleep pattern. Common disruptive influences on sleep include caffeine-containing drinks (such as cola drinks and coffee), stress and worry, illicit drugs and alcohol.

Sleep can be affected by physical problems, such as pain or breathing difficulties, and by psychiatric disorders such as anxiety, ADHD, autism, depression and mania (see Chapters 10, 11 and 17). Problems getting off to sleep, interrupted sleep and early waking are sometimes

associated with anxiety and depression, though some young people with depression complain of excessive sleep. There are conditions that specifically affect sleep, such as sleepwalking. Nightmares can occur after severe stresses in post-traumatic stress disorder (see Chapter 24). When sleep disturbance is part of another physical or psychiatric problem, one way to help is to treat the underlying disorder. However, there are also some general principles to help improve 'sleep hygiene' – see the table below.

Sleep hygiene techniques

Make the bedroom conducive to sleep	Encourage	Avoid
• comfortable bed • correct temperature • dark, quiet room • lack of stimulation • avoid negative associations – e.g. punishment in bedroom at bedtime • reassuringly familiar setting – e.g. teddies, posters	• bedtime routines to 'wind down' – e.g. bathing, stories, parents in room (young children) and relaxation techniques (older children) • consistent bedtime and waking-up times • thinking about problems and plans some time before going to bed • regular daily exercise	• over-excitement near bedtime – e.g. computer games • caffeine – e.g. cola, tea, coffee, especially late in the day • large meals at night • excessive daytime napping • too much time awake in bed (if so, try some time to relax in another room and then return)

It is worth trying these techniques with all sleep problems, but some situations may warrant a visit to the GP.

When to visit the GP

A GP should be considered if the sleep difficulty:

- fails to respond to sleep hygiene techniques
- is very marked
- causes significant distress
- significantly impairs everyday life

- is associated with mood changes, hyperactivity or attention problems
- follows from a very severe life change

GPs may refer young people with severe or complex sleeping problems to specialized clinics, and they may carry out more detailed assessments using sleep diaries, sleep monitoring or 'brain-wave' recordings.

What is Chronic Fatigue Syndrome (CFS)/Myalgic Encephalopathy (ME)?

Few medical conditions generate such controversy that there is even debate about the name. Myalgic encephalopathy (ME) and chronic fatigue syndrome (CFS) both refer to the same disorder and set of symptoms. Most doctors prefer the term CFS, as fatigue is undoubtedly the central component and we do not know that a physical disorder causes it; the term ME is thought to be ambiguous. Many patients, however, prefer the term ME, as it implies the disorder is due to some illness affecting the muscles or the brain. As this chapter aims to be as clear and unambiguous as possible, we will use the term CFS.

Fatigue is a normal everyday experience following physical exercise, psychological stress, mental exertion or a sleepless night – though too much sleep can also lead to fatigue. Persistent fatigue is associated with either a tendency to be sedentary or conversely with being physically active, and with depressive symptoms. In CFS, the main patient experience is one of poor physical health and of physical symptoms leading to substantial impairment.

Biological abnormalities may well occur in the condition (for example, in some cases glandular fever precedes CFS, and some immune and hormonal abnormalities are sometimes associated with it), but no single physical cause or pathology has yet been identified. Evidence so far suggests that CFS involves a complex interaction between physical, psychological and environmental factors, all of which need to be considered and worked on as part of treatment.

The controversy about CFS stems from the fact that the medical profession still does not understand it well and the symptoms can be diverse. However, despite the range of opinion on the matter, there was enough known for the National Institute for Health and Clinical Excellence (NICE) to produce consensus guidelines using evidence and best clinical practice principles in 2007.

What does CFS feel like?

Different people with CFS will have different experiences, but at its core is a severe fatigue or tiredness occurring after comparatively little effort for at least three to six months. Everyday activities, such as walking, going to school, concentrating on work and talking to friends can become a real challenge. At its extreme, patients are bed-bound and even tasks such as using cutlery or sitting up can be exhausting. Other physical symptoms are common and often precede the fatigue. For example, patients have headaches, sleep problems, muscle or joint pain, a sore throat or sore glands, flu-like symptoms, and feel dizzy or sick. Many young people, especially if severely affected, develop emotional disorders, with symptoms of anxiety and depression.

Lack of activity and prolonged rest can lead to physical problems, particularly in young people. Muscles can lose their bulk, making activity more difficult and so encouraging rest, which further atrophies the muscles. Prolonged rest can affect sleep, making the person tired and prone to rest during the day, and so further affecting sleep at night. A disturbed sleep/wake cycle may also affect diet if it leads to nibbling on food between naps rather than having regular meals. A poor diet may in turn contribute to the tiredness. One of the aims of treatment would be to try to break these 'downward spirals'.

Are home and school affected?

CFS can disrupt family life, which revolves increasingly around the young person's symptoms and altered lifestyle. Children can become anxiously dependent on their parents, who become highly attentive and emotionally involved with their child's condition. This is particularly problematic in adolescence, a time when teenagers would normally be exercising increasing independence.

Schoolwork can be particularly difficult if the CFS is affecting attention, concentration and memory. The young person tends to miss a lot of school and get behind on schoolwork, and may feel that friends are getting on with life without her, and so feel left out and frustrated. This is particularly distressing if the young person puts high expectations on herself or is sensitive and a worrier, conscientious or perfectionist – common tendencies in people who get CFS. Once a child starts missing school, returning becomes increasingly hard, as confidence with work or with friends is lost.

What can be done to help?

The family needs to visit their GP, who may then advise a referral to a paediatrician to make sure that every possible physical cause has been excluded. This will involve a physical examination, and possibly urine and blood tests. Self-help manuals are available. Depending on the severity of the illness, and the needs of the patient and their family, professionals such as physiotherapists, nurses or psychiatrists may need to be involved. Most people with CFS do not go into hospital, but this may be helpful if symptoms remain severe despite community treatment and if a specialized unit is available.

As the symptoms of CFS are similar to those of some other common physical and psychiatric disorders (such as depression or anxiety), these need to be ruled out before a diagnosis of CFS can be made, particularly as there is no specific test that can identify CFS itself. Even when CFS is diagnosed, depression and anxiety are still common and need to be checked so that suitable treatment is provided.

Exploring mental health issues can be a sensitive area for the family – parents may fear that this implies a dismissal of the symptoms as 'all in the child's mind'. It is important that you understand the relevance of a psychiatric assessment. These investigations will be kept to a minimum and will be completed as quickly as possible to ensure the young person starts treatment promptly. The clinician will discuss how best to manage the problem, rather than debating whether the problem is physical or psychological.

Some families may have high levels of parental distress and emotional involvement with the child's problem, and treatment should help the family understand that they should not just be concentrating on the physical symptoms. It will also help the family change the way they interact with each other in order to support the child in a positive way.

There is no one way of managing CFS that helps everyone, but NICE has identified three types of treatment that are safe, supported by research, and can complement each other. All may involve goal-setting, diary-keeping and questionnaires. Regular exercise usually improves fatigue and also mood.

Graded-exercise therapy aims to involve the patient in a daily physical activity routine that starts from the current level, gently and gradually building up over a number of weeks towards an ultimate goal via a series of shorter-term goals.

Activity management involves planning time so that there is a good balance of daily activity, short rest breaks and sleep. Relaxation techniques may help during rest breaks, and 'sleep hygiene' strategies may help promote healthy sleeping patterns (see table, p. 330).

Cognitive behavioural therapy (CBT) is a type of talking treatment commonly used in other medical and psychiatric disorders (see p. 351). In CFS, CBT may incorporate both the above therapies as part of the 'behavioural' component. The 'cognitive' component of the treatment helps the young person become aware of and understand their own thoughts, beliefs and behaviour relating to their fatigue and activity/rest patterns, which can help to identify factors that are perpetuating the illness. For example, the young person may have the belief that exercise damages muscles and that prolonged rest is helpful, or she might believe that she should feel guilty for asking for help. Research has also shown that young people with CFS and their parents may underestimate what fatigue levels are actually normal, and therefore overestimate their own.

CBT would aim to change such unhelpful beliefs by educating the young person and teaching her strategies to challenge negative thinking patterns and promote coping. By understanding the symptoms better, the young person may not worry about or focus on them so much. Cognitive therapy can also help with more deeply rooted core beliefs about perfectionism or self-worth, which may be acting to maintain the illness.

Medication, complementary and other therapies

There is little evidence that medication, dietary supplements or restriction diets help CFS, but a healthy balanced diet with regular meals is important. NICE reports there is not yet enough evidence on complementary medicine. Any complementary therapist involved should be registered and have experience of CFS.

Tips for parents, families, teachers, and friends

- Those living with young people with CFS can help by being sympathetic and acknowledging just how ill CFS makes someone feel, but at the same time encouraging and supporting them in gradually increasing their activity levels.

- Paradoxically, too much rest and sleep are as bad for fatigue as excessive activity.
- Large swings between rest and activity are unhelpful in CFS. Increases in activity are best planned and implemented in a step-by-step fashion.
- Many young people with fatigue come to recognize that everyday stresses (such as getting on with friends and school peers, managing schoolwork, stresses at home) and anxiety are very closely linked to feelings of fatigue. Learning to deal with those stresses can have an important beneficial influence on CFS.

How long does it last?

In severe cases, recovery may take months or years, and some people continue to experience more fatigue after recovery. However, most young people get better over time and do recover, returning to school and normal activities.

Dr Aaron Vallance and Professor M. Elena Garralda

INFORMATION

SUPPORT ORGANIZATIONS

Association of Young People with ME: Helpline: 08451 23 23 89. *www.ayme.org.uk*

The Young ME Sufferers Trust: *www.tymestrust.org*

WEBSITES OUTSIDE THE UK

Australia
www.mecfs.org.au

Canada
www.fm-cfs.ca

New Zealand
www.anzmes.org.nz

FURTHER READING

Chalder, Trudie, and Hussain, Kaneez, *Self-help for Chronic Fatigue Syndrome: a guide for Young People*, Blue Stallion Publications, 2002.

24 Trauma, Stress and Adjustment

Anna was eighteen months old when she witnessed her father murder her mother. She was found, fourteen hours later, clinging to her mother's body. She was initially withdrawn and 'frozen' when placed with relatives. Later, she became demanding and clingy, easily upset and difficult to comfort or reassure. Her sleep (and that of her carers) was broken by nightmares and her days by prolonged 'tantrums'. With the dedicated support of her carers, she gradually settled into her new home, but at the age of six could still get anxious about separations and disturbed by loud noises.

Andy was eight and in the back seat when his mother's car was involved in a road traffic accident. Mother was unhurt, but Andy was shocked and suffered minor injuries. Afterwards, he seemed to recover quite well, but remained fearful of riding in a car or crossing the road. With a short course of treatment, he made a complete recovery.

Mary was six when she and her granny were hit by a car as they crossed the road. Granny was killed; Mary was shaken but unhurt. Mary became very timid about going out, had nightmares and flashbacks, and felt responsible for Granny's death. When she was eleven, she received three sessions of specialist trauma treatment. She reported that she now felt as though a mountain had been lifted off her shoulders. She was no longer reliving the accident and no longer felt responsible for her granny's death.

Robert, a popular boy and a keen athlete, was fourteen when he was attacked by a gang of youths on his way home from school. His phone was stolen, but he was unhurt. His family and school were very supportive and he quickly recovered. However, six months later, he was attacked again, this time suffering a broken arm. There were complications with his arm and he was unable to continue with his sporting activities. He lost his confidence and became anxious about going out of the house. Two years later, in spite of good support from his family, he was still having nightmares and was avoiding friends and school activities. At this point, Robert was referred for specialist treatment. He soon stopped reliving the attacks and began to recover his confidence and to resume friendships and interests.

Irina, a refugee from Kosovo, was eight when war engulfed her country. Her village was torched and she saw many friends and neighbours killed. She was lucky to escape alive. In the UK, she suffered from severe nightmares and flash-backs, headaches and sweating. Then, the family were refused asylum and a pupil at her school was killed in a knife fight. Irina's symptoms got worse. Her treatment started when she was thirteen and continued, on and off, until she was seventeen. For a long time she could not bear to think about the atrocities she had witnessed. Treatment was mainly supportive. Eventually, when she felt able to work on the traumas, she returned to the clinic, asking for help with her frightening memories. After six months of trauma-focused treatment she reported that she was no longer having terrible dreams every night, her headaches and sweats were gone, and she felt hope for the future.

What is trauma?

We often speak loosely about an experience being 'traumatic', meaning that it has upset us. But a truly traumatic experience is one that is not only shocking but leads to the symptoms of stress (see below). Being involved in a car accident or fire, being mugged or bullied, are some examples of traumatic experiences. Burglaries, medical procedures or witnessing a death can also be traumatic. Traumatic stress reactions can affect not only individuals but whole communities after major catastrophes like floods, terrorist attacks and war.

It used to be thought that children were little affected by trauma –

'too young to understand'. However, we now know that children and young people can be badly affected.

What does trauma feel like?

When someone has experienced a very frightening event, it is normal for them to be upset and to take a while to recover. Children and young people will all react very differently, depending on their age, level of understanding, temperament and the amount of support they receive.

As children try to understand what happened and 'get their heads round' their traumatic experience, the following reactions are common:

- Being jumpy, easily startled and watchful. They can also be easily upset or 'over-excited' and find it difficult to calm down.
- Sleep problems, refusing to go to bed, wanting to sleep in their parents' bed.
- Intrusive memories related to the event unexpectedly popping into their mind.
- Feeling as if the traumatic event is actually happening again in flashbacks or nightmares.
- Repetitive play or drawing about the event that doesn't seem to be for fun.
- Not wanting to think, talk or be reminded about the event.
- Fear of being separated from parents – even for school or going out to play with friends.
- Regressive behaviour – e.g. bedwetting or thumb-sucking again.
- Being unable to concentrate or seeming to be in 'another world' (dissociating).

- Being irritable, angry or easily upset. Crying over 'little things'.
- Complaining of physical symptoms like headaches and stomach aches.

What can be done to help?

In the first few weeks after a traumatic event, children and young people worry less about what is happening to them if you help them to see that their reactions are normal and understandable. We know that 'good support' after a traumatic experience can do a lot to help recovery and that it can actually prevent longer-term mental health problems. Here are some suggestions that you may find helpful:

- Try to make things as normal as possible. A frightening event often makes people jumpy and insecure. We all feel safer when we know what to expect. You can help your child feel safer by sticking to his normal routines as much as possible.
- If the event has been in the news, or affected the whole community, it may be important to protect the child from being exposed to too much media coverage, such as TV pictures with upsetting images. If you do watch the news, then watch it together, so the child can ask questions about it if he needs to. If he has been directly involved in an event that has been covered by the media, you may need to think about protecting him from intrusive media interviewing.
- Be available to talk with your child, as and when he is ready. Sometimes parents and carers try to protect children by avoiding talking about the event. They worry that they will upset them unnecessarily or make things worse. Some people hope that, if they keep quiet, their child will forget all about it. In fact, a child is likely to want to make sense of what has

happened, and may need adult help with this. Let him know that you think his questions and concerns are important and appropriate. Some children communicate more readily using dolls or toys, or drawing pictures rather than using words. Try to provide opportunities, support and encouragement to help your child to talk about it when he's ready. Sharing his experience can help a child feel understood and supported. This can also help to reduce the bad memories. It helps to replace the raw 'reliving' intrusive memories with more ordinary 'story-type' memories that feel more distant and 'in the past'.

- Do look after yourself. Adults can also be affected by the trauma. If you are upset by what has happened, it may be more difficult to talk with your child about *his* experience or to give him as much support as you normally would. It may be helpful to talk to another adult or to your GP about how to get the support that you need. If you are a teacher, you may find it helpful to discuss with your staff group how best to manage the situation in school.
- Listen to your child's questions and provide honest information. Often, the lack of basic factual information is what lies behind a child's concerns. Try to answer questions simply, honestly and in a way that is appropriate to his age and understanding.
- Help your child to come up with a 'story' that explains what happened. A story incorporating the points below should leave him feeling safer. Even younger children can really benefit from being given a story to explain what happened.
    - It helps the child to make sense of the event and reduces some of the unpleasant feelings, such as fear, anger and sadness.

- The story can help correct misunderstandings and provide reassurance – e.g. some children wrongly believe that what happened was their fault; others are confused about important facts.
- If children have a story prepared, they can talk to others about what has happened, if they want to.
- Thinking things through with your child can also help him realize that, although bad things can happen, they don't happen so often that we need to be scared of them all the time.

If someone has died, explain what this means. It often takes time to accept a death as a fact, especially if it was sudden. Young children do not understand that death is permanent, that it happens to everyone and that it has a cause. At about the age of six, they are only beginning to grasp this. Some young children will seem to understand that the person has died, but then keep asking if the person is coming back. Often, such questions are a child's way of asking for reassurance. So it's important to be patient and take time to explain it in clear language (for example, it's clearer to say that 'Mummy has died' than to say 'Mummy has gone away'). For a young child, you may need to do this more than once. You may also need to explain in simple terms what this means, for example, 'Mummy's body was badly hurt. So now it doesn't work any more. The doctors tried hard but could not make her better.' In this kind of situation, it will also be important to reassure the child about who will now look after him and keep him safe.

When to seek professional help

Fortunately, most children, even those exposed to trauma, are quite resilient; they will recover and go on with their lives. However, for some recovery will be less straightforward. If the signs of stress persist for more than three or four weeks, the child may be developing some form of post-traumatic stress disorder. If so, he will need professional help. You can ask your GP or the school doctor to make a referral to your local specialist service.

De-stressing techniques

Traumatic experience often leaves survivors feeling hyper-alert and tense. Physical activities that promote a sense of calm and self-control, such as yoga, walking or Tai Chi, can be helpful for adults and for older children. Relaxation exercises, massage and aromatherapy can help with learning how to calm the body tensions that often follow a traumatic experience.

Medication

This can help in some cases. In the immediate aftermath of a trauma, some medication can help to improve sleep or reduce anxiety. However, talking treatments are much more effective than medication.

Psychological treatments

Often the most effective treatment involves working with parents to enable them to understand the child's difficulties better and helping them to provide the support and security that the child needs. If a child has symptoms of post-traumatic stress disorder, then cognitive behavioural therapy (CBT; see p. 351) and eye-movement desensitization and reprocessing (EMDR) are the most effective treatments.

People often delay seeking help, not knowing that treatment is both available and effective. Of course, most people do recover in the normal way after a few weeks. But for those who do not, symptoms can continue for many years, causing distress and disability. So getting help at an early stage can save a lot of grief. But, as the cases of Mary and Irina at the start of this chapter show, treatment can also be effective even when symptoms have been troublesome for a long time.

Dr Guinevere Tufnell

INFORMATION

SUPPORT ORGANIZATIONS

National Child Trauma Stress Network: provides a large and valuable source of information and resources relating to trauma and children. *www.nctsn.org*

Children & War: created to ensure that more solid knowledge about children can be gathered, and then used to improve the care of all children affected by war and disaster. *www.childrenandwar.org*

The UK Trauma Group: provides a useful list of local UK services and other links. *www.uktrauma.org.uk*

Winston's Wish: helps children rebuild their lives after the death of a parent or sibling, enabling them to face the future with hope. Helpline: 08452 03 04 05. *www.winstonswish.org.uk*

FURTHER READING

Harris-Hendriks, Jean, Black, Dora, and Kaplan, Tony, *When Father Kills Mother: Guiding Children through Trauma and Grief* (2nd edn), Routledge, 2000.

Rose, Richard, and Philpot, Terry, *The Child's Own Story: Life Story Work with Traumatized Children*, Jessica Kingsley, 2005.

Terr, Lenore, *Too Scared to Cry – How Trauma Affects Children and Ultimately Us All*, Basic Books, 1990.

Yule, William, and Gold, Anne, *Wise Before the Event: Coping with Crises in Schools*, Calouste Gulbenkian Foundation, 1993.

WEBSITES OUTSIDE THE UK

Australia
www.betterhealth.vic.gov.au

Canada
www.vac-acc.gc.ca

New Zealand
www.mentalhealth.org.nz

I thank David Trickey, Richard Baillie and Lucy Serpel for permission to use material adapted from their leaflet *After the Event: Supporting Children after a Frightening Event* (UCL Institute of Child Health, Great Ormond Street Hospital for Children, July 2006).

Part Six

Treatments and Therapies

25 Treatment for Children and Adolescents in Child Mental Health

Childhood is a time of rapid physical, emotional, social and moral development. There are major changes in behaviour because of what is learned and expected of children both at home and at school.

However, children are not small adults. Child behaviour that may be part of the normal range at one stage of development can become a problem if it occurs too early, or carries on too long. The way out of this problem for the child is not necessarily to reverse the things that led to the problem in the first place.

Often when children have mental health problems they have more than one, so sometimes more than one treatment may be necessary at the same time. Treatments should not interfere with the child's life, but it is important that they work. However, what works at one age may not be the right treatment when the child is a bit older.

Nearly all child mental health treatment is offered in the community or in hospital outpatient departments – only rarely do children need admission to hospital. While many problems are minor and can be easily overcome by timely help, some are much longer-lasting (a bit like diabetes in physical medicine) and need longer-term strategies.

People sometimes blame parents for their child's problems. Often this is unfair and these outsiders may make matters worse through ignorance or lack of understanding. Parents are often the best people to help things get better. Treatments can in many cases be offered in a family setting and with the support of the parents. Smaller interventions here can often lead to large changes.

When thinking about the effect of mental health difficulties on your child, you – and the professionals involved – will need to think about the effects that these problems are having in all areas of the family's lives, and try to think of things to do that will help.

Problems and solutions spread like ripples on a pond – changes in one area can lead to many changes elsewhere.

Behaviour therapy (BT)

Behaviour therapy is very useful for children of all ages and also for adults. It got itself a bad name in the early days as it was 'accused' of being based on work with animals, such as rats, mice and dogs. There was indignation that human beings might also respond to rewards and avoid things that they did not like (so-called punishments). The truth of the matter is that we are all motivated by rewards, such as attention, praise or a pay rise, and try to avoid punishments such as being told off. We do not like our efforts to be ignored.

The central idea of BT is that children want attention and will do almost anything good or bad to get it. When they get attention they feel better. Reward programmes aim to reward a child for behaving in a particular way. It is crucial that the reward is something that the child actually wants. A common trap is to choose big rewards that are too far into the future. Smaller, more frequent rewards are more effective. Such things as specific, labelled praise (for instance, 'I really liked the way you helped me with clearing up your toys'), or allowing the child to choose the dessert for supper or spend time on a computer game are much more effective for younger children than, say, the promise of a new bike in a few months' time. Teenagers may prefer to work for longer-range rewards, but still need lots of praise along the way. Rewards may need to be changed, otherwise they can become 'boring', and they need to be phased out when the child has learned a new skill, while you continue to offer explicit praise for positive behaviour.

BT is very useful as it can be applied at all stages throughout childhood and to a wide variety of difficulties. It can be used at home and in school.

Two of the most common myths about BT are that reward programmes are a form of bribery and that the child does not learn anything because all you are doing is changing their behaviour and 'not getting to the root of the problem'. Many parents have tried using a reward programme, such as a star chart, by themselves and have given up. This happens because, although the principles are simple, applying them takes some skill and persistence and may need the help of a child mental health professional.

So what sort of problems can be helped by these techniques? They include anxiety-based difficulties, tempers and helping children to do what they are asked, as well as mild to moderate hyperactivity. They can help behaviour problems in children with global learning difficulties, or those with autism and related difficulties.

There are increasing numbers of combined treatment approaches that use behavioural techniques as part of their toolkit – for example, child management training for parents. This usually begins with work helping to rebuild the parent–child relationship so that the child does not have to behave badly to get attention. It helps the parents and child to enjoy their time together. It also helps the parents be more effective and reduces their own anxiety and stress. When their relationship is better, they can move on to strategies for management of particular problems.

Cognitive Behavioural Therapy (CBT)

This is the most well-known and widely practised structured 'talking'-based therapy. It can be useful in the treatment of a range of mental health, emotional and behavioural difficulties, for example:

- anxiety problems
- obsessive compulsive disorder (OCD)
- low self-esteem
- post-traumatic stress disorder (PTSD)
- depression
- some eating disorders
- some aspects of psychosis

CBT is usually carried out with older children and adolescents, as they are more able to describe their thoughts and to understand and practise CBT techniques.

The therapy is based on the concept that thoughts, feelings and behaviour are linked together and influence each other. By working to change or balance one of these three components the others improve too.

A young person or child might have a negative thought which 'snowballs' into a huge problem. For example, worries about walking into the school assembly hall may lead to overwhelming feelings of dread because he imagines that he will faint in front of the entire school and everyone will laugh or think that he is stupid. As a result, the child may begin to avoid assembly or even going to school at all. Another child may feel upset as a result of her friend not smiling at her in class. This may lead to the thought that her friend dislikes her, a belief that nobody likes her, that she's boring and ugly, and to feelings of depression and hopelessness. This in turn may also lead to avoiding going to school completely.

The aim of CBT is to break out of these unhelpful patterns. For instance, a child who is afraid of fainting in assembly might be asked to keep an anxiety diary for a week and note his thoughts and feelings, as well as his behaviours. He will be asked to note when he feels his anxiety levels increasing as the time for assembly approaches. He will probably have been given relaxation technique training, as well as being asked to put himself in a gradually more anxiety-provoking situation. He will have had to work on the thoughts that accompany the anxieties and get himself to challenge his catastrophic thinking, realizing that the worst does not usually happen.

In CBT, the young person can be trained in self-talk to manage his anxiety, and can be taught 'coping thoughts' that he can use at those times when he begins to get into an anxiety cycle. He will be encouraged to use graded practice of these techniques and careful pacing so that he does not extend himself and cause a relapse.

Similarly, a child who thinks that nobody likes her will be coached to challenge these thoughts. She will be encouraged to engage socially and will be given some coaching if her social skills need attention.

In both these cases, the work of CBT is practical, using the child to build up evidence for themselves that the feared catastrophe is not about to happen, and that they can cope.

In CBT treatment the young person usually meets with a therapist once a week to talk about things. Sometimes the therapist will use worksheets or a workbook to help structure the treatment and there is always homework to do between sessions. Some services offer CBT to a group of young people. Both individual and group therapy have been shown to work. CBT can be hard work, but the benefits are skills that can last a lifetime and help protect against similar problems in the future. Sometimes, in the very beginning, a person might feel worse before things start to improve; in such cases the support and understanding of family, teachers and friends can be a great help.

The number of CBT sessions varies quite widely. For simple problems, six to ten sessions are usually sufficient. More complex problems can take many months. Usually sessions are started on a weekly basis and then gradually spread out. Sometimes booster sessions are built into the programme, which are scheduled for several weeks after the last formal session of a course of treatment.

Interpersonal therapy (IPT)

This therapy is useful for the treatment of depression in adolescents, but it is not normally used for children under the age of eleven. It is usually carried out over twelve weekly sessions and involves three phases. The therapist starts by getting to know the young person and defining the symptoms and problems; this includes building up a picture of the young person's relationships in the family and in a wider social context (first phase). The middle phase is concerned with the young person's specific problems and helping to solve them. While continuing to work with the young person, the therapist might also involve other people, such as family members, depending on the exact nature of the problems. The third phase of treatment is aimed at consolidating and ending the therapy.

IPT is particularly well suited to adolescents who are depressed because most depression in adolescence is related to problems in the young person's friendships and other important relationships. IPT has an evidence base to support its effectiveness.

Dialectical behaviour therapy (DBT)

Emotional instability, repeated self-harm, frequent suicidal ideas and impulsiveness are some of the specific problems that DBT helps with. Although it is not suitable for younger children, there is some evidence that it works with adolescents. It uses a combination of behavioural, cognitive and meditative techniques, along with practical-skills training. It is delivered through both individual sessions and group skills training (both usually weekly). There is always homework between individual and group sessions, and often telephone support is available between individual therapy sessions. DBT requires a high level of commitment on the part of the young person; many of the skills can be quite difficult at first and take a lot of practice.

Family therapy (or systems therapy)

The central idea in this approach is that children and young people grow up in families who provide love, comfort and challenge. In today's society, with high rates of family separation and new families being formed, feelings about each other become even more complicated. Family systems can be understood in a variety of ways, ranging from how people act towards each other, to the stories that each parent's family has about itself as well as those in the present family, to the effects of other external pressures. It is important that the therapist and family share an understanding of what the problem is.

In families with younger children therapy tends to focus more on behavioural techniques. For families with teenage children, more emphasis is placed on the different perceptions of the meaning of behaviour among different family members.

Sometimes family therapy can seem to focus on issues that are not the ones that the parents are troubled about. If this happens, the sensible thing to do is to discuss it with your therapist. It is an effective therapy with an increasing evidence base.

Family therapy has been shown to be helpful with behavioural problems among younger children. It is helpful with eating disorders (see p. 242) and with substance abuse (see p. 232) in adolescents. It also helps to reduce misunderstandings and false beliefs within the family or unhelpful behaviours that continue to affect the child's difficulties.

Psychodynamic therapy

For younger children this usually takes the form of child psychotherapy or play therapy. The idea here is that the child's play describes psychological conflicts that underlie the problem behaviours. Through play and interpretation, the therapist helps the child resolve her worries so that she can get on with the business of normal development. For adolescents, the sessions may be more about talking things through.

The young person will usually be seen once or twice each week at regular times, usually over a long period. The parent is likely to be asked to see another clinic worker on a regular basis. Sometimes parents become frustrated at the limited information that the therapist working with the child is willing to share about what actually happens in the sessions. This, however, is to protect your child's confidentiality and encourage her trust. Often the therapist will work out with the child how to share a difficult issue with parents when they both think this is necessary.

Although the evidence base is not as firm as for some of the other therapies considered here, psychodynamic therapy is still seen by experienced clinicians as able to help with complex emotional difficulties, such as threatened adoption breakdown, sexual and other trauma, etc., that may not respond to other approaches.

Art therapy

Creative therapies are specialist interventions and are not widely available in a community setting; most are found in in-patient or specialist units. These therapies do not involve 'talking' and are therefore particularly useful for children and young people whose verbal skills are limited – for example those with learning difficulties or autistic spectrum disorder, or following traumatic events that the young person cannot bear to talk about.

Art therapy usually takes place over a medium to long time frame, involving weekly sessions lasting 30–60 minutes. The therapist uses art materials and the artistic expressions of the young person to work through issues. Although very little research has been done to measure how effective art therapy is, many people vouch for how helpful it can be in situations where talking directly is too difficult for the child.

Common myths about art therapy

- '**Art therapy is totally unstructured**'. Art therapy might seem unstructured to an observer, and will not feel restrictive to the patient. However, the therapist will spend a lot of time between sessions thinking about the child and the creative work being done, making plans and introducing new creative work in a way that does not inhibit the child.

- '**There is little evidence to support it, therefore art therapy doesn't work**.' As is the case with many treatments in child and adolescent mental health, there is limited research evidence to confirm that they work. This, however, does not mean that they are ineffective. The effect of art therapy is particularly difficult to measure and compare to other treatments, but many experts agree that it helps some children a great deal.

Medication

The use of medication for children with mental health problems continues to be controversial among members of the public and among some health professionals. Concerns have ranged from general distaste and fears about 'altering children's minds' to worries about the long-term effects of medication on the developing brain and body.

Many medicines have to be prescribed 'off label'. This means that the pharmaceutical companies have not carried out separate safety trials and trials of effectiveness in children. It also means that the doctor has to take joint responsibility with parents for the use of such medicines. However, there are increasing numbers of good trials showing that medicines can help some serious child mental health difficulties and specialist doctors are becoming more willing to prescribe. As a general rule, it is wise to have the support of a specialist child psychiatrist or paediatrician rather than a GP alone when prescribing medicines for mental health problems. This is not always possible, but it is advisable.

It is not possible or appropriate here to go into all the conditions in which medication can be helpful, or the particular medicines that are used; however conditions include: marked ADHD, serious depression, obsessive compulsive disorder, bipolar disorder, psychosis and the short-term management of acute anxiety. See the discussion of medication for the various conditions and difficulties described in Chapters 9–24.

All medicines have side-effects. Your specialist doctor should discuss these with you together with the benefits. He should also discuss alternative treatments, including psychological interventions and other medicines. Usually a medicine is given as part of a treatment package that will include a psychological intervention. Medication can create a window of opportunity for psychological treatments to work. It can speed up recovery and reduce the distress for the child or young person and for parents.

Dr Habib Behi and Dr Brian Jacobs

SUPPORT ORGANIZATIONS

Young Minds: national charity committed to improving the mental health and emotional well-being of all children and young people. Tel: 0808 802 5544 (parents' information service) or 0207 336 8445 (general). *www.youngminds.org.uk*

Association of Child Psychotherapists: the professional organization for child psychotherapy in the United Kingdom. *www.acp.uk.net*

British Psychological Society: *www.bps.org.uk*

CSIP: children, young people and families programme. *www.camhs.org.uk*

WEBSITES OUTSIDE THE UK

Australia and New Zealand

Royal Australian and New Zealand College of Psychiatrists: *www.ranzcp.org*

Canada

Canadian Academy of Child and Adolescent Psychiatrists: *www.cacap-acpea.org*

26 Transition to Adulthood

THE CHANGE FROM CHILDHOOD to adulthood, which we call 'adolescence', involves the most rapid stage of mental development in our lives. Adolescents have spent their childhood learning facts – either aided by support, encouragement and a secure home, or hindered by ridicule, threat and insecurity – from their families and environments.

In the years of transition to adulthood, young people have to cope with:

- developing abstract thinking
- developing a sense of identity
- coming to terms with the overwhelming pressures of sexuality
- deciding on a life course
- developing and maintaining new relationships
- learning to respect themselves

Avoiding transition

Why does society in general have a 'down' on adolescents when they need so much support? Historically, complaints about youth go back to Roman times.

It might be because anxiety is our driving force. We are anxious first of all about survival, about safety, about having a roof over our heads, having enough to eat, and then about impressing our peers and being respected. All these anxieties are heightened when we feel threatened by younger, fitter and clearer-thinking replacements.

Anxiety makes us want to control young people in order to reduce that anxiety. However, as children grow up we recognize that we are less and less able to control them. Our anxiety increases, and therefore we – as a society – tend to distance ourselves, becoming less involved with them, or not providing for them. As a result, it is not surprising that services for adolescents, including mental health services, often fall through the gap between children's and adult services.

Transition in mental health services

In the past, the responsibility for managing the mental health problems of young people up to the age of sixteen fell on Child and Adolescent Mental Health Services (CAMHS). For people over eighteen, the responsibility lay with Adult Mental Health Services.

However, which services were to care for sixteen- and seventeen-year-olds – the transitional group – was a constant bone of contention. Some adult services refused to have anything to do with them, while CAMHS insisted that their services were only for those at school, or stopped at age sixteen.

In some areas, professionals compromised to ensure that these young people were cared for, but in others their needs were not met. The first real attempt to address the problem was for young people with psychotic disorders when, in 1999, the Department of Health suggested setting up specialist Early Intervention Teams for people aged between fourteen and thirty-five. Although only forty-one such teams had been established by 2004, they are now becoming an integral part of mental health services.

This still left young people with mental disorders other than psychosis suspended uncomfortably on the boundary between CAMHS and Adult Mental Health Services. However, in 2004 the government, through the National Service Framework for Children, Young People and Maternity Services, stated clearly that 'Child and Adolescent Mental Health Services are able to meet the needs of all young people including those aged sixteen and seventeen.' Despite a lack of funds to take on these young people, many CAMHS have since considered it their responsibility to do so, now working with young people up to eighteen and often afterwards.

CAMHS and Adult Mental Health Services

There is still a boundary issue between CAMHS and Adult Mental Health Services and young people now have to negotiate that boundary at eighteen.

Although both CAMHS and Adult Mental Health Services are multidisciplinary (involving healthcare professionals from different disciplines), they work quite differently. CAMHS tend to work with the young people themselves and with their families. The young person will continue to live at home or in an understanding environment, which will help him to develop.

In contrast, adult services tend to concentrate on managing the illness. CAMHS involve families and schools in the therapeutic process, whereas adult services use individual treatments (such as medication) and care, along with support networks.

These are obviously gross generalizations, but how the services are run tends to influence how professionals in different services see problems. Young people and their families can find it difficult and distressing to move between these two systems.

Different services will have different priorities. For example, some services may concentrate on neurodevelopmental disorders, such as ADHD and autistic spectrum disorders; these often make up a large part of the workload of CAMHS.

However, Adult Mental Health Services are often overwhelmed looking after people with psychosis and depression, as well as with personality disorder. They do not have the time, for instance, to assess whether a young adult would benefit from continued prescription of stimulant medication.

Similarly, unless a person with autism also has a clear psychiatric disorder, Adult Mental Health Services are unlikely to become involved. This can be very distressing for the young adult, who is often not able to cope on his own. There is an urgent need for the development of neurodevelopmental services for adults in the future.

In-patient care

The Children's National Service Framework (Department for Education and Skills & Department of Health, 2004) quite rightly made it clear that young people under the age of sixteen requiring psychiatric admission should not be placed on adult psychiatric wards. However, because of the scarcity of adolescent beds, sixteen–seventeen-year-olds are often found a place that is some way from home. Alternatively, they could be placed on an adult ward that is nearer home. The development of independence of sixteen- and seventeen-year-olds is now clearly recognized. They cannot be placed on psychiatric wards, even with the consent of their parents, if they do not consent themselves. Without their consent, they cannot be admitted unless their disorder is such that they require detention under mental health legislation as it applies in different countries.

Conclusion

Moving from CAMHS to Adult Mental Health Services would be difficult enough for anybody. Support is essential for those made vulnerable by their psychiatric disorder, whose fear of transition may worsen their condition or make them uncooperative. Support over the boundary is essential.

Mental health professionals in both adult services and CAMHS must make sure that transition is as smooth and seamless as possible for these vulnerable young people. This is not always easy, but depends on good working and respectful relationships between professionals in both services.

Dr Greg Richardson

INFORMATION

REFERENCES

Department of Health, *The National Service Framework for Mental Health*, Department of Health, 1999.

Department of Health, *The National Service Framework for Mental Health – Five Years On*, Department of Health, 2004.

Department for Education and Skills & Department of Health, *The National Service Framework for Children, Young People and Maternity Services: the Mental Health and Psychological Well-being of Children and Young People*, Department of Health, 2004.

Erikson, Erik, 'Eight Ages of Man', in *Childhood and Society*, W. W. Norton and Co. Inc., 1963.

Golombek, H., Wilkes, J., and Froese, A. P., 'The Developmental Challenges of Adolescence', in Steinhauer, P., and Rae-Grant, Q. (eds), *Psychological Problems of the Child and His Family*, Macmillan, 1978; 29–48.

27 How to Get Help

MANY OF THE CHAPTERS in this book address the best ways for parents and families to seek help for their child in relation to emotional, behavioural or psychiatric disorders. Each chapter looks at the different treatments and therapies available, as well as at other sources of help and further reading.

It is absolutely normal to be concerned about your child if things seem to be going wrong, whatever his age. Younger children are often very aware of their own feelings, but may not be able to express them. Older children may feel that you are interfering in their lives. However, in the first instance it is important to talk to them and try to find out what is happening. You need to involve them, as much as possible, in any decision that you may make.

Listening to your child sounds simple, but sometimes it is the quality of the listening that counts more than anything. It is important not to feel that your child's problem is all your fault. Try to listen with the heart and not just the ears.

Talk to someone you trust about your concerns. This may be your partner, a friend or relative, or even your local religious leader.

It can be difficult to accept that your child may have a mental health or behavioural problem and it can take a lot of courage to make the decision to get help. It can feel like a very lonely experience. However, if you do have any concerns, you should:

- talk to your GP or health visitor (if relevant) – they should know about the special services in your area for children, young people and families
- talk to your child's school – they may be able to help sort out difficulties, provide extra support and make allowances for your child
- find out about other organizations that give information and support in your local area
- contact social services to find out what support is available for your family

Most young people will recover from mental health problems without having to go into hospital. A number of specialist services in the community provide various treatments, including counselling and other talking treatments. It is important that the counsellors or therapists are trained to deal with the problems of children or adolescents.

How can I see a psychiatrist?

Your GP, health visitor, school doctor, clinic doctor, paediatrician, educational psychologist or social worker will be able to discuss any concerns and arrange for an appointment with the local Child and Adolescent Mental Health Service (CAMHS) if necessary.

Specialist services

If you are referred to a CAMHS, you may see a child and adolescent psychiatrist. These are medically qualified doctors who specialize in understanding and working with children and young people with mental health problems.

National Health Service (NHS) child and adolescent psychiatrists mainly work in:

- Child and Adolescent Mental Health Services (CAMHS)
- outpatient clinics in hospitals
- specialized in-patient units
- child and family services
- young people's services
- outreach services (e.g. in schools, nurseries, day centres)

Child psychiatrists work as part of a multidisciplinary service that may include other child mental health professionals, such as:

- child psychologists
- child psychotherapists
- family therapists
- children's psychiatric nurses
- social workers
- non-verbal therapists, e.g. art therapists

The CAMHS team is there to work with parents, in partnership, to help sort out the difficulties that you bring to them. They understand that parents can feel that nobody appreciates what it is like to have a child with problems.

Most of their work with children, young people and their families is done through outpatient appointments while the child continues to live at home. They are sometimes asked to provide expert opinion to the courts about child-welfare issues.

Child and adolescent psychiatrists deal with a wide range of mental health problems, as described in the chapters of this book. A large part of their work is to identify the problem, understand the causes and advise about what may help. Children have a variety of different emotional and behavioural problems – some of these are shortlived, while others are harder to deal with and need specialist help and/or treatment.

Seeing a psychiatrist or other mental health professional about your child's difficulties can be a daunting experience for a lot of parents. You may feel anxious and worried. So it might be helpful to take a friend or relative along with you.

As a parent, you will be asked a lot of questions by the person who sees you in order to:

- gather information (carry out an assessment)
- help determine the nature of the problem (diagnosis)
- decide what should happen next (treatment)

To help prepare you for this interview, the Royal College of Psychiatrists has produced a checklist for parents of children with mental health problems (see Support Organizations below for the website). This checklist provides you with some questions that you might want to ask about your child's:

- problem and/or diagnosis
- understanding of the problem and/or assessment
- treatment and/or help needed

Consent to treatment

Children under the age of sixteen can be given medical treatment for a mental health problem when a parent consents to it. If a child is in care, then the local authority has the responsibility. However, some children under sixteen are deemed under law to be mature and intelligent enough to understand the nature and implications of the treatment and can give consent themselves. This is known as 'Gillick competent'. Children over sixteen are considered as adults and will make their own decisions about their treatment.

Deborah Hart

SUPPORT ORGANIZATIONS

Young Minds: national charity committed to improving the mental health and emotional well-being of all children and young people. Tel: 0808 802 5544 (parents' information service) or 0207 336 8445 (general). *www.youngminds.org.uk*

Checklist for parents of children with mental health problems can be downloaded from *www.partnersincare.co.uk*

Editors and Contributors

Editors

Professor Sue Bailey OBE has been a child and adolescent psychiatrist for nearly thirty years, working especially with young people in the criminal justice system. Her focus is on multiprofessional input to support families facing all sorts of difficulties, to work in partnership with them to find safe solutions to problems. As Registrar of the Royal College of Psychiatrists, she leads on user and carer involvement, public education and policy. As a professor she is involved with international organizations that share the same aim of well-being and prevention of mental health problems in children across the EU.

Dr Mike Shooter CBE was a consultant in child and adolescent psychiatry for twenty-five years, working with deprived families in the valleys of South Wales. He is a former president of the Royal College of Psychiatrists, having previously been its Registrar and Director of Public Education. He is the current chair of Young Minds, Children-in-Wales and the Mental Health Foundation, and sits on the board of several other organisations.

Dr Martin Briscoe is a consultant psychiatrist in Exeter. He is the website editor for the Royal College of Psychiatrists and helps to produce their public information material.

Vanessa Cameron is chief executive of the Royal College of Psychiatrists. She has been interested for many years in working towards combating stigma and raising awareness of mental health issues.

Liz Fox is press officer at the Royal College of Psychiatrists. Having been a journalist for five years, she now works with the media to promote the work of the College and improve understanding of psychiatry and mental health issues.

Deborah Hart is head of communications and policy at the Royal College of Psychiatrists. She is committed to producing accessible information for the general public. She has been involved in a number of national campaigns to raise awareness of mental health problems and to reduce the stigma of mental illness.

Dr Margaret Murphy is a consultant child and adolescent psychiatrist working in Cambridge. She has a special interest in working with adolescents, particularly those young people who have experienced a severe mental illness. In addition, she has published research in the field of autism and genetics and is involved in the teaching and training of medical students and junior psychiatrists.

Dr Ros Ramsay is an adult psychiatrist working as a consultant at the South London and Maudsley NHS Foundation Trust. She is a member of the Royal College of Psychiatrists' Public Education Committee and works on the production of information for service users and carers.

Dr Philip Timms is a consultant psychiatrist with the START team – a homelessness outreach team – in South East London. He has edited the Royal College of Psychiatrists *Help is at Hand* series of leaflets for twelve years and chairs the College Public Education Editorial Board.

Dr Ann York is a child and adolescent psychiatrist working for South West London and St George's Mental Health NHS Trust in South West London. She has written information for families and young people on a range of mental health problems. Since April 2007, Ann has worked for two days a week as Child and Adolescent Mental Health Services Medical Adviser to the Department of Health in England.

Contributors

Professor Sue Bailey (Introduction, 'Antisocial Behaviour: Conduct Disorder and Delinquency') – see above.

Dr Margaret Bamforth ('Parenting and Families') has practised as a child adolescent psychiatrist for twenty-two years. Her special interest is infant mental health and she worked with colleagues to provide an innovative service to parents of young children. Other interests include autism and ADHD. She has also worked with the Royal College of Psychiatrists to develop materials that inform professionals, parents and children about mental health difficulties in childhood. She is married with three grown-up sons.

Dr Habib Joseph Behi ('Mood and Behaviour'; 'Treatments and Therapies') is a specialist registrar in child and adolescent psychiatry in the North Wales NHS Trust. He graduated from the University of Wales College of Medicine in 2000 and has since achieved a Diploma in Psychological Medicine and the MRCPsych. Dr Behi has run a number of community youth projects and he and his wife look after children as foster carers. He has an interest in writing mental health information that is accessible to young people.

Dr Helen Bruce ('Tics and Obsessions') is a consultant child and adolescent psychiatrist at East London NHS Foundation Trust and

Honorary Senior Clinical Lecturer at Barts and the London School of Medicine and Dentistry. She qualified from St Thomas's Hospital, University of London, and trained in both adult and child psychiatry at the Royal London and Great Ormond Street Hospitals, London. Her special interests include the transition areas between adult and child psychiatry.

Professor Tanya Byron ('Foreword') is Professor in the Public Understanding of Science. She is also a consultant clinical psychologist, broadcaster, journalist and the author of a number of bestselling books, including *The House of Tiny Tearaways* and *Little Angels.*

Dr Nisha Dogra ('Culture and Society') is a senior lecturer and honorary consultant in child and adolescent psychiatry at the University of Leicester and Leicestershire Partnership NHS Trust. She has been involved in medical education and diversity research. Her clinical interests are quality improvement in Child and Adolescent Mental Health Services (CAMHS), having been awarded a Leader for Change Award by the Health Foundation in 2007, and service development.

Dr Mona Freeman ('The Brain and Brain Development'; 'Coping with Problems'; 'Worries and Anxieties') is a consultant child and adolescent psychiatrist at the Tavistock and Portman NHS Foundation Trust in North London. She has contributed to several public education projects in the field of mental health and was awarded the Laughlin Prize by the Royal College of Psychiatrists in 2003.

Professor Elena Garralda ('Sleep, Fatigue and Chronic Fatigue Syndrome') is professor of child and adolescent psychiatry at Imperial College London, and honorary consultant in child and adolescent psychiatry with Central and North West London NHS Foundation Trust. Her research and clinical interests include the interface between physical and mental health problems in children and adolescents, and clinical services outcome research.

Dr Zoe Gilder ('Parenting Skills in Adolescence') is a final-year specialist registrar in child and adolescent psychiatry, currently working in the Community Child and Adolescent Mental Health Service in Sunderland.

Professor Simon Gowers ('Eating Problems, Weight Problems and Eating Disorders') is professor of adolescent psychiatry at the University of Liverpool and consultant to the Cheshire & Merseyside Eating Disorders Service for Adolescents (CHEDS). He has researched widely into the aetiology and treatment of eating disorders and chaired the NICE guideline group which reported on the management of eating disorders in 2004.

Dr Lucy Harrison ('Dealing with Loss') is a consultant child and adolescent psychiatrist in central Lancashire who has published research on bereavement experiences in children and adolescents.

Deborah Hart ('How to Get Help') – see above.

Dr Victoria Holt ('Atypical Gender Development in Children and Adolescents') is a consultant child and adolescent psychiatrist at the Tavistock and Portman NHS Foundation Trust in North London, specializing in gender identity disorder in children and adolescents.

Dr Anandhi Inbasagaran ('Eating Problems, Weight Problems and Eating Disorders') is a consultant child and adolescent psychiatrist in Central Team, Royal Liverpool Children's NHS Trust. She trained in child psychiatry in Mersey region, including a research and teaching post in the CHEDS eating disorders services, Chester.

Dr Brian Jacobs ('Treatments and Therapies') is a consultant child and adolescent psychiatrist with the South London and Maudsley NHS Foundation Trust, where he runs a neuropsychiatry outpatient service and a child psychiatry in-patient unit, both in the national and specialist portfolio of services. He has run parenting work in the community and classroom skills work with teachers in schools, as well as social skills work with children. He has carried out research in these areas. Trained as a family therapist and as a psychoanalyst, he has a particular interest in treatment approaches in child mental health and has written on this.

Dr Bob Jezzard ('Emotional Health and Well-being'), now retired, is a child and adolescent psychiatrist by profession. Throughout his clinical career he worked mainly with adolescents and also with local authority services, particularly for children and young people in care and for those with behavioural, emotional and social difficulties in need of special education. For the latter part of his career he was a senior policy adviser for children's mental health at the Department of Health in London.

Dr Dinah Jayson ('Children with Special Educational Needs'; 'ADHD and Autistic Spectrum Disorders') is a consultant child and adolescent psychiatrist working for Trafford NHS Healthcare Trust and Trafford Children and Young People's Service. She has contributed to several public education and anti-stigma projects in the field of mental health and published a book on understanding children's behaviour (family doctor BMA publication).

Dr Clare Lamb ('Mood and Behaviour') is a consultant child and adolescent psychiatrist with the North Wales Adolescent Service, North Wales NHS Trust. She has contributed to a number of national projects and policy documents, including the National Service Framework policy on Early Intervention Services for first-episode psychosis and NICE guidelines for bipolar disorder. She is the co-author of Royal College of Psychiatrists documents on workforce and capacity requirements for specialist CAMHS and mental health service needs for transition-age adolescents.

Dr Graeme Lamb ('Tics and Obsessions') is a consultant in child and adolescent psychiatry in East London NHS Foundation Trust. He qualified from Cambridge University and trained in child and adolescent psychiatry on the Royal London rotation. He is lead clinician at Newham Child and Family Consultation Service and has a particular interest in ADHD, as well as teaching and training.

Dr Ruth Marshall ('Drugs and Drink') is a consultant child and adolescent psychiatrist at Central Manchester University Hospitals NHS Foundation Trust. She has a keen interest in adolescent substance misuse and has contributed to books on this subject.

Dr Paul McArdle ('Parenting Skills in Adolescence') is a consultant child and adolescent psychiatrist and senior lecturer working at the Fleming Nuffield Unit, a Tier 4 regional day and in-patient unit, based in Newcastle upon Tyne.

Dr Theresa McArdle ('Mental Health of Young Offenders') is a specialist registrar in child and adolescent psychiatry. Prior to retraining in psychiatry, she had been a consultant paediatrician since 1994. She also spent several years involved in research in West Africa with the Medical Research Council. Her interests currently include young offenders and people with autistic spectrum disorders. She lives in Liverpool with her family.

Dr Iain McClure ('Self-harm and Attempted Suicide') is a consultant child and adolescent psychiatrist at the Royal Hospital for Sick Children, Edinburgh, Scotland. He is also an honorary senior research fellow at Heriot-Watt University and an honorary senior clinical teacher at Dundee University. He chaired the SIGN guideline on *Autism Spectrum Disorders in Children and Young People*, published in 2007 (www.sign.ac.uk), and regularly writes reviews connected to mental health for the *British Medical Journal*.

Dr Margaret Murphy ('Choosing a School and Problems at School'; 'Sexuality and Sexual Problems') – see above.

Dr Clare O'Donnell ('Parenting and Families') trained as a psychiatric social worker at Manchester University. She completed further PG diplomas in child mental health at both the University of Manchester and the University of Salford. Clare has worked in both adult and children's services within several local authorities' Social Care agencies. She is currently spending time in Estonia, where she plans to continue her interests in child mental health at Tallinn University.

Dr Greg Richardson ('Transition to Adulthood') is a consultant in child and adolescent psychiatry in York, with responsibilities to an adolescent in-patient service and to community CAMHS. He was chair of the child and adolescent faculty of the Royal College of Psychiatrists and has previously been chair of the Northern and Yorkshire Division. He is joint editor of a CAMHS operational handbook.

Dr Mike Shooter ('Introduction'; 'Understanding Child and Adolescent Development') – see above.

Dr Indra Singam ('Choosing a School and Problems at School') is consultant child and adolescent psychiatrist to the Darwin Centre for Young People, a sixteen-bed acute adolescent unit, and also to an outpatient CAMHS, both in Cambridge.

Dr Sue Storey ('Abuse, Neglect and Domestic Violence') is a consultant child and adolescent psychiatrist in Islington Community CAMHS, North London. She enjoys being involved in the training of junior doctors and other professionals; this includes supervision on complex cases and teaching on aspects of child psychiatry such as child abuse, childhood depression and family therapy.

Dr Taryn Tracey ('Sexuality and Sexual Problems') studied medicine at King's College London and undertook general psychiatry training on the St Bartholomew's and the Royal London rotational training scheme. She became a member of the Royal College of Psychiatrists in 2006 and is currently doing her higher specialist training in child and adolescent psychiatry in Cambridge. Her interests are in the relationship between antisocial behaviour and mental ill-health in young people, the effects of trauma on the young mind and concepts of resilience.

Dr Guinevere Tufnell ('Trauma, Stress and Adjustment') is a consultant child and adolescent psychiatrist at the Traumatic Stress Clinic at Great Ormond Street Hospital in London. She has contributed to several public education projects in the field of mental health, and is the originator of the popular *Mental Health and Growing Up* factsheets for parents and teachers.

Dr Aaron Vallance ('Sleep, Fatigue and Chronic Fatigue Syndrome') is an honorary clinical lecturer in child and adolescent psychiatry at Imperial College London. His interests include medical education, such as designing courses for medical students. His areas of research include depression in young people.

Index

abuse *see* child abuse
aches and pains 45–6, 131, 171, 179
ADD *see* attention deficit disorder
ADHD *see* attention deficit hyperactivity disorder
adolescents 18, 19, 27, 97–8
  abnormal behaviour 102–4
  and anger management 107
  brain development 52, 98
  communicating with 100–2, 105–6
  helping 104–8
  and importance of honesty 105, 109
  with mental health problems 104, *see* mental health disorders
  neglected 27–8, 167
  normal behaviour 99–100
  overprotected 28, 47, 67
  punishing 106–7
  and sense of identity 13, 98–9, 100
  setting rules and boundaries for 100, 106–7
  staying friends with 105–6, 107–8
  transition to adulthood 360–1
  violence in *see* violent behaviour
  see also peer groups; sexuality
adoption/adoptive parents 25–6, 61, 86, 88–9, 94
  understanding children's behaviour 87–8, 89–93
Adult Mental Health Services 362, 363
after-school clubs 127
aggression/aggressive behaviour 108, 170, 171, 292, 293, 307,
  see also violent behaviour
agoraphobia 132
alcohol abuse *see* substance abuse
alternative care 83–8, 172
amphetamines 234, 236
'anal' personalities 12
anger, handling 107
animals, cruelty to 23
anorexia nervosa 244, *see* eating disorders
antidepressants 36, 182, 206, 274, 280
antipsychotic drugs 274, 308
antisocial behaviours 292, 295–6, 304, *see also* conduct disorders
anxiety 18, 30, 33, 34, 35, 132, 143, 176–7
  causes 179–80
  and crime 298, 304, 305, 308
  general 177–8
  and medication 182
  panic attacks 178
  physical symptoms 179
  and sleep problems 329–30
  social 178
  and tics 254
  treatments for 181–2, 352
  triggers 178, 180
  see also phobias; post-traumatic stress disorder; separation anxiety

art therapy 357
artificial food colouring 194
ASD *see* autistic spectrum disorders
Asperger's syndrome 43–4, 196, 198, 202
atomoxetine 193
attachment theory 13–14, 69, 169
attention deficit disorder (ADD) 185
attention deficit hyperactivity disorder (ADHD) 33–4, 35, 184–5, 188–90, 299
  and autism 197
  causes 38, 187–8
  and conduct disorder 293
  and crime 185, 188, 194, 298, 304, 305, 307
  diagnosing 43, 186–7, 190
  and diet/food 188, 193, 194
  getting help and support 191–2
  help needed at school 194
  and learning difficulties 128, 129
  long-term outcome 190, 194
  medication for 37, 193, 294
  and sleep problems 329
  tips for parents and teachers 191–3
  treatments 188, 190, 193, 362
attunement 69–70
autism/autistic spectrum disorders 20, 33, 34, 35, 195–7, 200
  assessments 201–2, 203, 207
  causes 200–1
  and complementary therapies 206–7
  and crime 304, 308
  diagnosing 197–8, 202–3, 207
  getting help and support 203–5, 207–8, 362
  and learning difficulties 128, 129
  medication 206
  problems and solutions 198–200
  and rituals and routines 198, 208
  and schooling 37, 44, 204–5, 207
  and sleep problems 329
  tips for parents 207–8
babies 62–4
  communication with 67–8
  difficulties with 76–7, *see also* postnatal depression
  and fathers' role 64–6
  inability to love 70–1
  parental response to 68–70
bedwetting 23, 170, 171
behaviour therapy (BT) 350–1
benzodiazepines 236
bereavement *see* death and bereavement
binge-drinking 233
bipolar affective disorder 35, 154, 264, 271–2
  and complementary therapies 274
  medication for 274
  preventing relapses 275
  symptoms 272–3
  and talking therapies 274
  tips for families etc. 275
birth order 21
bonding 69
'bottom-shufflers' 10
boundaries, setting 76, 100, 106–7
Bowlby, John 14
brain, the 49–52
  in abused children 169
  and ADHD 187–8
  changes at puberty 52, 98
breakfast clubs 127
breathlessness 179
BT *see* behaviour therapy
bulimia nervosa 244, *see* eating disorders
bullying 29, 31, 134–6, 179, 277, 302
  by abused children 170
  cyber 134, 136–7
  and eating problems 244, 245
  signs of 135
  by your child 137–8
buprenorphine 238

caffeinated drinks 194, 329
CAMHS *see* Child and Adolescent Mental Health Services
cannabis 39, 232, 233–5, 306
carers, children as 229
CBT *see* cognitive behavioural therapy
central core (brain) 49, 51
CFS *see* chronic fatigue syndrome
Chance UK 164
Chess, Stella 76
child abuse 38, 163–6, 307
  and ADHD 188
  and crime 297
  and domestic violence 168, 171
  emotional 167, 168, 169, 171
  general effects of 168–9
  help and treatment 172, 173
  longer term effects 171–2
  physical 166, 167, 168, 169, 170
  sexual 166, 168, 169, 170
  signs of 169–71
  tips for families, teachers and friends 172
  see also neglected children
Child and Adolescent Mental Health Services (CAMHS) 173, 181, 187, 205, 293, 307
  and self-harming children 284, 289
  transition to Adult Mental Health Services 361–4
Child and Mental Health Services (CMHS) 108
childcare 82, 127
'child-centred' behaviours 72, 73–4
'child-directive' behaviours 72, 74–5
Child Protection Advisers 172
Children Act 1989 84, 172
Children Centres 60
Children's Social Care Services (CSCS) 83, 84–5, 87, 94, 164, 172
chocolate 194
chronic fatigue syndrome (CFS)/myalgic encephalopathy (ME) 331–6
chronotherapy 329
cigarettes 232
Climbié, Victoria 165
clomipramine 261
clonidine 252, 255
clumsiness *see* developmental coordination disorder
cocaine/crack cocaine 232, 234, 235, 236, 306
cognitive behavioural therapy (CBT) 227, 238, 255, 260, 335, 345, 351–3
  and anxiety problems 176, 181
  and mental health disorders 269, 274, 275, 279
cognitive development 11–12, 18
Coles, Robert 9
'comfort eating' 242, 244
commands, use of 74
communication
  with ADHD children 191–2
  autistic children 197–8, 202
  with babies 67–8, 79
  with teenagers 100–2, 105–6
'Communities that Care' schemes 299
co-morbidity 34–5, 293, 294
compulsions 258; *see* obsessive compulsive disorder
concentration, poor 129, 170, 186–7
conduct disorders 170, 293–4, 298, 304, 305, 307
  treatments 294–5
confused thoughts 266
consent to treatment 363, 368
contact arrangements 81
contraception 30, 44–5, 143, 314–15, 316
cooperative play 29
coping skills 22, 53–4, 67
coprolalia 253
cortex 49, 51
crawling 10

crime/criminal offences 1, 34, 292, 295, 306
and ADHD 185, 188, 194, 298, 304, 305, 307
help and treatment needed 299–300
and mental health 297–8, 304, 305–8
and substance abuse 295, 304–5, 306, 307–8
those at risk of 295–8
see also 'gang culture'
critical parents/criticism 66, 71, 75, 105, 134, 145, 147, 155, 167, 192, 280
cruelty to animals 23
crying at night (babies) 66
CSCS *see* Children's Social Care Services
cultural issues 15, 28–9, 30, 53, 97, 166, 210–17
and inter-country adoption 89
cyberbullying 134, 136–7

DAMP (disorder of attention, motor coordination and perception) 186
DBT *see* dialectical behaviour therapy
DCD *see* developmental coordination disorder
death and bereavement 22, 101–2, 153, 179, 218–22, 277, 297
understanding concept of death 16, 222, 288, 344
delinquency 292, 293, *see* crime
delusions 266, 273
depression 32, 33, 34, 35, 143, 264, 276–8
and bullying 134, 277
of carers/parents 167, 173, *see also* postnatal depression
and crime 297, 304, 305, 308
hereditary 38
medication for 280
psychotic symptoms 278–9
and school refusal 132
and self-harm 289
signs of 278, 307
and sleep problems 329–30
and substance abuse 279–80
and tics 254
tips for families etc. 280
treatments 182, 206, 279, 280, 352, 354
see also bipolar manic disorder
descriptive commenting 73
developmental coordination disorder (DCD) 146–8
diagnoses 34–5, *see also specific disorders*
dialectical behaviour therapy (DBT) 355
diazepam 236
disabilities
babies with 70, 76
children with 128, 142, 226, 227, 278
and sexuality 315–16
discipline 75–6, *see also* boundaries
distractibility 186–7
divorce and separation 61, 80–1, 102, 179, 220, 242, 277
do's and don'ts 222–4
and self-harm 286
dogs, fear of 175–6
domestic violence 46, 134, 168, 172, 173, 296, 297, 305
and child abuse 166, 167, 168, 171
dopamine 187
'downers' 236
Down's Syndrome 143
drugs *see* medication
drugs, recreational 236; *see also* substance abuse
DSH *see* self-harm, deliberate
dyscalculia 128, 145
dyslexia 128, 144–5
dyspraxia 128, 146–8
and ADD 186

E *see* ecstasy
Early Intervention Teams 361
eating disorders 28, 35, 39, 243, 244–6
and abuse 170

self-help 248
tips for families etc. 248–9
treatment and therapies 246–8, 352, 356
ecstasy 234, 236
Edinburgh Postnatal Depression Scale (EPDS) 78, 79
Educational Welfare Officers 132, 133
emotional abuse 167, 168, 169, 171
'emotional intelligence' 155, 156
'emotional literacy' 19–20, 31, 155–6
'emotional well-being' 151
development programme for 156
differences in 154–5
and mental health 152–3
negative 153–4, 157–9
positive 154, 159
emotions, management of 156–7
E-numbers 194
EPDS *see* Edinburgh Postnatal Depression Scale
Erikson, Erik 13, 18
Every Child Matters (government programme) 60
exam stress 102, 103, 133–4, 272
Extended Schools 60
eye contact, abnormal 197
eye movement desensitisation and reprocessing 345

faddiness 242
fairness, concept of 29
family, the 25–8, 59
family therapy 294, 355–6
fathers, role of 64–6
fatigue 328
see also chronic fatigue syndrome
fears *see* anxiety; phobias
feeding difficulties 243–4, 245, 246
fidgeting 179, 186
fire, fascination with 23
fizzy drinks 194
fluvoxamine 261
foetal alcohol syndrome 40
foster carers/parents 25, 61, 85, 89, 90, 94
private 86–7
and Special Guardianship Orders 85
understanding children's behaviour 87–8, 90–3
Fowler, James 15, 18
Freud, Sigmund 12
friends: as care-givers 83, 84, 87
FRIENDS (programme) 159
friendships 61, 91, 98, 100, 115, 310–12
and children with eating problems 248, 249
difficulty in making 2, 29, 43, 122, 131, 170, 171, 178, 188, 267, 277, 354
parental attitudes to 28, 29–30, 312
see also 'gang culture'; peer groups
frontal lobes 49, 98, 187

gambling 101
'gang culture' 28, 138–9, 298
gender identity disorders 319–23, 326
associated difficulties 323
help and treatments 323–6
genetic causes for disorders 38, 179
Gilbert, Francis: *The New School Rules* 119–20
'Gillick competent' 44–5, 368
glial cells 49, 50
'good enough' parents 8, 66–7
government policies 60
'graded exposure' 181
grandparents 25, 54, 59, 61, 81, 84

hallucinations 266, 273
hallucinogenics 236
help and support, getting 365–6, *see also specific disorders*
hereditary disorders 38
heroin 232, 235, 236, 238, 306
holiday playschemes 127

homosexuality 31, 213, 312–13, 326
hormone blockers 321, 325–6
hospital stays 14, 24, 30–1
hugs and cuddles 74
hyperactivity 186, 305, *see* attention deficit hyperactivity disorder
hyperkinetic disorder 185
hypothyroidism 143

identity
  cultural 211–15
  establishing sense of 13, 19, 20, 98–9, 100
  see also gender identity disorders
ignoring unwanted behaviours 71, 74
illness 181, 219, 220
  children 24, 53, 54, 128, 131, 224–7, 278
  and hospital stays 14, 30–1
  parental 53, 88, 179, 229
  see also aches and pains; psychosomatic problems
imitation: as positive attention 74
impulsiveness/impulsivity 187, 355
Individual Education Plans 130
inherited disorders 38, 179
in-patient care 363
insomnia *see* sleep problems
interpersonal therapy (IPT) 354
IQs 142

Kanner's syndrome *see* Asperger's syndrome
Kennell, John 69
Klaus, Marshall 69

language(s), learning 51
  delay in 128, 198, 202
laws and legal matters 61, 84, 109, 128–9, 131, 136, 140, 172, 368
learning difficulties 35, 127–31, 142
  and crime 294, 298, 304, 305, 307
  and mental health 129
  and tics 254
  and truancy 132
  see also dyscalculia; dyslexia; dyspraxia
learning disabilities 131, 142–3
legal matters *see* laws
lesbianism 312–13, *see also* homosexuality
limbic system (brain) 49
lithium carbonate 274
'looked after' children 84–5
lorazepam 236
LSD 236

manic depression *see* bipolar affective disorder
marriage rates 79–80
masturbation 30
ME *see* chronic fatigue syndrome
medication 36–7, 358; *see also specific disorders*
melatonin 328
mental health disorders 32–6, 157–8
  and crime 302, 305–9
  diagnoses 34–5
  help and intervention 34, 36, 159, *see* mental health treatments
  parents with 228–9
  see also specific disorders
mental health treatments 36–7, 349–50
  art therapy 357
  behaviour therapy 350–1
  dialectical behaviour therapy 355
  family therapy 355–6
  interpersonal therapy 354
  medication 36–7, 358
  psychodynamic therapy 356
  systems therapy 355–6
  see also cognitive behavioural therapy
methadone 238
mixed-race children 214
mobile-phone bullying 134, 136

mood changes 263
Morris, Lynn 79
motivation, lack of 266–7, 270
moving house 220
multisystemic therapy (MST) 294, 299, 308
myalgic encephalopathy *see* chronic fatigue syndrome

nagging 106
name-calling 134, *see also* bullying
negative attention 71, 72
neglected children 27–8, 167, 168
neurodevelopmental problems 142, *see* attention deficit hyperactivity disorder; autistic spectrum disorders
neurones 49, 50, 51
newborn babies 62–4
  bonding with 69
  inability to love 70–1
nightmares 330
'No', use of 74–5
numbers, difficulty with *see* dyscalculia

obesity 244, 245, 247
'object constancy/permanence' 11, 18
obsessions 258; *see* obsessive compulsive disorder
obsessive compulsive disorder (OCD) 254, 255, 257–60
  treatments 260, 261, 352
occipital lobes 49
OCD *see* obsessive compulsive disorder
ODD *see* oppositional defiant disorder
OFSTED 94, 120
old parents 26
omega-3 fish oils 193, 206, 270, 274
oppositional defiant disorder (ODD) 193, 293, 307
orlistat 247
over-activity 186
over-eating 244, 246
overprotective parents 28, 47, 67, 180
over-talkativeness 186

pain, dealing with 226–7
panic attacks/disorder 178
paracetamol 283, 287, 289
Parent Support Advisors (PSAs) 133
'parental responsibility' 109
parenting groups 71, 76
'parenting plus' 87–8
parenting programmes 108–9, 307
parents 303, 306, 307
  'good-enough' 8, 66–7
  and inherited disorders 38, 179
  relationship with babies 63–4, 67–71, 76–7
  relationship with children 59, 61, 64–6, 72–6
  relationship with teenagers 100–2, 104–8
  see also critical parents; domestic violence; overprotective parents and specific disorders
parietal lobes 49
PECS *see* Picture Exchange Communication System
peer groups 11, 13, 19, 23, 28, 29–30, 31, 100, 293, 297, *see also* 'gang culture'
'personality' 21
'personality disorders' 21, 298
phobias 175–6, 177
physical abuse 166, 167, 168, 169, 170
physical development 10–11, 16
Piaget, Jean 11, 18
Picture Exchange Communication System (PECS) 203
play therapy 356
playing with children 74
pornography 166
positive approaches 71, 72–4
postnatal depression 70, 77–9

post-traumatic stress disorder 180, 330, 338–42
and crime 298, 304, 305, 307, 308
helping children with 342–4
seeking professional help 344–5, 352
praise, importance of 72, 73, 350
pregnancy
and substance misuse 39–40, 51, 172, 187
teenage 26, 28, 82, 314
premature babies 70
preservatives, food 188, 194
PRUs *see* pupil referral units
PSAs *see* Parent Support Advisors
psychiatric wards 363
psychiatrists 366–8
psychodynamic therapy 356
'psychopaths' 23
psychosexual development 12
psychosis 143, 264–7, 299, 304, 305
and depression 278–9
drug-induced 234–5
treatments 267, 352, 361
psychosocial development 12–13
psychosomatic problems 227–8, *see also* aches and pains
punishments 27, 72, 75, 106, 107, 108, 166, 350
pupil referral units (PRUs) 131, 132, 164

questions
children's 11–12
parental 75

reading difficulties 128, 304, *see also* dyslexia
relationships 310–12, *see also* sexuality
parental *see* parents
Residence Orders 84, 86
'resilience' 54, 158, 159, 188
reward programmes 350–1
risk 46–7
risperidone 255
Ritalin (methylphenidate) 37, 193, 194
running away 28

St John's wort 274, 280
sanctions, use of 76, 106–7
schizophrenia 35, 259, 264, 267–8
assessments 269
and food supplements 270
and medication 269
psychological and social interventions 269–70
tips for families etc. 270
School Action/School Action Plus 130
school refusal/phobia 131–2, 163–5
schools 31
applying for places 116–18
choosing 115, 118–22
independent 118, 120
interacting with 139
'league tables' 119
refusal to go to *see* school refusal
sex education 101, 314
starting primary 122–4
starting secondary 37, 44, 124–6
and truancy 1, 132–3
see also bullying; exam stress; teachers
SEAL (Social and Emotional Aspects of Learning) 156
self-esteem 13, 27, 29, 30, 35, 154, 304
and ADHD 188, 194
and eating disorders 243, 244, 245, 246, 247
raising 54, 147, 148, 159, 249, 352
self-harm, deliberate (DSH) 1, 31, 33, 285–7, 297, 303, 305
by abused children 170, 171
among Asian girls 29
and bullying 134
causes 285–7
in juvenile prisons 305

and need for responsible adult 288–9
specialist help 289–90, 355
and substance abuse 285, 286
'self speak' 191
SEN *see* Special Educational Needs
separation *see* divorce and separation
separation anxiety 14, 17, 132, 177, 180
sertraline 261
sex education 101, 314
sexual abuse 166, 168, 169, 170, 296
sexual offences 292, 297, 300, 308
sexuality 19, 30, 101, 310–11
and drugs and alcohol 315
inappropriate behaviour 170
pressure and promiscuity 313–15
and young people with disabilities 315–16
and young people with learning difficulties 143
see also homosexuality
sexually transmitted diseases 30, 45, 313, 314, 315
sharing, concept of 29
siblings
death of 219, 220
jealousy of 2, 41–2, 137
sibutramine 247
Skynner, Robin 65
'sleep hygiene' techniques 330
sleep problems 171, 176, 179, 328–31
sleeping in parental bed 40–1, 180
smacking 165
smiles 68, 73
smoking 232
'smothering' children *see* overprotective parents
social anxiety 178
social communication difficulties 197
social phobia 132
social skills training 294, 300, 308
sodium valproate 274
soiling 170
Special Educational Needs (SEN) 128–9, 130, 139
Special Guardians/Guardianship Orders 85–6
special schools 130–1, 142
speech *see* language(s)
spelling difficulties 128
spiritual development 14–15, 18
SSRI antidepressants 182
stage theories 15–17
step-parents 25, 61, 66, 81
Stern, Daniel 68, 79
stories, social 204
strangers, talking to 171, 187
stress 46, 51, 78, 165, 219
and chronic fatigue syndrome 336
and de-stressing techniques 345
exam 102, 103, 133–4, 272
reactions to 137, 152, 153, 155, 157, 168–9, 179, 277, 329
see also post-traumatic stress disorder
substance abuse 100, 101, 232–6, 293, 299, 303–4
by abused children 170, 171
and crime 295, 297, 298, 306–7, 308
and family therapy 238, 356
giving help and support 236–7, 240
medication for 238
and mental health problems 305
in pregnancy 39–40
as self-harm 285, 286
signs of 239
and sleep problems 329
talking treatments 237–8
suicidal thoughts/attempted suicide 1, 31, 32, 33, 34, 282–4, 285
and bullying 134
in juvenile prisons 305
signs of intent 287
treatments 284, 355
see also depression
Sure Start 60, 71

synapses 50
systems therapy 355–6

talking treatment *see* cognitive behavioural therapy
tantrums *see* temper tantrums
tartrazine 188, 194
TEACH (Teaching and Education of Autistic Children and Handicapped Children) 204
teachers 31
  complaints about 139–40
  contacting 139
teaching children (parents) 75
teenagers *see* adolescents
temper tantrums 18–19, 76, 154
  of abused children 170, 171
  and anxiety 179
termazapam 236
'terrible twos' 13, 18–19, 27
Thomas, Alexander 76
tics 197, 251–6
  behaviour therapy for 350–1
'time out' 72, 75–6
Tourette's syndrome 251, 253–4, 255–6
trauma 340, *see* post-traumatic stress disorder
treatments *see* mental health treatments
truancy 1, 132–3, 171
trust 13, 15, 69, 70, 106
  and self-harm 288, 289, 390
Twain, Mark 97

unresponsivness 197, 198
'uppers' 236
urinary infections 170

valium 236
violent behaviour 23, 108, 264, 292, 294, 295, 296–7, 300, 304
  of abused children 107, 171
  from boyfriends of teenage girls 312
  and multi-agency interventions 296
  towards parents 300
  see also domestic violence; 'gang culture'

walking 10
weight problems 246, *see also* obesity
Winnicott, Donald 8, 66
withdrawn children 2, 104, 137, 164, 170, 171, 221, 234, 263, 266–7, 279, 338
'working mothers' 82–3
writing difficulties 128, *see also* dyslexia; dyspraxia

Young Carers 229
Young Minds 152
Youth Justice System 295, 298, 299, 304